Modern Language Association of America

Approaches to Teaching
World Literature

Joseph Gibaldi, Series Editor

1. Joseph Gibaldi, ed. *Approaches to Teaching Chaucer's* Canterbury Tales. 1980.
2. Carole Slade, ed. *Approaches to Teaching Dante's* Divine Comedy. 1982.
3. Richard Bjornson, ed. *Approaches to Teaching Cervantes'* Don Quixote. 1984.
4. Jess B. Bessinger, Jr., and Robert F. Yeager, eds. *Approaches to Teaching* Beowulf. 1984.
5. Richard J. Dunn, ed. *Approaches to Teaching Dickens'* David Copperfield. 1984.
6. Steven G. Kellman, ed. *Approaches to Teaching Camus's* The Plague. 1985.
7. Yvonne Shafer, ed. *Approaches to Teaching Ibsen's* A Doll House. 1985.
8. Martin Bickman, ed. *Approaches to Teaching Melville's* Moby-Dick. 1985.
9. Miriam Youngerman Miller and Jane Chance, eds. *Approaches to Teaching* Sir Gawain and the Green Knight. 1986.
10. Galbraith M. Crump, ed. *Approaches to Teaching Milton's* Paradise Lost. 1986.
11. Spencer Hall, with Jonathan Ramsey, eds. *Approaches to Teaching Wordsworth's Poetry.* 1986.
12. Robert H. Ray, ed. *Approaches to Teaching Shakespeare's* King Lear. 1986.
13. Kostas Myrsiades, ed. *Approaches to Teaching Homer's* Iliad *and* Odyssey. 1987.
14. Douglas J. McMillan, ed. *Approaches to Teaching Goethe's* Faust. 1987.
15. Renée Waldinger, ed. *Approaches to Teaching Voltaire's* Candide. 1987.
16. Bernard Koloski, ed. *Approaches to Teaching Chopin's* The Awakening. 1988.
17. Kenneth M. Roemer, ed. *Approaches to Teaching Momaday's* The Way to Rainy Mountain. 1988.
18. Edward J. Rielly, ed. *Approaches to Teaching Swift's* Gulliver's Travels. 1988.
19. Jewel Spears Brooker, ed. *Approaches to Teaching Eliot's Poetry and Plays.* 1988.
20. Melvyn New, ed. *Approaches to Teaching Sterne's* Tristram Shandy. 1989.
21. Robert F. Gleckner and Mark L. Greenberg, eds. *Approaches to Teaching Blake's* Songs of Innocence and of Experience. 1989.
22. Susan J. Rosowski, ed. *Approaches to Teaching Cather's* My Ántonia. 1989.
23. Carey Kaplan and Ellen Cronan Rose, eds. *Approaches to Teaching Lessing's* The Golden Notebook. 1989.
24. Susan Resneck Parr and Pancho Savery, eds. *Approaches to Teaching Ellison's* Invisible Man. 1989.
25. Barry N. Olshen and Yael S. Feldman, eds. *Approaches to Teaching the Hebrew Bible as Literature in Translation.* 1989.
26. Robin Riley Fast and Christine Mack Gordon, eds. *Approaches to Teaching Dickinson's Poetry.* 1989.
27. Spencer Hall, ed. *Approaches to Teaching Shelley's Poetry.* 1990.

Approaches to
Teaching Shakespeare's
The Tempest
and Other
Late Romances

Edited by
Maurice Hunt

The Modern Language Association of America
New York   1992

Library of Congress Cataloging-in-Publication Data

Approaches to teaching Shakespeare's The Tempest and other late
   romances / edited by Maurice Hunt.
     p. cm. — (Approaches to teaching world literature ; 41)
   Includes index.
   ISBN 0-87352-707-0 ISBN 0-87352-708-9 (pbk.)
   1. Shakespeare, William, 1564–1616 — Tragicomedies.
   2. Shakespeare, William, 1564–1616 — Study and teaching.
   3. Shakespeare, William, 1564–1616. Tempest. 4. Tragicomedy — Study
and teaching. I. Hunt, Maurice, 1942–   . II. Series.
PR2981.5.A67   1992
822.3'3 — dc20   92-14830

Cover art of the paperback edition: Illustration from *Compositions from
Shakespeare's* Tempest, by Sir Joseph Noel Paton, London, 1877. Courtesy of
the Print Collection, Miriam and Ira D. Wallach Division of Art, Prints, and
Photographs, The New York Public Library, Astor, Lenox and Tilden Foundations.

Published by The Modern Language Association of America
10 Astor Place, New York, New York 10003-6981

To the memory of
Elmore and Irene Hunt

CONTENTS

PREFACE TO THE SERIES

In *The Art of Teaching* Gilbert Highet wrote, "Bad teaching wastes a great deal of effort, and spoils many lives which might have been full of energy and happiness." All too many teachers have failed in their work, Highet argued, simply "because they have not thought about it." We hope that the Approaches to Teaching World Literature series, sponsored by the Modern Language Association's Publications Committee, will not only improve the craft — as well as the art — of teaching but also encourage serious and continuing discussion of the aims and methods of teaching literature.

The principal objective of the series is to collect within each volume different points of view on teaching a specific literary work, a literary tradition, or a writer widely taught at the undergraduate level. The preparation of each volume begins with a wide-ranging survey of instructors, thus enabling us to include in the volume the philosophies and approaches, thoughts and methods of scores of experienced teachers. The result is a sourcebook of material, information, and ideas on teaching the subject of the volume to undergraduates.

The series is intended to serve nonspecialists as well as specialists, inexperienced as well as experienced teachers, graduate students who wish to learn effective ways of teaching as well as senior professors who wish to compare their own approaches with the approaches of colleagues in other schools. Of course, no volume in the series can ever substitute for erudition, intelligence, creativity, and sensitivity in teaching. We hope merely that each book will point readers in useful directions; at most each will offer only a first step in the long journey to successful teaching.

Joseph Gibaldi
Series Editor

PREFACE TO THE VOLUME

This volume would not have been possible without the help of the ninety-three teachers of Shakespeare's late romances whose names and academic affiliations appear in the list of contributors and survey participants at the end of the book. Part 1, "Materials," depends heavily on information gleaned from survey participants' completed questionnaires. The eighteen teachers whose essays make up part 2 were chosen from this sizable group of instructors and invited to describe a distinctive approach to teaching one or more of the plays traditionally called Shakespeare's late romances—*Pericles*, *Cymbeline*, *The Winter's Tale*, and *The Tempest*. The nature and distribution of the approaches reflect the interests and opinions of the larger pool of respondents. More essays are devoted to *The Winter's Tale* and *The Tempest* because they are assigned more often than are the other romances.

Some readers will be disappointed not to find *Henry VIII* and *The Two Noble Kinsmen* treated in this volume. The practical problem of adequately covering the four late romances in the number of pages allotted for books in the Approaches series led to the decision not to solicit essays on these plays. Nevertheless, many of the pedagogies described apply to *Henry VIII* and *The Two Noble Kinsmen*, and many of the resources cited in the "Materials" section contain chapters on these plays or present methodologies that apply to them. Other readers may be troubled by my calling *Pericles*, *Cymbeline*, *The Winter's Tale*, and *The Tempest* romances. In fact, the original title of this volume was "Teaching Shakespeare's *Tempest* and Other Late Plays." But most of the teachers and critics of these plays call them romances in print if not in their minds or conversation. Certainly the reader aware of the plays' non- or antiromantic features will find sympathetic chords struck by several essayists in this book. Finally, it seemed best to call the four plays late romances to indicate that plays such as *Timon of Athens* and *Henry VIII* are not major topics.

I have incurred many debts in preparing this volume, most notably to James Barcus and William Cooper, respectively chairman of the English department and dean of the College of Arts and Sciences at Baylor University. They were instrumental in helping me secure a summer sabbatical and research grants for writing and editing this book. I owe special thanks to my colleague Robert Ray for valuable advice. Janet Sheets and David Sherwood, Baylor reference librarians, helped me locate not only copies of lesser-known studies of the romances but also elusive information for ordering videocassette versions of the plays. My wife, Pamela, and Alison, Jeffrey, Andrew, and Thomas were patient with me when the tasks of compiling this volume took precedence over our family life. My parents, to whose memory the book is dedicated, always encouraged my pursuit of the Bard, even when they (like my younger self) were not always certain of the value of the chase.

MH

Part One

MATERIALS

Editions

Complete Editions of Shakespeare

Of those instructors who teach the romances from a complete edition of Shakespeare's works, the majority prefer the texts edited by G. Blakemore Evans and introduced by Hallett Smith in *The Riverside Shakespeare*. By more than a two-to-one margin, they choose this edition over David Bevington's *Complete Works of Shakespeare*, arguing that it provides valuable illustrations and that "the notes are the least prudish." Others state that "its fairly elaborate apparatus makes it particularly appropriate for majors or those who may pursue further study" and that "the glosses are clear and the introductions geared to raising questions of interpretation." One respondent notes, "I like its secondary material, trust its editorial judgments, and, given that the Spevack *Concordance* is keyed to the Riverside, consider it the American scholar's 'Text of Record.'" Another teacher mentions that it contains *The Two Noble Kinsmen* (whereas the Bevington edition does not). A third instructor praises the Riverside for including variant readings from texts other than Evans's primary one for a play. Nevertheless, the Riverside's inclusion of variant readings in brackets and its mixture of modern and Renaissance spellings are criticized by teachers for unnecessarily distracting students' attention. Moreover, the bibliographies require updating.

This last charge cannot be brought against the Bevington edition (4th ed., 1992), the second most popular complete edition among teachers surveyed. One respondent comments that she has "found no other text with such useful footnotes for undergraduates" and such satisfactory introductory materials and bibliographies. Those instructors critical of Evans's variant readings and mingling of spellings may prefer the Bevington edition, in which the spelling is "more modernized." In addition, "the general introduction is quite rich and informative on Shakespeare's life and the Elizabethan age." One teacher points out that the Bevington edition is also less expensive than the Riverside. Others comment on the book's "pleasant typeface," "balanced critical introductions," and "reliable, readable, and full" footnotes and appendixes.

Only a small minority of respondents preferring a complete Shakespeare use other editions. Five teachers employ *The Complete Pelican Shakespeare* and two *The Complete Signet Classic Shakespeare*. While those favoring Signet gave no reason for their choice, the Pelican users remark that the general editor, Alfred Harbage, "numbers only those lines that are footnoted," a fact "that clues students when to look at the bottom of the page." Another respondent prefers teaching *The Tempest* out of the Pelican because Northrop Frye edited the text.

Single Editions

A respondent who prefers the Riverside's version of the romances states, "I don't like students using the New Arden *Tempest* because I find Kermode's magisterial introduction tends to prejudice interpretation." Such an opinion, however, represents an anomaly. Along with the Signet Classic editions, the New Arden editions are the favorite texts among instructors preferring to teach out of individual volumes. In fact, the popularity of the two series is almost equally divided, with twenty-five respondents favoring the New Arden texts and twenty-four those of the Signet Classic editors.

Teachers most often recommend the Signet Classic editions for their primary sources and critical essays. In *Pericles*, edited by Ernest Schanzer, selections include excerpts from John Gower's *Confessio Amantis* (bk. 8) and Laurence Twine's *Pattern of Painful Adventures* (chs. 11–15) and commentaries by G. Wilson Knight (from *The Crown of Life*), John F. Danby (from *Poets on Fortune's Hill*), Kenneth Muir (from *Shakespeare as Collaborator*), Carol Thomas Neely ("*Pericles*: Incest, Birth, and the Death of Mothers"), and Sylvan Barnet ("*Pericles* on the Stage"). The Signet *Cymbeline*, edited by Richard Hosley, offers selections from Boccaccio's *Decameron* and Holinshed's *Chronicles* and commentaries by Knight (from *The Crown of Life*), Bertrand Evans (from *Shakespeare's Comedies*), Northrop Frye (from *A Natural Perspective*), and Hosley ("*Cymbeline* on Stage and Screen"). The Signet Classic texts of *Pericles* and *Cymbeline* appear in a single large paperback volume (along with *The Two Noble Kinsmen*, edited by Clifford Leech). Frank Kermode has edited the Signet *Winter's Tale*, which reprints selections from Robert Greene's *Pandosto* and commentaries by Simon Forman, Samuel Taylor Coleridge, E. M. W. Tillyard (from *Shakespeare's Last Plays*), Knight (from *The Crown of Life*), Wolfgang Clemen (from *The Development of Shakespeare's Imagery*), Neely ("*The Winter's Tale*: Women and Issue"), and Barnet ("*The Winter's Tale* on the Stage"). Robert Langbaum has edited the Signet *Tempest*, which includes excerpts from William Strachey's *True Repertory of the Wrack*, Sylvester Jourdain's *Discovery of the Barmudas*, the Council of Virginia's *True Declaration of the Estate of the Colony in Virginia*, Montaigne's "Of the Cannibals," and Ovid's *Metamorphoses*, as well as commentaries by Coleridge (from *The Lectures of 1811–12*), Tillyard (from *Shakespeare's Last Plays*), Bernard Knox ("*The Tempest* and the Ancient Comic Tradition"), Reuben A. Brower ("The Mirror of Analogy: *The Tempest*"), Lorie Jerrell Leininger ("The Miranda Trap: Sexism and Racism in Shakespeare's *Tempest*"), and Barnet ("*The Tempest* on the Stage"). In addition to basic textual notes and bibliographies, each Signet edition includes the editor's introduction to the play as well as a brief general introduction, by Barnet, to Shakespeare's life, times, and theater.

By reading Ovid, Montaigne, Coleridge, and Tillyard in the Signet Classic *Tempest*, students "come to understand what a collaborative venture writing and interpreting a play of Shakespeare's is." Several respondents single out the Signet Classic *Winter's Tale* for special praise, mentioning Neely's essay in particular (which also appears in her *Broken Nuptials in Shakespeare's Plays*). Because Signet Classic editions "incorporate contemporary, theoretically driven approaches," they are especially recommended for out-of-class writing assignments. One teacher comments that "the reliable texts, solid introductions, and conveniently reprinted critical and source materials assist meeting-to-meeting discussions and allow research assignments to proceed easily." The Signet edition is the "ideal text for a Great Books course," concludes one instructor. Respondents find the Signet editions particularly useful in undergraduate Shakespeare courses. As one teacher states, "the scholarly apparatus and introductions are more than sufficient at the beginning level" and the books are "handy and inexpensive."

Kermode's introduction to the New Arden *Tempest* remains the most celebrated modern preface to the text of a Shakespeare play. It has become a model for a balanced, objective essay concisely reflecting a breadth of scholarly learning. But the New Arden introductions to *Pericles*, *Cymbeline*, and *The Winter's Tale*, written during the 1950s and early 1960s, may in places be critically outdated in a way that Kermode's is not. For example, in 1982 F. David Hoeniger published an article revising his 1963 estimate of Gower's role. Be that as it may, Hoeniger's introduction for *Pericles*, J. M. Nosworthy's for *Cymbeline*, J. H. P. Pafford's for *The Winter's Tale*, and Kermode's for *The Tempest* each describe the play's text, list dates of performances and printing, and examine major sources and historical trends of criticism. Each also puts forward the editor's critical interpretation of the special issues of the play. Hoeniger tackles the authorship problem of *Pericles*, offering a tentative solution, while Nosworthy reviews the old issue of the relation of *Cymbeline* to Beaumont and Fletcher's *Philaster*. All four New Arden editions contain appendixes. Hoeniger reprints extracts from Twine's *Pattern of Painful Adventures*; he also presents the evidence for John Day's coauthorship of parts of *Pericles*, furnishes conjectural reconstructions of vexed episodes, and suggests rearrangements of problematic verses. Nosworthy reprints extracts from Holinshed's *Historie of Scotland*, *Frederyke of Jennen*, and Thomas Underdowne's *Aethiopian Historie* and includes an analysis (contributed by Harold F. Brooks) of act 3, scene 1 of *Cymbeline* and certain passages from *The Mirror for Magistrates*. He also describes the play's stage history and two of its lyrics. Pafford reprints the complete 1595 version of Greene's *Pandosto*, describes the stage history and music and songs of *The Winter's Tale*, and analyzes four of the play's stylistic bêtes noires, including the passages about affection and nature's bastards. Kermode reprints relevant sources (Strachey's *True Repertory of the Wrack*, Jourdain's *Discovery of the Barmudas*, the Council of Virginia's *True Declaration*, Montaigne's "Of the Cannibals," and Ovid's *Metamorphoses*); analyzes Ariel as daemon and fairy; and describes the music of *The Tempest* and the play's Jacobean staging.

With only one exception, advocates of the New Arden editions recommend them for graduate Shakespeare classes. One teacher praises the quality of the text and notes but finds them "too advanced for nonmajor undergraduates." The New Arden editions are "good for seminars because there's more time to use the critical apparatus," a second instructor notes. A third teacher echoes this opinion, adding that the appended source materials contribute to the effectiveness of the New Arden texts in a seminar context. "Until the Oxford paperbacks appear," one respondent judges, "the Arden is the least condescending edition." Prospective users should be aware, however, that paperback New Arden editions sometimes disintegrate because of the "infuriatingly inadequate" gluing of the spine. The notes are the single most recommended feature of the New Arden editions. They are praised for the useful cross-references to the other plays, for the "especially rich" notes on language, and for the "technical details they contain that students need to know." It appears that a series combining the selection of critical essays and source materials seen in the Signet Classic editions with the quality of the notes in the New Arden volumes would find a wide market.

Teachers surveyed cite five additional paperback series of the individual romances. The series and the number of respondents recommending them are New Penguin (8), Bantam (6), Pelican (5), Oxford (3), and Washington Square (1).

The New Penguin editions of *Pericles* (ed. Philip Edwards), *The Winter's Tale* (ed. Schanzer), and *The Tempest* (ed. Anne Righter [Barton]) place textual commentaries and notes after the play texts. *Pericles* includes a useful map of the hero's wanderings among the ports and waters of the ancient Mediterranean; *The Winter's Tale* reprints the scores and lyrics of three of the play's six songs; *The Tempest* appends the music (score and lyrics) for "Full fathom five" and "Where the bee sucks" as well as the possible score of the music for one of the play's two dances. The Bantam editions appear in two volumes — a single edition of *The Tempest* and a collected edition of all four romances. The texts of the plays originally appeared in 1980 in Bevington's *Complete Works of Shakespeare*, but they have been reedited and substantially revised in every respect. Each romance includes selections from primary sources, an essay on the play in performance, and an annotated bibliography. Pelican paperbacks of *Pericles* (ed. James G. McManaway), *Cymbeline* (ed. Robert Heilman), *The Winter's Tale* (ed. Baldwin Maxwell), and *The Tempest* (ed. Frye) contain revised texts from the 1969 *Complete Pelican Shakespeare*. Users of the Pelican editions prefer them for the "ease of reading, consistency of editing, and the quality of the introductions and notes." One teacher of *The Tempest* suggests that "Frye's elegant introduction is good for a sophomore survey of English literature." Edited and introduced by Louis B. Wright and Virginia A. LaMar, the Washington Square paperbacks of *The Winter's Tale* and *The Tempest* include woodcuts and engravings of subjects relevant to passages in the plays and feature keys to "famous lines." The references for further reading, however, are badly out-of-date.

The text of Stephen Orgel's Oxford Shakespeare *Tempest* "is easily the best," according to one user. This edition is "good for exploring textual and other matters in greater depth." Orgel's introduction discusses the play's central issues, especially its Renaissance political context; the motifs of renunciation and resolution; and the relevance of magic, epic and history, and the Stuart masque for its images and events. Appendixes provide material on navigation for act 1, scene 1, and reprint the music and score of "Full fathom five"and "Where the bee sucks," as well as selections from the Strachey letter, Montaigne's "Of the Cannibals" and "Of Cruelty," and Ovid's *Metamorphoses* (in the English version of Arthur Golding). Several respondents look forward to the publication of Orgel's *Winter's Tale* in this series. Oxford editions may soon displace the unrevised New Arden texts.

Anthologies

Of the late romances, only *The Tempest* has been anthologized in texts appropriate for undergraduate literary surveys or introductions to literature. Frank Kermode includes the play in volume 1 of *The Oxford Anthology of English Literature*, prefaced by a brief introduction and complete with the music and score of "Full fathom five" and "Where the bee sucks." Robert Lamm, Neal Cross, and Dale Davis feature *The Tempest* in volume 2 of *The Humanities in Western Culture*, a basic anthology intended for freshmen and sophomores, and make possible the intertextual discussion of cultural issues by reprinting excerpts from Castiglione's *Courtier* and More's *Utopia* and the whole of Montaigne's essay on cannibals. *The Winter's Tale* ought eventually to find a place in a college anthology of literature.

The comments of two teachers deserve quotation as a conclusion to this survey of editions. A well-known Shakespearean writes, "I like to have students using different editions. Nothing better teaches them that the texts are edition-made than a roomful of people saying 'mine is different.'" Similarly, a Shakespearean known for her emphasis on the performance art of the plays remarks, "I like to have my students select their own texts, as long as the text is marked with act, scene, and line numbers. In this way, we naturally become aware of editors' emendations and additions. In a sophomore class I can't get into textual issues very much, but the variety in the texts causes issues to come up rather nicely." Granted the number of different texts of the romances, students allowed to choose their own editions stand a good chance of developing a lively classroom discussion.

Required and Recommended Student Readings

A significant minority of teachers surveyed believe that any required or recommended student reading detracts from time spent with the plays themselves. "At the undergraduate level," one instructor writes, "I insist on two or three *full*, careful readings of the play rather than readings of secondary critical sources." "Don't let people find substitutes for their responses and values," suggests a prominent close reader. A third teacher offers an alternative to assigning critical and background readings: "I assign productions to watch. The 'text' is a *script*. For special projects I do assign critical readings and often include a survey of production reviews from *Shakespeare Quarterly*."

Instructors who use a complete Shakespeare often assign only the separate introductions to the romances. Those who use the Riverside edition usually have students read the general introduction, which is concerned with Shakespeare's life, company, stage, and play texts. Teachers using Signet Classic paperbacks generally assign one or more of the sources and critical essays appended to the play text.

Beyond these groups, the great majority of respondents assign student readings that range from a few to twenty or thirty for a graduate class. What for one instructor are required readings for students are for another required only for instructors. Naturally this statement may be read in reverse. The following discussion lists the readings most often recommended for students and first focuses on critical readings of the romances as a group before identifying readings of individual plays.

The four most frequently mentioned book-length student readings are E. M. W. Tillyard, *Shakespeare's Last Plays*; G. Wilson Knight, *The Crown of Life: Essays in Interpretation of Shakespeare's Final Plays*; Derek A. Traversi, *Shakespeare: The Last Phase*; and Northrop Frye, *A Natural Perspective: The Development of Shakespearean Comedy and Romance* (as well as the section on romance from Frye's *Anatomy of Criticism*). These war-horses remain vital, even though they have fallen out of fashion with some teachers. In each romance Tillyard finds "the same general scheme of prosperity, destruction, and resurrection" (26), while Traversi discovers "at the heart of each . . . the corruption of an organic relationship between breakdown and reconciliation, between the divisions created in the most intimate human bonds . . . by the action of time and passion and the final healing of those divisions" (2). For both Tillyard and Traversi, the romances transcend the tragedies but owe their origins to them, especially to certain scenes in *King Lear* and *Antony and Cleopatra*. Likewise, Knight and Frye complement each other, with Knight standing closer to Tillyard and Traversi. For Knight, the romances exist within a potentially tragic context: "Their plots . . . reflect the poet's intuition of immortality and conquest within apparent death and failure" (13). Nevertheless, like Frye, Knight celebrates the romances as myth and miracle. Unlike Tillyard and Traversi, Frye links the romances to Shakespearean comedy by showing their adherence to, and variation from, a basic comic pattern derived from myth and ritual. Robert G. Hunter's *Shakespeare and the Comedy of Forgiveness* provides an appropriate conclusion to this set of readings. Like Tillyard and Traversi, Hunter traces a potentially tragic pattern of sin, suffering, and remorse; unlike Frye (whom he mentions as furnishing a contrast to his own approach), Hunter anchors romance events of forgiveness and reconciliation not in myth but in medieval religious drama and the ideas of Aquinas, Luther, and the *Book of Homilies*. A recent publication heavily indebted to Hunter's work is Cynthia Marshall's *Last Things and Last Plays: Shakespearean Eschatology*, an analysis of all four romances in the light of Elizabethan and Jacobean doctrines of apocalypse.

Frye's notion of romance is self-confessedly general, even vague. Students can gain a more specific understanding of the late plays as romances by reading Howard Felperin's *Shakespearean Romance* and Douglas L. Peterson's *Time, Tide, and Tempest: A Study of Shakespeare's Romances*. The appendix in Felperin's book, entitled "The Fortunes of Romance," surveys "the critical and sometimes theatrical history [of romance] from the viewpoint of developing romance theory" (viii). In reconstructing "the system of ideas" that informs "the 'restorative' pattern of the romances" (xii), Peterson explores an epistemological dimension of the genre of dramatic romance. E. C. Pettet's *Shakespeare and the Romance Tradition* and Carol Gesner's *Shakespeare and the Greek Romance* supplement Felperin's and Peterson's works. Pettet analyzes the late romances as based on medieval chivalric romance and traces its transformations in the comedies of John Lyly, Robert Greene, and Shakespeare himself, while Gesner reveals the plays' affinities with Heliodorus's *Aethiopica*, Achilles Tatius's *Clitophon and Leucippe*, Longus's *Daphnis and Chloe*, and other Greek romances. Barbara A. Mowat's *Dramaturgy of Shakespeare's Romances* enables students to understand how the playwright re-created his own comedy and tragedy into the tertium quid of romance. Mowat also complements Gesner's study by associating the late plays with the conventions of Greek romance. In *Shakespeare's Romances: A Study of Some Ways of the Imagination*, Hallett Smith resembles earlier critics in arguing that the romances are a "natural growth of Shakespeare's experience in writing comedy and tragedy" (x). Along with John F. Danby's *Poets on Fortune's Hill*, Smith's study incidentally gives students the clearest, most detailed grasp of the importance of Sidney's *Arcadia* for the romances.

For an understanding of the romances as tragicomedy, students could not do better than to read Joan Hartwig's *Shakespeare's Tragicomic Vision*. Marvin T. Herrick's *Tragicomedy: Its Origin and Development in Italy, France, and England* and Nancy K. Maguire's *Renaissance Tragicomedy:*

Explorations in Genre and Politics provide students with working definitions of the genre and its conventions. Of special interest are Herrick's chapter 7, "English Tragicomedy before Beaumont and Fletcher," and, in the Maguire volume, Mimi Still Dixon's "Tragicomic Recognitions: Medieval Miracles and Shakespearean Romance" and Mowat's "Shakespearean Tragicomedy." Kenneth Muir describes the romances as tragicomedies in *Shakespeare's Comic Sequence* and finds that the pattern of the plays resembles both Giovanni Battista Guarini's and John Fletcher's formulas for tragicomedy.

Assigned readings in the following books deepen students' appreciation of the growth of the romances out of Shakespearean comedy: Bertrand Evans, *Shakespeare's Comedies*; John Russell Brown, *Shakespeare and His Comedies*; and R. A. Foakes, *Shakespeare: The Dark Comedies to the Last Plays — From Satire to Celebration*. Foakes regards the romances as developing out of the satirical comedy of Shakespeare, Jonson, and Marston and the satirical tragedy of these three playwrights and Tourneur. Both Norman Rabkin, in *Shakespeare and the Common Understanding*, and Philip Edwards, in *Shakespeare and the Confines of Art*, illuminate for students the paradoxical representation of art in the romances as simultaneously nonsensical or artificial and all-powerful, the vehicle of memorable wisdom.

Those teachers wishing to focus on gender relations and questions of sexual and human identity might assign chapters of Coppélia Kahn's *Man's Estate: Masculine Identity in Shakespeare*, Marianne Novy's *Love's Argument: Gender Relations in Shakespeare*, and Carol Neely's *Broken Nuptials in Shakespeare's Plays*. (Selections from Neely's book are reprinted in two of the three Signet Classic editions of the romances.) Neely especially clarifies the incestuous overtones of certain romances, as well as the question of incest and issue in *The Winter's Tale*. Novy's chapter 9, "Transformed Images of Manhood in the Romances," complements Kahn's chapter 7, "The Providential Tempest and the Late Shakespearean Family." Additional studies of gender relations are cited below in the descriptions of often assigned student readings on individual late plays.

Two popular overviews are Frank Kermode's *William Shakespeare: The Final Plays* and Robert Adams's *Shakespeare: The Four Romances*. Kermode's brief survey, containing accounts of what happens in the plays, is particularly ideal for freshmen, sophomores, and non-English majors. Adams's pragmatic approach analyzes "the texts with a minimum of methodological apparatus" (ix). A Norton publication, Adams's book appears to have been expressly designed for use as assigned reading for students and nonscholars. The most recent overview of the late romances, one ideal for new teachers of the plays, is Elizabeth Bieman's *William Shakespeare: The Romances*, a volume in the Twayne's English Authors Series. Bieman establishes the transformational pattern of Greek romance as the basis for her Jungian and post-Jungian interpretations. Emphasizing family relationships,

Bieman examines the initiation rituals that baptize the heroes and heroines into mature sexuality. The plot summaries are also useful for students.

An assignable book-length study of *Pericles* is nonexistent at this late date in Shakespeare studies. Derick R. C. Marsh makes *Cymbeline* the center of his argument in *The Recurring Miracle: A Study of* Cymbeline *and the Last Plays*, which highlights the complex "miraculousness" of the play in a spirit (if not in a manner) reminiscent of G. Wilson Knight's. A volume on *Cymbeline*, written by Roger Warren, has appeared in the Manchester Shakespeare in Performance series. Also available is Peggy Muñoz Simonds's *Myth, Emblem, and Music in Shakespeare's* Cymbeline: *An Iconographic Reconstruction*. In addition to considering chapters on these plays in previously mentioned books such as those by Knight, Traversi, Felperin, and Peterson, teachers of *Pericles* and *Cymbeline* may want to make assignments based on the following essays. "Sidney and the Late-Shakespearean Romance" — chapter 3 of Danby's *Poets on Fortune's Hill: Studies in Sidney, Shakespeare, Beaumont and Fletcher* — remains one of the best explications of *Pericles*, especially for its adaptation of Sidneyan romance. Written in 1967, Thelma N. Greenfield's article "A Re-examination of the 'Patient' Pericles" is still popular. Readings for *Cymbeline* might include Coburn Freer's chapter on the play in *The Poetics of Jacobean Drama*, in which he admirably demonstrates how the stylistics of *Cymbeline* create dramatic character; Homer Swander's "*Cymbeline* and the 'Blameless Hero'"; Robert Y. Turner's "Slander in *Cymbeline* and Other Jacobean Tragicomedies"; and Arthur Kirsch's "*Cymbeline* and Coterie Dramaturgy."

Although badly in need of reprinting, S. L. Bethell's Winter's Tale: *A Study* offers students a reading that stands somewhere between Knight's and Frye's approaches to the romances. Bethell provides a Christian interpretation of the play's pattern of sin, repentance, and restoration. Charles Frey's *Shakespeare's Vast Romance: A Study of* The Winter's Tale and Fitzroy Pyle's Winter's Tale: *A Commentary on the Structure* represent the most comprehensive studies to date. Frey includes historical views and reviews of the play in addition to describing the "larger clusters of scenic rhythms, features of style, patterns of actions, and the like that mark out the distinctive orchestration, or drive of *The Winter's Tale*" (114). Students learn about gender relations in *The Winter's Tale* from Neely's essay, from Peter Erickson's *Patriarchal Structures in Shakespeare's Drama*, and from "Courageous Wives: *The Winter's Tale*," chapter 6 of Irene G. Dash's *Wooing, Wedding, and Power: Women in Shakespeare's Plays*. The most highly recommended essay for helping students grasp Shakespeare's use of the principal source of this play is S. R. Maveety's "What Shakespeare Did with *Pandosto*: An Interpretation of *The Winter's Tale*," in Waldo F. McNeir and Greenfield's *Pacific Coast Studies in Shakespeare*. Muir has edited a casebook on *The Winter's Tale*, while Ronald P. Draper and Wilbur Sanders accommodate the play to undergraduates with short volumes in, respectively, the Text and

Performance series and Twayne's New Critical Introductions to Shakespeare. Bill Overton's book on *The Winter's Tale* and David Daniell's volume on *The Tempest*, in the series The Critics Debate, survey the major critical approaches to the plays and contain bibliographies keyed to the various methods examined. This format is useful in suggesting topics for papers or other essays to students.

The two most often recommended book-length studies of *The Tempest* are D. G. James's *Dream of Prospero* and Gary Schmidgall's *Shakespeare and the Courtly Aesthetic*. Like many earlier commentators, James traces *The Tempest* to Shakespeare's tragedies, especially *Lear*. Chapters 3 on magic and 4 on the New World clarify these subjects in the play. Schmidgall explicates *The Tempest* with reference to the new courtly art developed by Ben Jonson and Inigo Jones. Donna Hamilton's *Virgil and* The Tempest: *The Politics of Imitation* newly assesses the art and politics of *The Tempest* and examines the political context of the play and its relation to the *Aeneid*. The collection of essays entitled *Twentieth Century Interpretations of* The Tempest, edited by Hallett Smith, reprints selections from several previously mentioned studies and includes an excellent antiromantic reading by Bonamy Dobrée. Critical and performance-art readings specially created for undergraduates are John Russell Brown's *Shakespeare:* The Tempest, David L. Hirst's book in the Text and Performance series, and D. J. Palmer's *Shakespeare*, The Tempest: *A Casebook*. Tom McCavera's study for Twayne's New Critical Introductions to Shakespeare will appear in 1992.

The most often assigned feminist essay on the play is by Lorie J. Leininger, entitled "The Miranda Trap: Sexism and Racism in Shakespeare's *Tempest*" (published in *The Woman's Part: Feminist Criticism of Shakespeare*, ed. Lenz, Greene, and Neely, and reprinted in the Signet Classic *Tempest*). Classes stressing the psychoanalytic interpretation of *The Tempest* will want to read David Sundelson's "(So Rare a Wonder'd Father): Prospero's *Tempest*" (in Schwartz and Kahn's *Representing Shakespeare: New Psychoanalytic Essays*). The most often cited new-historicist treatment is Paul Brown's " 'This Thing of Darkness I Acknowledge Mine': *The Tempest* and the Discourse of Colonialism" (in Dollimore and Sinfield's *Political Shakespeare: New Essays in Cultural Materialism*). Other essays clarifying the play's colonizing dimension are Alden Vaughan's "Shakespeare's Indian: The Americanization of Caliban"; Meredith Skura's "Discourse and the Individual: The Case of Colonialism in *The Tempest*"; and Trevor Griffiths's " 'This Island's Mine': Caliban and Colonialism." For a non-new-historicist approach to this aspect of the play, teachers might assign "The New World Savage as Stranger; or, 'Tis New to Thee,' " chapter 4 of Leslie Fiedler's study, *The Stranger in Shakespeare*.

As background reading for the romances, teachers assign certain chapters of Muir and Samuel Schoenbaum's *New Companion to Shakespeare Studies*, which deals with subjects such as the playhouses, actors and staging,

Shakespeare's reading, Shakespeare the Jacobean dramatist, Shakespeare and music, and Shakespeare and the thought of his age. Muir and Schoenbaum is more useful for the romances than Stanley Wells's *Cambridge Companion to Shakespeare Studies* (the more recent version of this text). John Andrews's *William Shakespeare: His World, His Work, His Influence* comprises fifty-nine fairly comprehensive essays by various hands on various subjects. Of particular interest to students of the romances are the essays by G. R. Elton, "The State: Government and Politics under Elizabeth and James"; Michael MacDonald, "Science, Magic, and Folklore"; Wylie Sypher, "Painting and Other Fine Arts"; John Dixon Hunt, "The Visual Arts in Shakespeare"; and John Russell Brown, "Shakespeare's Tragicomedies and Romances." Advanced students desiring a history of the period might consult Roger Lockyer, *The Early Stuarts: A Political History of England, 1603–1642*. Especially written for undergraduates, Isabel Rivers's *Classical and Christian Ideas in English Renaissance Poetry: A Students' Guide* admirably introduces and explains fourteen important topics, such as the golden age and the Garden of Eden, the pagan gods, Platonism and Neoplatonism, stoicism, Protestant theology, humanism, and allegory. (Assignable readings in the sources of the late romances are described in the next section, "The Instructor's Library.")

Material on Shakespeare's staging and principles of performance art appears in J. L. Styan's *Shakespeare's Stagecraft* and John Russell Brown's *Shakespeare's Plays in Performance*. Brown illustrates the comic performance art of the romances, especially that of *The Tempest*. Most often recommended for a grasp of theatrical issues is *The Revels History of Drama in English: Volume 3, 1576–1613* (Barroll et al.). J. Leeds Barroll writes on the social and literary context of the drama of this period, Alexander Leggatt on the companies and actors, and Richard Hosley on the playhouses (including the First Globe and the Second Blackfriars).

Finally, certain readings in world literature are sometimes assigned to illuminate aspects of the romances. Among these works are Pico della Mirandola's *Oration on the Dignity of Man* (for characterizing the positive and negative potentialities of Prospero's character); Thomas Elyot's *Governor* (for a model of Renaissance rule violated by Cymbeline, Leontes, and Prospero); John Davies's *Orchestra* (for a theory of dance applicable to the dancers of *The Winter's Tale* and especially *The Tempest*); Machiavelli's *Prince* (for political issues in the romances, especially *The Tempest*); Castiglione's *Courtier* (for violated Renaissance courtesy in *The Winter's Tale* and *The Tempest*); and Virgil's *Aeneid* (for the context of certain episodes and speeches of *The Tempest*).

The Instructor's Library

Reference Works

The standard annotated bibliography of books, articles, and reviews on Shakespeare's plays is issued by the Shakespeare Association of America as an annual number of *Shakespeare Quarterly*. Nancy Michael's *Pericles: An Annotated Bibliography* and Henry E. Jacobs's *Cymbeline: An Annotated Bibliography* have appeared as Garland Shakespeare Bibliographies. For material published before 1958, after which the annual listings in *Shakespeare Quarterly* and the *MLA International Bibliography* suffice, consult *A Shakespeare Bibliography* (1930) and the *Supplement for the Years 1930–1935*, both by Walter Ebisch with the assistance of Levin L. Schücking, and Gordon Ross Smith's *Classified Shakespeare Bibliography, 1936–1958*. Especially useful in the classroom are David M. Bergeron's *Shakespeare: A Study and Research Guide*, a bibliographical tool that contains a section on writing a research paper on a Shakespearean subject, and Stanley Wells's *Shakespeare: A Bibliographical Guide*. In a chapter in the Wells volume, Michael Taylor keys the references in his survey of play texts and critical commentary on the late romances to items in a select bibliography.

Samuel Schoenbaum's *Shakespeare's Lives* and *William Shakespeare: A Documentary Life* separate facts from fabrications. Because autobiographical speculation still buzzes about *The Tempest*, this separation remains important. An older collection of material is found in E. K. Chambers, *William Shakespeare: A Study of Facts and Problems*. Chambers's *Elizabethan Stage* (4 vols.) is a standard reference work for questions pertaining to such matters as the revels office, the control of the stage, the acting companies, and staging at court. Marvin Spevack's *Harvard Concordance to Shakespeare* is the most authoritative reference work of this kind.

Other standard reference works include Alexander Schmidt's *Shakespeare-Lexicon* and C. T. Onions's *Shakespeare Glossary*; Morris P. Tilley's *Dictionary of the Proverbs in England in the Sixteenth and Seventeenth Centuries* and R. W. Dent's *Shakespeare's Proverbial Language: An Index*; and *The Geneva Bible: A Facsimile of the 1560 Edition*.

Background Studies

This section describes historical, cultural and intellectual, and background studies of topics important for the romances. The broadest historical swaths are cut by Fernand Braudel in *The Perspective of the World*, volume 3 of *Civilization and Capitalism: Fifteenth–Eighteenth Century*, and by Perry Anderson in *Lineages of the Absolutist State*. Social and political histories of Renaissance England have been written by Keith Wrightson, *English Society, 1580–1680*; Christopher Hill, *Reformation to Industrial Revolution: A Social and Economic History of Britain, 1530–1780*; Godfrey Davies, *The Early Stuarts, 1603–1660*; and J. P. Sommerville, *Politics and Ideology in England, 1603–1640*. Hill includes chapters on religion and intellectual revolutions of the Elizabethan and Stuart periods. Sommerville's study updates that of Davies.

The two best works for getting a sense of what it was like to live day to day in Shakespeare's London are William Ingram, *A London Life in the Brazen Age: Francis Langley, 1548–1602* and Russell Fraser, *Young Shakespeare*. While these books do not extend to the period of the romances, they capture details of quotidian life that generally hold true for that time also. Of special importance for the romances are Lawrence Stone's *Crisis of the Aristocracy: 1558–1641* and *Family, Sex, and Marriage in England, 1500–1800*. Stone's studies have become required reading for Shakespeareans interested in questions of Renaissance patriarchy, gender relations, the value attached to the nuclear family, the place of women, different attitudes toward sex, and the aristocracy's view of these and other cultural matters. (Nevertheless, David Cressy has demonstrated that Stone's findings sometimes require major qualification.) For Renaissance popular culture, Anthony Fletcher and John Stevenson's *Order and Disorder in Early Modern England* is excellent.

At this late date in Shakespeare studies, E. M. W. Tillyard's *Elizabethan World Picture* is useful for teachers either as an example of the analogical reasoning prevalent in the period and important for the dramatist or (as one respondent put it) as "a collection of static assumptions to be destabilized" by gender-based, new-historicist, and cultural-materialist approaches. Still of interest are the first chapters of Basil Willey, *The Seventeenth Century Background* — "The Rejection of Scholasticism" and "Bacon and the Rehabilitation of Nature." Herschel Baker's *Wars of Truth* traces the decay of Christian humanism in the early seventeenth century. The chapter titles of Hiram Haydn's study *The Counter-Renaissance* indicate its greater relevance to the romances: "The Vanity of Learning"; "Montaigne"; "Universal Law Repealed"; "Magic and the Secrets of Nature"; "Empiricism and the Facts of Nature"; "Toward 'A True Model of the World': Francis Bacon" are all topics of special significance to *Cymbeline*, *The Winter's Tale*, and *The Tempest*. One respondent observes that, in general, the romances (with the possible exception of *Pericles*) depict various "rebellions against the broad central tradition of Christian humanism" — Haydn's subject. Teachers interested in additional intellectual-background studies should consult William R. Elton's *Shakespeare's World: Renaissance Intellectual Contexts*, a selective, annotated bibliography for the years 1966–71.

David Hirst's *Tragicomedy* offers background reading for teachers concerned with this generic approach to the romances. Teachers seeking a better knowledge of the structures of the romances should read the appropriate sections of James E. Hirsh's *Structure of Shakespearean Scenes* and Mark Rose's *Shakespearean Design*. Hirsh illustrates Shakespeare's scenic architecture with reference to twenty-five different scenes from the romances, while Rose presents a superb diagram of the scenic symmetry of *The Tempest*. Those interested in the plays as romances might consult Roderick Beaton, *The Medieval Greek Romance*, which provides a bridge between Gesner's and Pettet's studies. Wylie Sypher's classic *Four Stages of Renaissance Style* and Frank J. Warnke's *Versions of Baroque* explore contexts for understanding the mannerist and baroque features of the romances. The best background studies for the pastoral art of the romances are Renato Poggioli's *Oaten Flute* and Andrew V. Ettin's *Literature and the Pastoral*. Enid Welsford's *Court Masque* and selected masques of Ben Jonson illuminate masquelike scenes of *The Winter's Tale* and *The Tempest*. Jonson's *Masque of Queens*, in Stephen Orgel's *Ben Jonson: The Complete Masques*, is especially recommended, mainly because it includes the first full-blown Jonsonian antimasque, a feature of this subgenre recently identified in the latter two Shakespearean romances.

Teachers interested in colonial and imperial dimensions of *The Tempest* would do well to read Stephen Greenblatt's essay "Learning to Curse: Aspects of Linguistic Colonialism in the Sixteenth Century," in Fredi Chiappelli's *First Images of America*; Boies Penrose's "Early Colonization of North America," in his *Travel and Discovery in the Renaissance, 1420–1620*; and Richard Marienstras's "Elizabethan Travel Literature and Shakespeare's *The Tempest*," in his *New Perspectives on the Shakespearean World*. Marienstras's study is also useful for clarifying, in the words of one instructor, the "legal and social implications of the 'foreign' in Shakespeare's England" as well as "the concepts of 'far' and 'near' and how their definitions affected Tudor and Stuart Britain." Instructors desiring a better grasp of new historicism should read the essays by Greenblatt and Louis Montrose in H. Aram Veeser's *New Historicism*.

Those wishing background for a feminist or gender-oriented approach to the romances might consult Linda Woodbridge's *Women and the English Renaissance*, Katherine Usher Henderson and Barbara F. McManus's *Half Humankind: Contexts and Texts of the Controversy about Women in England, 1540–1640*, and Ian Maclean's *Renaissance Notion of Woman*.

Theatrical Studies

Two essential background works on Shakespeare's dramaturgy, stage, and acting practices are Bernard Beckerman's *Shakespeare at the Globe, 1599–1609* and Irwin Smith's *Shakespeare's Blackfriars Playhouse*. Since certain romances may have been acted at both the Globe and Blackfriars, these studies complement each other. While mainly updating Beckerman's work,

Peter Thomson's *Shakespeare's Theatre* contains a chapter about the decision of the King's Men to repossess the second Blackfriars playhouse and about the differences between the Globe and Blackfriars stages. Herbert Berry's *Shakespeare's Playhouses* describes the design and use of the Theatre in Shoreditch and the stage and boxes of Blackfriars and contains three chapters on the Globe concerning its documents and ownership, a lawsuit, and reviews of performances after Shakespeare's death. Berry also has a handlist of documents pertaining to the Theatre in Shoreditch. For a general overview of companies, players, playhouses, staging, and audiences, instructors highly recommend Andrew Gurr's *Shakespearean Stage, 1574–1642*. Gurr's *Playgoing in Shakespeare's London* and Ann Jennalie Cook's *Privileged Playgoers of Shakespeare's London, 1576–1642* provide fascinating information on playgoing and the makeup of Shakespeare's audiences. Gurr's chapter on the mental composition of playgoers is especially suggestive. Finally, J. L. Styan's *Shakespeare Revolution* includes an essay on the ways different generations have performed the romances, which is also the subject of Dennis Bartholomeusz in The Winter's Tale *in Performance in England and America, 1611–1976*.

Source and Textual Studies

The authoritative collection of sources and analogues for the romances is Geoffrey Bullough's multivolume *Narrative and Dramatic Sources of Shakespeare*, volume 6 for *Pericles* and volume 8 for the other romances. In his Oxford Shakespeare *Tempest*, Orgel points out that selected passages from Virgil's *Aeneid* are missing from Bullough's collection of sources and analogues for this play. This absence constitutes the only major criticism of Bullough's work. For other collections of sources, see the earlier review of the Signet Classic and New Arden editions of the romances.

A basic understanding of the text of a Shakespearean play is provided by G. Blakemore Evans's essay "Shakespeare's Text," in *The Riverside Shakespeare*. More advanced treatments of the subject appear in W. W. Greg, *The Editorial Problem in Shakespeare: A Survey of the Foundations of the Text*, and in Stanley Wells and Gary Taylor, *William Shakespeare: A Textual Companion*. Also useful is Charlton Hinman's two-volume *Printing and Proofreading of the First Folio of Shakespeare*, mainly because the authoritative texts of *Cymbeline, The Winter's Tale*, and *The Tempest* derive from this original edition of collected plays. Only *Pericles* (not included in First Folio) appeared in a quarto volume, which unfortunately represents one of the most vexed bibliographic problems in all Shakespeare.

Teachers may examine the First Folio texts of three of the last romances in Hinman's *First Folio of Shakespeare: The Norton Facsimile*. Instructors wishing to compare a version of *Pericles* in a student edition with the complete 1609 quarto text should consult Michael J. B. Allen and Kenneth Muir's

Shakespeare's Plays in Quarto: A Facsimile Edition of Copies Primarily from the Henry E. Huntington Library. The most complete accounts of this problematic quarto text are given by F. D. Hoeniger in the New Arden *Pericles* and by Wells and Taylor in *William Shakespeare: A Textual Companion.* Wells and Taylor supply the most comprehensive scene and line textual notes and lists of quarto or folio stage directions not only for *Pericles* but also for the other three romances.

Critical and Linguistic Studies

Studies placing the romances in the context of Shakespearean tragedy are Orgel's "New Uses of Adversity: Tragic Experience in *The Tempest*"; John P. Cutts's *Rich and Strange: A Study of Shakespeare's Last Plays*; and Robert Uphaus's *Beyond Tragedy: Structure and Experience in Shakespeare's Romances.* Cutts argues that Shakespeare "outgrew" the genre of romance in the process of writing the late plays and that their realistic elements make them nonromantic, while Uphaus identifies five ways the plays represent and enact a realm of experience "beyond tragedy." Although criticized for distorting Shakespeare through the lens of post–World War II pessimism, Jan Kott's reading of *The Tempest*, in *Shakespeare Our Contemporary*, complements the above studies by crystallizing the play's antiromantic elements. Kott finds tragic history sadly repeating itself at the end of the play. G. Wilson Knight's chapter "The Final Plays," in *The Shakespearian Tempest*, provides an antidote to darker views. In a more concentrated way than in Knight's *Crown of Life*, this essay reveals how music rectifies the tragic tempest afflicting romance characters. Approaching *The Winter's Tale* and *The Tempest* through audience response, Michael Goldman's *Shakespeare and the Energies of Drama* provides fine metatheatrical readings.

The most noteworthy collections of critical essays are Carol McGinnis Kay and Henry Jacobs, *Shakespeare's Romances Reconsidered*; John Russell Brown and Bernard Harris, *Later Shakespeare*; D. J. Palmer, *Shakespeare's Later Comedies*; and Richard C. Tobias and Paul Zolbrod, *Shakespeare's Late Plays.* Harold Bloom has assembled and introduced mainly familiar essays in *William Shakespeare's* The Winter's Tale and *William Shakespeare's* The Tempest for the Modern Critical Interpretations series. Of these books, the most helpful is the Kay and Jacobs volume, which includes articles by Norman Sanders, Northrop Frye, Howard Felperin, Cyrus Hoy, Joan Hartwig, Charles Frey, David Bergeron, and David Young. Particularly useful are Frye's "Romance as Masque," Hoy's "Fathers and Daughters in Shakespeare's Romances," and Young's "Where the Bee Sucks: A Triangular Study of *Doctor Faustus, The Alchemist,* and *The Tempest.*" Wells's "Shakespeare and Romance," Bernard Harris's " 'What's Past is Prologue': *Cymbeline* and *Henry VIII*," and Philip Brockbank's "*The Tempest*: Conventions of Art and Empire" recommend Brown and Harris's *Later Shakespeare.*

Brockbank's essay is cited repeatedly by Orgel in his introduction to the Oxford *Tempest*. Deserving more praise than it has received, Tobias and Zolbrod's volume *Shakespeare's Late Plays* includes papers by L. C. Knights on *The Tempest*, Muir on the theophanies of the romances, and Andrew Welsh on heritage in *Pericles*. This last essay is particularly perceptive.

The pastoral art of the romances has been richly served. A pioneering study of *The Tempest* as an American pastoral appears in Leo Marx's *Machine in the Garden*. Especially recommended are Thomas McFarland, *Shakespeare's Pastoral Comedy*; David Young, *The Heart's Forest: A Study of Shakespeare's Pastoral Plays*; and Edward Tayler, *Nature and Art in Renaissance Literature*. Young links the pastoral of the romances with an "inverted" pastoral, Lear's heath, providing another association between the romances and the tragedies. Tayler's chapter on *The Winter's Tale* focuses on the notorious art and nature debate of act 4, placing the pastoral aspect of that topic within classical, medieval, and Spenserian contexts. Chapters 6 and 7 of Rosalie L. Colie's *Shakespeare's Living Art* are especially good on the "hard" pastoral of *Cymbeline* and round out an understanding of this topic. Instructors who wish to consider the late romances — especially *The Tempest* — as antipastoral literature should consult Peter Lindenbaum's *Changing Landscapes: Anti-pastoral Sentiment in the English Renaissance*.

Psychoanalytic (and postpsychoanalytic) readings have also proved fertile ground for teachers of the romances. The most celebrated study is chapter 10 of C. L. Barber and Richard Wheeler's book *The Whole Journey: Shakespeare's Power of Development*. Like Coppélia Kahn, Barber and Wheeler get at the importance of the feminine through literary psychoanalysis and brilliantly demonstrate Shakespeare's reconstruction in the romances of the "sacred" family, especially woman's place in it. They also provide an excellent account of the romances' relation to *Antony and Cleopatra*, *Timon of Athens*, and *Coriolanus*. Other psychoanalytic approaches are found in David Sundelson's *Shakespeare's Restorations of the Father* and Kay Stockholder's *Dream Works: Lovers and Families in Shakespeare's Plays*. While Sundelson treats only *The Tempest*, Stockholder in three chapters applies dream theory to all four romances and regards each play's action as dreamwork. Murray Schwartz and Coppélia Kahn's *Representing Shakespeare: New Psychoanalytic Essays* includes an early version of Sundelson's essay on *The Tempest*; the chapter "The Providential Tempest and the Shakespearean Family" from Kahn's *Man's Estate*; and perhaps the best article of this kind on *Cymbeline*, Meredith Skura's "Interpreting Posthumus' Dream from Above and Below: Families, Psychoanalysts, and Literary Critics." In *Shakespeare's Other Language*, Ruth Nevo reads the romances in terms of postpsychoanalytic semiotics. Nevo's analysis of the logic of unconscious speech complements the discussion in Stockholder. Making phenomenology psychological, Thomas W. MacCary's chapter "The Late Romances," in his *Friends and Lovers: The Phenomenology of Desire in*

Shakespearean Comedy, concerns a life-consuming narcissism of the self within the plays' principal characters.

Regarding gender studies, Lisa Jardine's *Still Harping on Daughters: Women and Drama in the Age of Shakespeare* warrants mention here for its analysis of the romances (except for *The Tempest*), even though the book's treatment of heroic womanhood easily qualifies as cultural-background reading for the teacher of the late plays. Primarily intended as an analysis of feminine cosmic principles and archetypes of the feminine in *Pericles* and *The Winter's Tale,* Stevie Davies's *Idea of Woman in Renaissance Literature* incidentally includes an excellent analysis of the language of *Pericles* and the best available application of Greek and Eastern mythologies to this play. Peter Erickson, in *Patriarchal Structures in Shakespeare's Drama,* explores the political implications of gender and the limitations of reformed masculinity in *The Winter's Tale.* In a long chapter on the romances in *The Patriarchy of Shakespeare's Comedies,* Marilyn Williamson explicates the power inherent in family relationships in their historical context. Her work provides a transition to the next approach.

The most remarkable new-historicist readings of the romances to date are Bergeron's *Shakespeare's Romances and the Royal Family* and Leah S. Marcus's rich chapter on *Cymbeline* in *Puzzling Shakespeare: Local Reading and Its Discontents.* Locating the romances in the dynamics of James I's family, Bergeron alludes frequently to Jacobean royal history. Quite simply, Marcus's reading of *Cymbeline* as Shakespeare's qualified argument for James's union of Scotland and England dazzles. New historicism, like literary psychoanalysis, on occasion allegorizes components of the work (a tendency explicitly present in Marcus's reading). A. D. Nuttall's *Two Concepts of Allegory: A Study of Shakespeare's* The Tempest *and the Logic of Allegorical Expression* can help teachers decide if practitioners of this recent approach have committed the old sin of critics who allegorized *The Tempest* in terms of the mind's faculties or Shakespeare's autobiography. Complementing Marcus's localizing Shakespeare as a historical and cultural product is Francis Barker and Peter Hulme's "Nymphs and Reapers Heavily Vanish: The Discursive Con-texts of *The Tempest,*" an essay in John Drakakis's *Alternative Shakespeares.* Steven Mullaney concludes *The Place of the Stage: License, Play, and Power in Renaissance England* with a materialist analysis of romance, theatricality, and marketplace dynamics in *Pericles.* Teachers of the romances who prefer an alternative historicism (one neither new nor old) might read Frances A. Yates's *Shakespeare's Last Plays: A New Approach* and Glynne Wickham's "Romance and Emblem: A Study in the Dramatic Structure of *The Winter's Tale.*" Yates finds hermetic influences emanating from Giordano Bruno and John Dee, while Wickham argues that *The Winter's Tale* comments on the investiture of Henry Stuart as prince of Wales and heir apparent to a reunited England, Wales, and Scotland.

Descriptions of the magic (or "science") of *The Tempest* inevitably either mystify it by reference to Neoplatonic or theurgistic traditions or render it more familiar by comparing it to the contemporary practice of Renaissance jugglers and street magicians. The first strain originates in chapter 6 of Walter Clyde Curry's *Shakespeare's Philosophical Patterns*. In *Renaissance Magic and the Return of the Golden Age*, John Mebane develops this line of argument by emphasizing the occult tradition of hermetic and cabalistic magic in Prospero's art. Barbara H. Traister's *Heavenly Necromancers: The Magician in English Renaissance Drama* stresses the similarity of Prospero's magic to that of classical and medieval wizards and Renaissance entertainers. An account of more realistic analogues to Prospero's magic is given in Barbara Mowat's article "Prospero, Agrippa, and Hocus Pocus." By placing Prospero's magic within the context of metatheatrical criticism, Alvin B. Kernan in *The Playwright as Magician* provides another way of teaching the magic of *The Tempest*.

In *Shifting Perspectives and the Stylish Style: Mannerism in Shakespeare and His Jacobean Contemporaries*, John Greenwood describes the mannerist style of the romances. Alternatively, Patrick Cruttwell in *The Shakespearean Moment* defines the metaphysical style of these plays, placing Shakespeare's drama in the context of that style's cultural development at the end of the sixteenth and beginning of the seventeenth century. In *Shakespeare's Romance of the Word*, Maurice Hunt applies Baconian linguistics, J. L. Austin's and John Searle's speech-act theories, the Sapir-Whorf hypothesis, and linguistic contextualism to an analysis of the language of the romances. In chapter 7 of *Shakespeare's Wordplay*, M. M. Mahood shows how the wordplay of *The Winter's Tale* is a key to its deep structure. An excellent essay that makes the same point, this time in terms of the play's poetry, is Russ McDonald's "Poetry and Plot in *The Winter's Tale*." (McDonald's essay on the style of *The Tempest* appears in the 1990 volume of *Shakespeare Survey*, a collection of essays devoted primarily to the romances.) The authoritative study of the metrics of the romances appears in George Wright's *Shakespeare's Metrical Art*.

Aids to Teaching

Pericles, Cymbeline, and *The Winter's Tale* are on videocassette only in the BBC-TV/Time-Life series, but several video productions of *The Tempest* including one by the BBC are available. In the words of one survey respondent, David Jones's BBC *Pericles* "is magnificent. It captures the 'mystery' and 'distance' that are essential to the play." Teachers also praise Jane Howell's BBC *Winter's Tale* but with only a single exception consider John Gorrie's BBC *Tempest* uninspiring and "deeply flawed." Two other television versions on videocassette are the 1960 Hallmark Hall of Fame production, directed by George Schaefer and starring Maurice Evans, Lee Remick, and Richard Burton (as Caliban), and the 1983 Bard production, directed by William Woodman and starring Efrem Zimbalist, Jr., and William Bassett. According to a veteran commentator on film versions of Shakespeare's plays, "none of the 'complete' versions is particularly successful. TV has not proved a good vehicle for this script."

Several teachers recommend *Tempest*, an adaptation directed by Paul Mazursky and starring John Cassavetes, Gena Rowlands, Molly Ringwald, and Susan Sarandon; it helped one viewer recognize the strain of violence in Shakespeare's play. Another adaptation, *Prospero's Books*, directed by Peter Greenaway and featuring John Gielgud as Prospero, Michael Clark as Caliban, and Michel Blanc as Alonso, identifies Prospero as Shakespeare. He writes the play's text and speaks all the lines until the final act, when the characters, forgiven, are allowed to speak. *The Forbidden Planet* is a sci-fi takeoff on *The Tempest*, directed by Fred McLeod Wilcox and starring Walter Pidgeon and Leslie Nielsen. One instructor notes that, in focusing on the Hollywood adaptation's version of Freudian theory, a student "explained how the Renaissance understanding of psychology differs from that of the twentieth century and how contemporary theories change the way we understand Prospero's relationship with Miranda."

Caedmon audiocassette recordings of all four romances are available (see Sackler; Wood, in "Audiovisual Materials"). Recordings of all four plays by the Marlowe Society and Professional Players will be reissued on audiocassette by Decca Records, London.

Complete ordering information appears in the "Audiovisual Materials" section of the Works Cited listing.

NOTE: Citations in this volume are from the Evans edition, with the following exceptions: Aercke (Righter ed.), Campbell (Pafford ed.), Forker (Bevington ed.), Halio (Wells and Taylor ed.), Kinney (Langbaum ed.), Willson (Bevington ed.).

Part Two

APPROACHES

INTRODUCTION

With few exceptions, those instructors who teach two of the romances in a semester select *The Winter's Tale* and *The Tempest*, believing that their dramaturgy and motifs can more easily be linked to earlier Shakespearean plays than can corresponding elements in *Pericles* and *Cymbeline*. One teacher comments that for students *The Winter's Tale* and *The Tempest* produce "both a sense of Shakespeare's development — the totality of his work — and an awareness of the metacritical element of his art. The foregrounding of artifice is indispensable in raising questions of art and its relation to a reality most students take for granted." (Unless indicated, quotations are from survey respondents.) These romances "offer more opportunity for philosophical speculation and for interpretive range than do *Pericles* and *Cymbeline*." Many instructors teach the best known of the romances because the pattern of sin, suffering, repentance, and forgiveness seems clearer in them than in *Pericles* and *Cymbeline*. Others note the complexity of *The Winter's Tale* and *The Tempest*. One instructor remarks that *The Winter's Tale* compares within itself a worldview of classical Greece with that of the Christian Renaissance. This play offers an opportunity to focus on father-daughter relationships and to raise the issue of women's mobility in sixteenth- and seventeenth-century England. *The Tempest* allows students to understand "submerged social unrest in England" and the repercussions of "New World exploration and nascent colonialism and imperialism."

The Winter's Tale and *The Tempest* represent contrary dramatic experiences: "*The Tempest*'s concentration, political harshness, and bitter skeptical joy contrast with *The Winter's Tale*'s expansiveness, romance treatment of politics, and fullness of measured happiness." An instructor interested in Fletcherian tragicomedy considers *The Winter's Tale* the "best illustration of tragicomedy as a genre. This romance can be related to earlier romantic and problem comedies, so that students see the essential comic form of the genre as well as the potentially tragic complications. The comparative view of genre helps them make sense of *The Tempest*, which is not as clearly 'tragicomic' in structure as *The Winter's Tale*."

Some instructors who teach the two late plays in the same course pair *Pericles* with either *The Winter's Tale* or *The Tempest*. "*Pericles*, as the prototype or trial run for the later, greater plays, is good preparation for them." A respondent who teaches *Cymbeline*, *The Winter's Tale*, and *The Tempest* in the same course writes, "I usually present a working definition of a romance in dramatic form with *Cymbeline* and introduce Robert Uphaus's theory that *Cymbeline* is a parody of the traditional romance. I regret the omission of *Pericles* but feel I would need to go into complications of authorship and sources if I taught it." Teaching *Pericles* or *Cymbeline* (or both) with the greater romances has one advantage: "The romances taken as a whole provide the opportunity to observe in a nutshell the development of a genre." In this respect, unlike Shakespearean comedy, tragedy, or history, they lend themselves to the graduate or upper-division seminar.

Most instructors selecting only one romance for their Shakespeare course choose *The Winter's Tale* or *The Tempest*. The majority favor *The Tempest* for its fully realized artistry and its status as a relatively brief but rich summation of Shakespeare's intellectual interests and artistic practices. *The Tempest* "recapitulates and transmutes many earlier themes and devices" and provides an end (and resolution) to the revenge motif in previously assigned tragedies. Moreover, Shakespeare here "achieves a fusion of all the arts (what Apollinaire would call 'syncretic art')." This romance "best displays many of the thematics we will have studied (especially the notions of what it is to be human and the relation of word to action), and its high theatricality completes our examination of Shakespeare the poet who chose to be a playwright." Other reasons for selecting only *The Tempest* involve its "simplicity of plot," Shakespeare's use of the classical unities, his "knowledge of contemporary literature in contradistinction to his use of past sources," his "economical artistry," and the play's "political overtones of freedom and authority." Respondents also note that "*The Tempest* is a remarkable précis of Shakespeare's career," that it "raises issues of colonialism," and that there are three versions on videocassette, plus the "wonderful" 1982 San Francisco Ballet performance. One colleague prefers *The Tempest* because "it brings together the issues and motifs of the earlier romances and makes visible the ways in which the pressures of unresolved ideological conflicts force Shakespeare into the fairy-tale and magical worlds of romantic comedy."

Instructors teaching only *The Winter's Tale* in their Shakespeare course do so partly because the play contrasts well with *Othello*. One teacher regards *The Winter's Tale* "as a kind of answer to *Othello* (the latter play being especially valuable to black students)." *The Winter's Tale* "can strike home to students, who know what sexual jealousy and absolute rule are about." A few instructors consider this romance the most typical and successful of the late plays. With the exception of one instructor who makes the rococo art of *Cymbeline* the culmination of a sequence including the neoclassical *Julius Caesar* and baroque *Antony and Cleopatra*, none of the ninety-three respondents would select either *Pericles* or *Cymbeline* if limited to a single romance in the course.

When teachers systematically compare one or more of the romances with earlier works of Shakespeare's, the old argument that the romances grow out of certain scenes and values in *King Lear* and *Antony and Cleopatra* prevails. Certain transfiguring moments in these tragedies, notably the reunions of Lear and Cordelia and the apotheosis of Antony and Cleopatra's romantic love, provide the dramaturgy for father-daughter relationships and for unanticipated reunions in the romances. In addition to introducing the art-and-nature issue that figures prominently in certain romances, *Antony and Cleopatra* resembles the later plays in its "rhetoric and meditations on imagination and identity" and "intertwining threads of witchcraft and the monstrous." Comparing aspects of the romances with certain features of Shakespearean tragedy proves fruitful: "Tragedies that can naturally be juxtaposed to the romances include *Hamlet* (the sea 'journey' is crucial to reconstituting the main character we meet in act 5) and *King Lear* (Lear's experience on the heath is a kind of 'dark pastoral,' as David Young argues in *The Heart's Forest*)." Both *Hamlet* and *The Tempest* present "the theme of revenge and of principals who are playmakers." The first half of *The Winter's Tale* appears to reprise the seduction and fall of Othello: "I stress the difference between Leontes and Othello as jealous lovers and how Shakespeare's depiction of Leontes seems darker, even Calvinistic, since Leontes falls into utter depravity because of something in himself, not because of an outside agent such as Iago." *The Winter's Tale* is "a useful model for discussion of the 'sudden break' plot: in *Romeo and Juliet*, the death of Mercutio drops the curtain on comedy; Antigonus's demise sets the scene for comedy."

When Shakespearean comedy provides the basis for comparison, teachers generally link *The Tempest* with *A Midsummer Night's Dream* and *Measure for Measure*. All three plays chart the development of a stage-manager character with special powers. In *Dream* Shakespeare's emphasis on imagination and magic invites comparison with *The Tempest*. As one instructor notes, "Some useful comparisons can be made with *A Midsummer Night's Dream*: Oberon and Puck; Prospero and Ariel; the plays within; and Caliban, Stephano, Trinculo and Bottom and Company." "I begin with *Dream* and close with *The Tempest*," another respondent writes, "to take the class from the deceptive complexity of a four-plot but clearly hierarchic structure to the more baffling simplicity of Shakespeare's seemingly most unified play. Since we earlier do *Macbeth*, students also examine Shakespeare's interest in magic, as metaphor and fact." One teacher begins with *Twelfth Night*, then uses *The Winter's Tale* and *The Tempest* "to unify the course around the topos of the shipwrecked heroine and the themes of reunion and forgiveness." Several teachers assign *Much Ado about Nothing* and *Othello* to provide examples of other stagings of jealousy and the slandered-woman motif for comparison with those elements in *Cymbeline* and *The Winter's Tale*. Occasionally *Love's Labor's Lost* is paired with *Dream* for comparison with *The Tempest*. All three plays might be taught "largely as occasional, court-oriented plays," which make possible a discussion of "reflexive references to plays and playwriting."

Some respondents group the late romances and other Shakespearean plays so as to cut across the grain of genre. On issues of justice and tragicomedy, *The Tempest* might be compared with *2 Henry IV* and *Measure for Measure*. Moreover, "*The Tempest* compares interestingly with *Titus Andronicus*, *The Merchant of Venice*, and *Othello*, if a class reads Caliban as one of Shakespeare's aliens." "I have taught *The Tempest* in the context of the history plays," one teacher writes; "governance and servitude are common subjects, but the rifts of history and politics are healed by Prospero's renunciation of power as well as by the voluntary union of Ferdinand and Miranda." "I compare *Hamlet*, *Lear*, and *Troilus and Cressida* with *The Tempest*," another respondent concludes, "because it incorporates the tragic and satiric visions found in the problem play."

When asked to identify the problems facing teachers of the romances, respondents most often describe the difficulty of convincing students to take the "unrealistic" dramaturgy of the romance mode seriously. Here are some examples of respondents' phrasing of the main pedagogical challenge: "getting students to accept romance on its own terms is an obstacle, particularly since romance does not translate well to TV"; "students are so bound to the Aristotelian notion of action that it is hard to convince them of the theatrical effectiveness of 'slow' plays"; "the last plays are not congruent with students' realist or psychologistic assumptions about the nature of drama"; "students find the romance qualities unsettling, if not distasteful; they see the ending of *The Winter's Tale* as a cop-out or insist that the return of Hermione must be a dream sequence in Leontes's senile head"; "the hurdle is acknowledging the soap-opera plots, uncertainties of text and authorship, and undeveloped characters while seeing the plays as worthy of critical examination."

Making certain spectacles and highly artificial components of the late plays understandable in the classroom is equally problematic. These features include the masque of Ceres in *The Tempest*, the theoretical context in which Time appears and the sheep-shearing festival in *The Winter's Tale*, and the magical and mystical visions and the presence throughout of a medieval poet, Gower, in *Pericles*. Students often cannot distinguish the symbolic dimensions of the plays from the literal or realistic ones; they have difficulty developing "multileveled perspectives." Any Shakespeare play requires this kind of manifold awareness if it is to be comprehensively appreciated, and the romances, with their rich mixtures of realistic, romantic, and allegorical elements, especially demand this way of knowing.

Other challenges involve the language, characterization, and providential design of the romances. The pedagogical obstacle posed by the plays' providential design takes several forms, but religion invariably enters the picture. One instructor cites the struggle of students to comprehend the plays' focus on "the place of the supernatural or 'divine' in human lives." "It's difficult to expect a college senior to have thought enough about the world-historical effects of Christianity to understand many aspects of *Cymbeline*," a second teacher concludes. A third instructor cautions that, while the romances "are deeply spiritual plays, allegories of faith, if you will," they are "far from exercises in didactic Christianity." Because the plays are "serene, titanic, and bespeak a life of suffering and fulfillment," undergraduates must grope to appreciate them. One respondent judges that "students would need to have suffered more of the losses of growing up and growing old to be fully receptive to the visionary reach and alchemical poetics of Shakespeare's 'message.'"

Relatively more idealized and less "three-dimensional" than the characters of Shakespearean tragedy, the personages of the romances strain the ability of many students to suspend disbelief willingly. They "find it difficult to like some of the characters. They hate Leontes and think he does not get what he deserves." "Students often dislike Prospero," another respondent notes, "because they see him as manipulative and vindictive. Sometimes this dislike carries over to the play itself." Because Shakespeare's method of characterization in the romances is "less stringently 'organic,'" students may not grasp principles of romance characterization, to say nothing of the Renaissance notions of psychology on which some phases of character development are based. "Some students, conditioned to be dazzled only by the 'special effects' of technological magic, find it difficult to accept the method the women use to set things straight — call it 'natural magic,' after Shakespeare."

Teachers differ on whether the poetic language of the late plays is more difficult to teach than the poetry and prose of other Shakespearean plays. Those who find that the language of the romances presents special problems focus on its greater richness, especially its metaphoric condensation. "Though sonorous, the self-conscious poetry is a 'hard sell.'" For some, the romantic conventions contextualizing the language of the romances compound the difficulty. Nevertheless, "the enormous importance of auditory experience" for the characters in the romances, especially in *The Tempest*, makes overcoming students' discomfort with the language particularly important.

Other pedagogical impediments may be briefly mentioned. "It is most challenging to present the plays as actively engaged in the ideological debates of the period, without turning drama into flat allegory." Teachers cite the "background (Jamesian production at court)" and the "political dynamics — the problem of authority, familial and national." These relate to the general problem of teaching the baroque and to "the cultural contexts and knowledge (e.g., biblical, mythological) that an audience of Shakespeare knew intimately." One instructor mentions that "certain issues of gender and racism are particularly difficult: the father's anxiety in the father-daughter relationship, the importance of chastity before marriage, the fear of aging, the need to give up power and domination" and the "valedictory tone" of *The Tempest*.

The present volume addresses many of these challenges. Jay L. Halio's "The Late Plays as the Fulfillment of Shakespeare's Tragic Pattern," Robert F. Willson's "Enframing Style and the Father-Daughter Theme in Early Shakespearean Comedy and Late Romance," and Kay Stockholder's "Shakespeare's Magic and Its Discontents: Approaching *The Tempest*" help instructors link the romances to Shakespeare's earlier plays. Michael Mooney's "Defining the Dramaturgy of the Late Romances" suggests an approach to persuading realistically minded students to understand some of Shakespeare's romance conventions in the late plays. Bruce W. Young's "Teaching the Unrealistic Realism of *The Winter's Tale*" focuses on overcoming this obstacle through imaginative classroom discussion. "'An Odd Angle of the Isle': Teaching the Courtly Art of *The Tempest*," by Kristiaan P. Aercke, offers ideas for clarifying the baroque features of the play. The special characterization and character configurations of the romances are partly the subjects of Gary Waller's "The Late Plays as Family Romance," Dorothea Kehler's "Teaching the Slandered Women of *Cymbeline* and *The Winter's Tale*," and Cynthia Lewis's "Teaching 'A Thing Perplex'd': Drawing Unity from the Confusion of *Cymbeline*." Political and cultural dimensions — both Renaissance and modern — are illuminated by Donna Hamilton's "Shakespeare's Romances and Jacobean Political Discourse," Douglas L. Peterson's "The Utopias of *The Tempest*," and William Morse's "A Metacritical and Historical Approach to *The Winter's Tale* and *The Tempest*." Ways of teaching the performance art of the late plays are presented by Kathleen Campbell in "Making the Statue Move: Teaching Performance" and by Hugh Richmond in "Teaching *The Tempest* and the Late Plays by Performance." Herbert R. Coursen's "Using Film and Television to Teach *The Winter's Tale* and *The Tempest*" complements Campbell's and Richmond's approaches. Charles R. Forker's "Negotiating the Paradoxes of Art and Nature in *The Winter's Tale*," William W. E. Slights's "Trusting Shakespeare's *Winter's Tale*: Metafiction in the Late Plays," and Arthur F. Kinney's "Teaching *The Tempest* as the Art of 'If'" introduce especially original ways of approaching the two most frequently taught romances.

Each reader of these essays will have his or her own candidate for either the most practical or imaginative approach to teaching one or more of the late romances. Given the quality of these papers, he or she will perceive that a single essay often possesses both virtues.

THE LATE ROMANCES

The Late Plays as the Fulfillment of Shakespeare's Tragic Pattern

Jay L. Halio

At the crucial moment in the last act, when all other appeals have failed, Volumnia speaks to her son, Coriolanus. Silent and hard after greeting his mother, wife, and son, he listens, then rises to leave, saying, "I have sat too long" (5.3.132). But his mother detains him:

> Nay, go not from us thus.
> If it were so that our request did tend
> To save the Romans, thereby to destroy
> The Volsces whom you serve, you might condemn us
> As poisonous of your honour. No, our suit
> Is that you reconcile them. . . .   (132–37)

Volumnia's proposal carries the day; although Coriolanus knows how "dangerously" she has prevailed with him (189), he nevertheless yields and agrees to frame "convenient peace" (192). It is a stunning victory not only for Rome (which celebrates with gratitude and joy) but also for conciliatory mediation, which has been an undercurrent in Shakespeare's tragedies up to now. It surfaces at last in *Coriolanus* and leads directly to the principal theme of the late romances.

Conciliatory mediation appears as early as *Romeo and Juliet*. Defying ancient grudges and violent feuding between their families, the young couple fall in love and get married. Although their happiness is short-lived and they pay for their love with nothing less than their lives, at the end the sacrifice has not been entirely in vain. "All are punished," as the prince says (5.3.294), but old Capulet immediately reaches out to his erstwhile enemy:

> O brother Montague, give me thy hand.
> This is my daughter's jointure, for no more
> Can I demand.   (5.3.295-97)

Montague accepts reconciliation and goes further, promising a statue of Juliet in pure gold. Capulet promises one of Romeo to lie by his lady's, "Poor sacrifices of our enmity" (303). It is, the prince says, a "glooming peace" that the morning brings; but, finally, it is peace.

The peace of tragedy and the reconciliation of opposing forces that comes with it are not without great cost. The "sense of waste" that A. C. Bradley identifies as a chief element in our feelings at the end of a Shakespearean tragedy is acute (23). But, as Bradley and others show, Shakespearean tragedy does not leave us solely with feelings of loss. E. M. W. Tillyard identifies "a new order" at the end of *Othello* and *King Lear*; destruction is heavy, but it is followed by regeneration (*Last Plays* 16-17). The new order is cut short in tragedy: the principals of the drama are not permitted to benefit fully from what they have suffered and from what, through their suffering, they have perhaps earned. But the tragic pattern includes the significant upturn, however truncated or brief, that is the completion of the tragic curve, the fulfillment of tragedy. The pattern is more completely developed in the late romances than in the tragedies, which is one reason the late plays are sometimes called tragicomedies.

Critics now generally recognize that the late plays grow out of both the major tragedies and the comedies. As Barbara Mowat writes, "the similarity of fables, incidents, characters, and devices ties the Romances firmly to Shakespeare's work in the two major genres" (*Dramaturgy* 31). My purpose here is to show that the mature tragedies already tend toward the emphasis—if not the tone or dramaturgy—found in the last plays, as exemplified by the excerpt from Volumnia's speech. From *Julius Caesar* to *Othello* the tragic protagonist reveals an increasing awareness of alternatives to disaster. In *King Lear* he confronts them through the outspokenness of his loyal servant, Kent, but furiously rejects them. This awareness is a turning point in the tragedies, which from *Macbeth* onward present protagonists acutely conscious of what they have at stake as they make their fateful decisions. Unlike Brutus, Hamlet, or Othello, who should share that awareness but do not, or do so only partially and obliquely,[1] they elect to pursue a course of action they know may end disastrously. No providential agency of any kind intervenes, as it does in the major comedies, where, for example, Oberon and Theseus intercede on behalf of the young lovers, or, as in *Much Ado about Nothing*, where Dogberry and the Watch finally manage to expose the truth and avert ultimate catastrophe. Appeals to the gods in *King Lear* remain unheard or unanswered, as the tragic action relentlessly unfolds.

In the late romances, potentially tragic events only proceed up to a certain point. Either the protagonist learns to act rightly in the face of events or he is rescued from ultimate and complete ruin. In several plays, the agent of salvation is a daughter, a young woman unstained by the world's vices. Through negligence, naïveté, or academic absorption — actually, all those qualities — Prospero loses his dukedom in Milan and spends twelve years in exile on an island with only Miranda, Caliban, and Ariel for companionship, such as it is. Pericles sees through the riddle Antiochus presents, and he escapes just in time, only to find that he is not safe in his own kingdom and that he must continue in flight through further adventures and misadventures. These result in the presumed death of Thaisa, his wife, and the loss of Marina, his daughter. Imogen, in *Cymbeline*, falsely accused on two counts, seeks refuge in disguise in what seems to her a desert wilderness, though it is really a version of pastoral. Closest to the tragic paradigm is *The Winter's Tale*, in which the deaths of innocent or basically good people (Mamillius, Antigonus) occur before Leontes finally comes to his senses, thanks in large part to the oracle delivered from Delphi. Notwithstanding significant differences in linguistic development, psychology, and dramatic conventions (Mowat, *Dramaturgy* 6–21; Foakes 3), the late plays essentially begin where the tragedy begins. That they do not end where tragedy ends owes something to Shakespeare's enlarged vision in these plays, where he attempts to bring together major aspects of comedy and tragedy (which Socrates saw as two sides of the same coin) in a more comprehensive, complementary, and benign view of human existence (Hartwig 20, 31–33).

Some specific comparisons illustrate this point. Whatever else *Hamlet* is, it is first a play about revenge. In it Shakespeare explores more deeply than any earlier dramatist had done the far-reaching implications of the tradition of blood vengeance. Revenge tragedy was never again the same. As later plays like *The Revenge of Bussy D'Ambois* and *The Atheist's Tragedy* show, *Hamlet* permanently altered the genre. In *Hamlet*, however, the question of revenge is persistent and unrelenting: it gives the prince no rest, until he hits on the device to "catch the conscience of the king." Even after he catches Claudius out, or thinks he does (Horatio seems, but only seems, to corroborate Hamlet's conviction), Hamlet moves, not to an immediate and just revenge, but to the murder of the wrong man. Had he taken his revenge in the prayer scene, all might have been well (Bowers 744). Instead, he there becomes momentarily identical with the bloodthirsty revenger of the earlier drama, imaged forth in the figure of Pyrrhus in the first player's scene (2.2.453–95) and inveighed against by church and state alike. He therefore sheathes his sword, hoping to find Claudius at a fitter time:

When he is drunk asleep, or in his rage
Or in th'incestuous pleasure of his bed
At gaming, swearing, or about some act
That has no relish of salvation in't.
(3.3.89–92)

In these thoughts, Hamlet ironically comes dangerously near to damning himself (Joseph 129–33) and then kills Polonius. Only later, after the Ghost's last intercession, does Hamlet realize the full import of his deed:

For this same lord,
I do repent. But heaven hath pleased it so
To punish me with this, and this with me,
That I must be their scourge and minister.
(3.4.156–59)

Despite his later resolution (in the 1604 Quarto) to let his thoughts "be bloody, or be nothing worth" (4.4.57), Hamlet does not act again to further his revenge — or his ministry, to his mother or anyone else (Halio, "Hamlet's Alternatives" 182–85) — until he returns from his abortive sea voyage to England. Then it is questionable whether he acts or merely reacts to events others have set in motion.

Prospero also faces the issue of revenge, and for much of *The Tempest* he seems intent on taking vengeance against his enemies, Alonso, Antonio, and Sebastian. "By accident most strange," he tells Miranda, "bountiful Fortune / . . . hath mine enemies / Brought to this shore" (1.2.179–81). The time is at last ripe for him to deal with them, and he means to do so. By separating Alonso from his son, Ferdinand, and letting the father believe the son drowned, Prospero has already inflicted severe pain and remorse on Alonso. (Ferdinand is otherwise preoccupied, according to a different part of Prospero's plan.) All the malefactors, but also good old Gonzalo, are taunted by the illusory banquets and grotesque figures that Ariel conjures. Although the scene does relatively little to bring the recalcitrant Antonio and Sebastian to despair, the torments are real and they may be seen as precursors of worse to follow. As the banquet vanishes, Ariel in the form of a harpy warns the "three men of sin" that they are "most unfit to live" (3.3.53–58). For their "foul deed" against Prospero, he continues, "The powers, delaying not forgetting, have / Incensed the seas and shores, yea, all the creatures" against them (73–75). Only "heart's sorrow, / And a clear life ensuing" (81–82) can forestall their "Ling'ring perdition — worse than any death" (77).[2]

It is doubtful whether Antonio and Sebastian are entirely and genuinely penitent, despite the punishment that Ariel threatens (5.1.7–19), but there is no question about Alonso's penitence. Gonzalo's pity for all three so moves Ariel that he suggests Prospero's "affections" would become tender if he too beheld them. Ariel's compassion moves Prospero's, precisely as Claudius's attempt to pray failed to move Hamlet — or, rather, moved him in the opposite direction. Of course, Duke Prospero is far different from Prince Hamlet. Whereas Hamlet puzzled fruitlessly over the nobler course of action — sufferance or armed opposition (3.2.57–60) — Prospero, on Ariel's prompting, is fully cognizant of what he must do:

> Though with their high wrongs I am struck to th' quick,
> Yet with my nobler reason 'gainst my fury
> Do I take part. The rarer action is in
> Virtue than in vengeance. They being penitent,
> The sole drift of my purpose doth extend
> Not a frown further. (5.1.25–30)

Prospero feels constrained to frown a bit more at Antonio and Sebastian, whose intended treachery against Alonso might cause that king's frown — or worse — as well (128–30). But the play ends in general reconciliation, reunion, and (through the marriage of Ferdinand and Miranda) promises of generation and regeneration in Naples and Milan. In this the ending of *The Tempest* is quite unlike that of *Hamlet*, where the hope for regeneration of any kind lies not with Denmark's royal family or even Polonius's but with Fortinbras, the Prince of Norway. It is he who has Hamlet's dying voice to back his "rights of memory" to the kingdom that now at tremendous cost lies purged of its corruption.

The Winter's Tale is often compared with *Othello* and *Much Ado about Nothing*, of the plays in the two major genres, since all three deal with jealousy, deception, false accusation, and death, real or supposed. Although Mowat has argued forcefully against Tillyard's belief that the first half of *The Winter's Tale* is "seriously tragic" (Tillyard, *Last Plays* 41; Mowat, *Dramaturgy* 7–8), surely the momentum of the first three acts veers strongly toward the tragic mode. The love between Leontes and Hermione does not quite reach the idealized level of Othello's and Desdemona's — which, Mowat says, "raises the theme of jealousy to tragic intensity" (*Dramaturgy* 10) — but Hermione's devotion, seasoned over many more years, is the equal of Desdemona's. The situation is further complicated by the mutual devotion of Polixenes and Leontes for a still longer period, one that stretches back to their boyhood. If anything, Renaissance thinking placed love between friends on a higher level than that between the sexes. If Leontes's love for Hermione, Polixenes, or both, seems insufficiently emphatic or felt, the love of others for him is not. All the more striking, even terrifying, then, is his sudden and irrational enmity. Although his anguish may differ from Othello's (Mowat, *Dramaturgy* 11), it is no less real. Here Shakespeare allows the tragic curve to pursue its downward course further than in any other romance or in the parallel comedy *Much Ado about Nothing*. After Leontes blasphemes the oracle (3.2.137–40), he hears of Mamillius's death and watches Hermione swoon.

The parallel in *Othello* occurs as Othello reaffirms his belief in Desdemona's adultery only to hear Emilia disabuse him of his erroneous conviction immediately before Iago kills her (5.2.217–38). Like Leontes, Othello comes to his senses, but unlike Leontes he has no opportunity to repair any of the injuries he has done, and his repentance cannot restore Desdemona to life. What hope there is for a new order at the end of the tragedy lies mainly with Cassio, who is reinstated and appointed to rule over Cyprus in Othello's place. More important for the final impression the tragedy leaves, Othello fully recognizes his tragic error and the recognition leads to his growth as a character. As Tillyard says, "Othello in his final soliloquy [*sic*] is a man of a more capacious mind than the Othello who first meets us" (*Last Plays* 17). Othello's recognition also leads to his suicide. He dies kissing Desdemona, but the kiss, however poignant and, in the circumstance he describes (5.2.368–69), appropriate, is powerless to revive her.

Cordelia's kiss, in contrast, does help revive Lear. His awakening and his reconciliation with his daughter seem, like much else in the drama, to promise a happier outcome than Shakespeare permits. As Stephen Booth and Frank Kermode demonstrate, the play appears to end — or to be moving toward an ending — many times before its actual conclusion (Booth, *Indefinition* 33; Kermode, *Sense of an Ending* 18). Here Shakespeare altered all his sources[3] and, in doing so, seemed intent on repeatedly raising the audience's expectations only to dash them completely. Whether Lear dies kissing Cordelia as he tries to revive her is a matter for a theatrical director to decide,[4] since the text is silent; but in many respects the situation differs widely from the ending of *Othello*. In *Pericles*, however, when Marina brings her father out of his profound depression and despair, the awakening in *King Lear* is reprised. As in *The Winter's Tale*, the reunion of father and daughter is the prelude to a still greater wonder: Pericles's reunion with Thaisa, whom he had long thought dead. But like the death of Hermione, Thaisa's death was an illusion, and her restoration is a reality. Furthermore, in the nuptials of Marina and Lysimachus, as in those of Ferdinand and Miranda or Perdita and Florizel, the movement toward reconciliation is completed, promising a new and gentler generation (Traversi 206, 268).

The concluding situations of the late plays, and the feelings aroused by them, are thus quite different from those of the middle tragedies — *Hamlet* and *Othello*, say, or *King Lear*. But in subsequent tragedies Shakespeare gave greater prominence to the attitudes and ideas submerged in those darker, more terrible plays. Speaking of *Antony and Cleopatra* and of *Coriolanus*, Bradley notes that whereas the final impressions they make "can scarcely be called purely tragic . . . , at least the feeling of reconciliation which mingles with the obviously tragic emotions is here exceptionally well marked" (Bradley 84, qtd. in Tillyard, *Last Plays* 20–21). For Bradley, *Coriolanus* signals "the transition to the latest works, in which the powers of repentance and forgiveness charm to rest the tempest raised by error and guilt." Our feelings at the ending of *Coriolanus*, he says, more closely resemble those at the end of *Cymbeline* than those at the end of *Othello* (84).[5]

These are impressions, admittedly, but they are firmly founded upon demonstrable elements in the plays in question, as Bradley indicates. This is not to say that the romances are very close to the later tragedies in every respect. Important differences exist, and distinctions must be made, or we shall easily be led into "searching for excellencies and profundities which do not exist in the Romances, and, more seriously, into overlooking the excellencies and profundities which indeed are there" (Mowat, *Dramaturgy* 21). As Mowat shows, the "excellencies and profundities" in the last plays have a great deal to do with Shakespeare's altered approach to drama, his different use of symbolism and the supernatural, his greater willingness to take risks in developing and counterpointing what Tillyard calls the "planes of reality," or what others might term the modes of awareness and being in his drama.[6] That the romances in some ways grow out of the tragedies, to which they are clearly linked, does not signify that the late plays are simply an expansion of the earlier ones or merely a conjoining of tragedy and comedy. Tragic and comic elements are integral parts of the last plays, but governing all of them is another genre, or perhaps we should say concept — a concept that derives from the great romance tradition that was a vital part of Shakespeare's classical heritage.[7]

NOTES

[1]For example, after the play within the play, when Rosencrantz and Guildenstern come to summon Hamlet to his mother, they mention Claudius's "choler." Hamlet jokes sardonically and refers to the king's need for a doctor. Later, after he kills Polonius, he realizes that his proper role in Denmark is to be both "scourge and minister." See 3.2.290–94 and 3.4.157–61.

[2]Compare *Hamlet* 3.3.36–72. Claudius, in the prayer scene, recognizes that the only way to forgiveness is through sincere repentance, which includes not only remorse but the amendment of life.

[3]The reasons for this are not hard to find, and they are summed up in the concluding lines of the play.

[4]This is the way Nicholas Hytner staged it in the 1990 production of *King Lear* at the Royal Shakespeare Theatre.

[5]I expand on Bradley's notion of *Coriolanus* as a "drama of reconciliation" in "*Coriolanus*."

[6]Compare Joan Hartwig (5–9, 15–31), who discusses Shakespeare's new emphasis on artifice in the romances.

[7]The most extended discussion of Shakespeare's debt to the classical romance tradition is Carol Gesner, *Shakespeare and the Greek Romance: A Study in Origins*. See also Howard Felperin's opening chapter, "Golden Tongued Romance," in *Shakespearean Romance*, which also treats medieval romance, and Mowat's "Brief Notes on Greek Romance" (*Dramaturgy* 129–32).

Enframing Style and the Father-Daughter Theme in Early Shakespearean Comedy and Late Romance

Robert F. Willson, Jr.

Bernard Beckerman identifies a basic problem for teachers of Shakespearean drama, especially for those who are intent on discussing significant themes. His comments are particularly relevant in the poststructural climate of today's Shakespearean criticism:

> Narrative is not exclusive to drama, but shared by romance and epic, history and cinema. Episode or incident is also shared by more than one medium. It is when we come to enacted incidents that we begin to focus on drama. And it is when we concentrate on the distinctive style and form with which the incident is elaborated or structured that we begin to attend to the aesthetic of drama. Form is embedded in the Shakespearean text and though it permits, even more invites, variation, it also has a primary integrity of its own.
>
> ("Some Problems" 310)

The "primary integrity" of comic form in Shakespeare may be discovered by identifying and tracing the development of the playwright's structural method. That Shakespeare relies heavily on framing his comic plots, in both early and late models, is a given among interpreters of his work (R. Berry). In a related approach to representing comic action, he employs plays within to create a metatheatrical mood that further distances audiences from the action. The device offers numerous opportunities for parody as well as for commentary on the nature of his art. By examining these structural elements, we can better understand that Shakespeare regards comedy as the appropriate genre for exploring the relation between imagination and reason, illusion and reality, art and nature. As I attempt to demonstrate in this essay, Shakespeare holds fast to the notion that audiences should respond to comic illusion, especially when marriage, family reunion, and the promises of new life are represented, as if witnessing a miracle. Spectators must demonstrate their faith in the artist's power to "mend" their fears or apprehensions and so fulfill their desire for dreams to be realized.

In the late romances, as opposed to the early and middle comedies, Shakespeare frequently uses framing figures like Old Gower or Time to remind us that we are witnessing an old tale, an oft-told, reliable fable that reveals tested truths about human — and divine — nature. It is in the late romances as well that the plays within, now more elaborate and masquelike, are introduced by such stage magicians as Paulina and Prospero. Shakespeare appears enchanted with the idea that the artist possesses a godly energy capable of fashioning illusions that can inspire faith. By analyzing the use of frames and plays within in early comedies and romances — Beckerman's "enacted incidents" — we can better appreciate the playwright's growing sophistication as an artist and thinker concerning the relation between his craft and life.

It is likewise important to examine a salient character "structure" in the early comedies and late romances, father-daughter relationships. Shakespeare selects narratives in which the father is, for want of a better term, the blocking figure, the force threatening to prevent the marriage that will prompt our response of wonder. In the early comedies, these relationships are mostly superficial, serving as the occasions for rebellious or defiant daughters to satisfy their wills. But in the late romances this narrative device provides the central character interest; separated daughters and fathers must be reunited before happiness and order can be restored. Here too Shakespeare's art matures in its emphasis on regeneration as a central theme (Frye, *Natural Perspective*).

In *The Comedy of Errors*, the opening scene discovers the Syracusan merchant Egeon facing the dilemma of finding a thousand marks to ransom him from death at the hands of Duke Solinus of Ephesus. Separated from his family, which he believes lost, he seems to welcome death, an invitation further clouding the play's opening sky. What we discover in the enclosed action of the comedy is that Egeon's sons have not only survived but are present in Ephesus and able to ransom him. We see no more of Egeon until the final scene, when father, sons, mother, and servants are saved and reunited in a rush of discoveries and unmaskings. We might be excused for believing that we have entered the world of the late romances when Emilia, Egeon's wife, declares,

> Thirty-three years have I but gone in travail
> Of you, my sons, and till this present hour
> My heavy burden ne'er delivered.
>   (5.1.400–02)

The chief difference of course is that the play's action transpires over a period of twenty-four hours, not thirty-three years, and we are never unaware of the Plautine elements to which the effects of this comedy owe so much.

Nonetheless, the awareness of framed design helps students of Shakespeare's comedies and romances grasp the playwright's storytelling technique. Another example of framing in an early comedy occurs in *The Taming of the Shrew*, which invites spectators to view the wooing of Kate and Bianca as an enclosed interlude observed by the stage audience of Christopher Sly. Although the surviving play does not feature a closed frame — Kate's capitulatory speech serves as a resounding period — there is no escaping the conclusion that her taming is meant to be seen as a more thoroughgoing illustration of the same civilizing lesson being taught to Master Sly. Thus unlike the framing action of *The Comedy of Errors*, that of *Shrew* remains outside the play within: Sly does not wake to join the company of Paduan revellers as a long-lost relative. Yet we also recognize increased sophistication in the technique of framing, since Egeon's predicament is simply the structural pretext for entering and exiting the world of the comedy. In *Shrew*, by contrast, the interlude, though incomplete, presents an analogous form of taming, involves disguise, and presents a boy actor — the Page — playing the role of Sly-the-lord's lady.

Love's Labor's Lost cannot be called a framed play. It features no external choruslike character (Egeon) or onstage audience member (Sly) to remind us that the main action is enclosed, observed, judged. Yet Shakespeare does devise an internal playlet, the Nine Worthies interlude, to poke fun at the male lovers' pretensions to greatness as philosophers. The amateurish group of actors dominated by the braggart Don Armado and the pedant Holofernes seek to undertake "parts" for which they are unsuited and appear strikingly foolish in the process. The same could be said for Navarre, Longaville, Dumaine, and Berowne, especially since they have failed miserably as Petrarchan poets and as actors in the masque of the Muscovites. As David Bergeron observes, the men also reveal their blindness by delivering caustic comments on the Nine Worthies pageant performance, while the women sit quietly, "secure in their ironclad hold on reality" ("Plays within Plays" 162). This play within the play allows Shakespeare to parody bombastic Senecanism and to comment reflexively on the blindness of his male lovers to their exaggerated styles. And, instead of the closure we experience at the end of both *The Comedy of Errors* and *The Taming of the Shrew*, this comedy's finale offers no assurance of resolution in marriage. In fact, the news of the Princess's father's death and the penalties imposed on the men for breaking their word create a mood comparable to that of the problem plays.

The answer to the dilemma of suspended closure comes in *A Midsummer Night's Dream*, the comedy that harmonizes many of the structural and thematic problems noted so far. Here Shakespeare blends a frame action and a play within the play, both of which create an inspired mood of dream. The play's occasional nature and the event — a court wedding — for which it was probably written contribute significantly to its particular form, to be sure. But the Athenian daylight world, where the mature lovers Theseus and Hippolyta reign, contrasts sharply with the wood where the lovers, Titania, and Bottom, dream of adventures or horrors that both confound and transform their lives. When the royal pair come upon the sleeping pair of lovers in act 4, Theseus overrules Egeus, declaring that some superior power has determined which Jack will have which Jill.

Once this matter is settled, "Pyramus and Thisby" can serve as the fitting reception diversion for the Athenian newlyweds. That the mechanicals' performances transmute a potentially tragic story into a hilariously funny one only underscores the Athenian lovers' fellowship with Bottom and Company. The satiric effect is similar to that of the Nine Worthies pageant in *Love's Labor's Lost*, but here all the lovers, not just the men, are shown to be blind to their bombastic behavior in the wood. Theseus's rational explanation of the pastiche—"The best in this kind are but shadows" (5.1.211)—functions as only the rationalist's explanation of play-world events. It is Hippolyta's remarks about the lovers' forest-world adventures that adumbrate the intimate link between reality and illusion, the world and the stage:

> But all the story of the night told over,
> And all their minds transfigur'd so together,
> More witnesseth than fancy's images
> And grows to something of great constancy;
> But, howsoever, strange and admirable.
>   (5.1.23–27)

Hippolyta's observation about the metamorphic power of imagination signals Shakespeare's fascination with the subject of art and its relation to life (Belsey 189). Because the early plays are so indebted to Ovid, whose *Metamorphoses* recounts the sudden changes of state undergone by famous pairs of lovers, Shakespeare's youthful comedies place greater emphasis on the speeded-up process of maturation necessary for lovers whose marriages represent that "something of great constancy" Hippolyta speaks of. Kate is tamed, Navarre and his philosophers learn from the ladies how to speak true words of love, and Hermia discovers in her state of rejection a mirror image of Helena's—all these lessons are taught at breakneck speed and in lunatic, dreamlike, even nightmarish, imagined worlds. That order can be restored, indeed that the new order promises joy beyond belief in the form of unions destined to produce beautiful offspring, should provoke in us emotions of amazement and awe.

In choosing the adjective *admirable* Hippolyta points to the maguslike role of the playwright. The Elizabethan sense of this word is "a source of wonder," the thought-ravishing response of witnesses to a miracle. In an Ovidian world of lusty gods and goddesses, the transfigurations of human beings into beasts are indeed awe-inspiring, but they do not promise future happiness for the mortals involved. Such Ovidian tales as those involving Venus and Adonis rather reveal the tragic consequences of human defiance of the gods' wills. True, Adonis's blood nurtured the flower called love-in-idleness, whose juice plays a critical role in "curing" Demetrius of his distaste for Helena. But as Puck demonstrates in his misapplication of that potion, such elixirs can have malicious as well as beneficial effects.

The admirable consequences to which Shakespeare seems to be pointing us in the resolution of *A Midsummer Night's Dream* are of another order.

Perhaps it is best expressed by Bottom's response to his own reverie: "I have had a dream, past the wit of man to say what dream it was. Man is but an ass, if he go about to expound this dream" (4.1.203–05). These remarks anticipate those of Hippolyta: both observers deny the efficacy of reason to explain dreams and their consequences. They also underscore the importance of accepting the results of such dreams as happy accidents. Here the artist and providential forces appear to work hand in hand; the dreams of the lovers, Titania, and Bottom are fractional images of the larger play. Puck's epilogue (5.1.419–34) emphasizes how "this weak and idle theme" is "but a dream" yet a dream that likewise "mends." Just as the potion-induced sleep of the lovers has mended their quarrels and Egeus's complaint, so Shakespeare's comedy has "restored amends" in the audience by fulfilling our desire for a happy resolution of the threatening conflicts. In both instances criticism, the exercise of the faculty of reason, proves superfluous or ineffectual; only those who admit to the power of imagination or faith can join the community of "friends."

In the late romances Shakespeare returns to the question of art's role in mending his audience's imagination and the lives of his characters (Frye, *Fables* 112–14). Here too we find him using framing and play-within elements to represent comedy's reflexive qualities. Father-daughter conflicts are likewise central to the romances, taking on a much more significant role than they play in the early comedies. Admittedly, the conflicts in the comedies possess intensity. Baptista must find a husband for Kate before he can accept the many bids for Bianca's hand. His dilemma is serious, since Kate's shrewishness not only promises spinsterhood for her but threatens the peace of his household. Petruchio answers this father's prayers and, in effect, obviates any further exchange between father and daughter. Indeed, the parent-child relationship that drives the latter half of the play concerns father Vincentio and son Lucentio: Will Vincentio consent to Lucentio's choice of wife? When Kate responds to her husband's call with a lengthy apology for the "naturally" submissive role of wives toward husbands, she underscores her argument by employing triadic phrases like "thy lord, thy king, thy governor" (5.2.138) and "thy lord, thy life, thy keeper" (5.2.145) to show that her husband assumes in her mind the additional paternal functions of father and ruler. Kate the "moveable" (2.1.197) has now become a part of Petruchio's collection and at the same time has been transformed from a "woman mov'd" to an untroubled, beautiful "fountain" (5.2.142).

Egeus too must confront "a fountain troubled" (5.2.142) in the person of his daughter Hermia. She rejects his selection of husband in Demetrius and instead hangs upon Lysander, whom Egeus accuses of bewitching his previously dutiful child. This conflict is resolved in the fourth act when Theseus, observing the couples asleep in the wood, overrules Egeus, announcing that they will be married as part of his and Hippolyta's nuptial ceremonies. The aged and rigid father is not heard from again; he is notably absent from the reception festivities at court. Theseus, like Petruchio, has assumed the roles of husband, "father," and ruler, exemplifying as he does the model of flexibility or sensibility for such identities that Shakespeare appears to be promoting in the closes of the early comedies. Like Baptista, Egeus — and, in early tragedy, Capulet — serves a largely functional purpose, one suited to the style of a comedy that places heavy emphasis on plot. And although Kate proves a more complex heroine than either Hermia or Helena, we are left with the impression that her character type, like theirs, allows for little depth or sensitivity. Each comic father fulfills his plot function as the blocking figure, and each comic daughter moves on to become newly married wife and prospective mother. Parent and child may be reunited, but this symbolic recovery of family is not the central focus of these plays.

In the romances, father-daughter relationships occupy more of the emotional and dramatic center of the action. The separations and reunitings seem also to explore significant themes concerning rewards for faith or suffering. We of course understand that the potentially tragic consequences of separation in the romances must be linked to the darker worlds of the tragedies. In *Cymbeline* Imogen's marrying of Posthumus in defiance of her father's wishes recalls the behavior of daughters in *A Midsummer Night's Dream* and *Romeo and Juliet*. But evil forces of the kind found in the tragedies intervene. After Posthumus's banishment, Imogen is victimized by the schemes of Cymbeline's queen, whose son Cloten she was supposed to marry. Shakespeare makes Imogen into a heroine more mature than either Hermia or Juliet; hers is the resourcefulness of a Viola or Portia. In describing Cymbeline's anger at her hasty marriage to the "lowly" Posthumus, Imogen recalls the perceptiveness and poetry of even so elevated a figure as Cordelia. Describing to Pisanio the king's fury as she bade her husband farewell, she announces that

> ere I could
> Give him that parting kiss which I had set
> Betwixt two charming words, comes in my father,
> And like the tyrannous breathing of the north
> Shakes all our buds from growing. . . .
> (1.3.33–37)

Talk of blasted buds comes from characters like Friar Laurence in the early comedies and tragedies. By assigning to Imogen the wisdom of a chorus, Shakespeare suggests that this heroine of romance combines both strength and innocence in her character. Given the power of the forces arrayed against her, she requires these gifts *and* divine aid to win out.

It would likewise be difficult to comprehend the significance of Leontes's banishment of Perdita without recalling the estrangement of Lear and Cordelia (Barber 63). Indeed, the guilt-driven desire for forgiveness, which

Lear expresses so poignantly in his "Come, let's away to prison" speech (5.3.8–19), is similarly observable in Leontes's behavior on his daughter's return to Sicilia. It is as if Leontes, and to some extent Pericles and Prospero, are Lears who have defeated madness and earned the right to enjoy the return and spiritual support of their ever-true Cordelias.

Yet the romances are unmistakably comedies, and their father-daughter relationships are, not surprisingly, tied to the themes of marriage and regeneration. Moreover, the daughters of the romances are symbolically named and given goddesslike roles that suggest they are intended to be regarded as new Eves returning the fallen world to a state of Edenic innocence. Their fathers, then, following this allegorical paradigm, function as old Adams; although initially blinded by jealousy or revenge or suffering at the hands of fate, they prove capable of redemption through a resurgence of faith. Their recovery is prompted by daughters who also find mates of equally innocent natures — new Adams. Shakespeare presents an unequivocally optimistic vision at the close of these plays, hinting that the "brave new world" Miranda glimpses may yet be realized.

This vision is distinctly mythopoeic at the close of *Cymbeline*. The reuniting of the king's family, symbolic of the victory of virginal innocence embodied in daughter and sons, also marks the joining of the English lion and the Roman eagle. Imogen's "tender air," with the attendant pun on "woman" (*mulier*), sets the scene for an idyllic kingdom whose monarch and subjects have found the key to harmonizing personal joy and Rome's imperial vision. This regained Paradise has a particularly nationalistic — and Jacobean — character absent from the Edens of the other romances. Shakespeare here works with the same mythic clay he put to different uses in *King Lear*, where the reconciliation of father and daughter precipitated neither personal happiness nor a vision of the ideal state. In *Cymbeline*, moreover, the happy king can blame the troubles of his family and kingdom on "our wicked queen" and her cipher of a son, two melodramatized caricatures. Once these satanic forces are eliminated (with the aid of the heavens), a "Roman and British ensign wave / Friendly together."

Such a paradise seems unattainable as we enter the world of *Pericles*, where the hero faces the challenge of solving a riddle in order to win the hand of Antiochus's daughter. The situation faintly resembles the casket-choosing episode in *The Merchant of Venice*. Both Bassanio and Pericles must exercise heroic wit and insight to qualify as husbands for these richly endowed daughters. But Antiochus has undertaken an incestuous affair with his daughter, a fact that Pericles discovers as he deciphers the riddle. He glimpses not only the severed heads of the losers but also the darkest side of human nature. Shakespeare succeeds in positing the most unnatural of models for father-daughter relationships, one that pollutes the very well of life. As the stunned Pericles flees this sink of sin, he commences a Mediterranean odyssey full of hardship and loss; at his lowest ebb, he will be nursed back to spiritual health by a daughter serving in her natural role toward her father. In this first episode of what was probably his first romance, Shakespeare portrays the incestuous father-daughter affair as symbolic of corruption in the family and the state.

But the final scenes of *Pericles* delineate a tableau of restoration meant to inspire the same kind of admiration described by Hippolyta in her answer to Theseus. Marina, whose name signifies the sea where she was born, comes to her distempered father on a barge in the port of Myteline. She has resisted all attempts by bawds to destroy her virginity; in fact, her goddesslike innocence has helped her to convert employees and customers alike. One of these converts, the governor Lysimachus, summons Marina to cure the visiting prince through the power of her song. When the recovered Pericles realizes that his nurse is actually the daughter he had long thought dead, his words recall the state of wonder experienced by the lovers and Bottom in *A Midsummer Night's Dream*: "This is the rarest dream that e'er dull sleep / Did mock sad fools withal" (5.1.166–67). Here too we witness the magic by which dreams mend the lives of dreamers.

A similar response is provoked by Paulina in *The Winter's Tale*, when she unveils the "statue" of Hermione. Although the revealed figure is that of Leontes's wife, the return of Perdita ("the lost one") has set in motion a chain of events leading to this final, awe-inducing reunion. While Shakespeare does not portray the reuniting scene between Perdita and Leontes, he does employ certain gentlemen to report what they have seen. The First Gentleman describes how a "notable passion of wonder appear'd" (5.2.15–16) in those who witnessed the scene, keeping alive the concept of art's power to provoke awe in those who witness its miraculous effects. In the statue scene, Shakespeare creates even more impressive magic by breathing life into the apparently dead clay representing Hermione's shape. Not only is the onstage audience moved by what it sees; the theater audience, ignorant of Paulina's scheme, must also be shocked to see her come alive. This is the only instance of such deception in all of Shakespeare, yet his purpose is certainly not solely to deceive us. In the early comedies marriage celebrations function to reconstitute the community and to promise progeny who will redefine the older order; in the romances scenes involving reunited families serve a similar yet more comprehensive goal. As Paulina puts it, the viewers are required to "awake" their "faith."

Paulina's role in this ritual is that of the magus, the artist onstage. In the other romances, characters such as Cerimon (*Pericles*) and Prospero (*The Tempest*) play comparable roles. As her symbolic name suggests, Paulina performs an apostolic function, rekindling in all those who witness her artistry a belief in the essential benevolence of the heavens. She fashions the statue scene as a kind of play within the play on the theme of art improving, but working intimately with, nature. She has also managed to exemplify the ideal of service, keeping her lord and lady chaste until both were prepared to be rejoined. Paulina's devotion, perseverance, and recognition and acceptance of higher moral truth give her the power to perform miracles (Neely, "Triumph" 321–23). As Leontes touches his revived wife, he pays proper tribute to her godlike talent: "If this be magic, let it be an art / Lawful as eating." Paulina's reward is similarly the restoration of a mate, as she and Camillo, her male counterpart in the plot, are joined in marriage.

Yet Paulina remains a minor character, albeit one with extraordinary gifts. The character who has magical character talents and the facility for controlling the actions of characters in godlike style and yet who also occupies the significant position of ruler is Prospero from *The Tempest*. Indeed, in this play, Shakespeare's last solely written dramatic work, the comic playwright seems to have come full circle in his treatment of the genre of romantic comedy. *The Tempest* and *A Midsummer Night's Dream* share so many features of mood, imagery, and characterization that one is tempted to believe the later play a revision of the earlier one. Both comedies proceed along similar plot lines involving lovers, spirits, and mechanicals; the controlling figures in each play confront challenges to their authority; these rulers are served by familiar spirits who carry out their instructions yet assert independent personalities; the lovers in these comedies, seduced as it were by their senses, regard each other as gods or goddesses; and both plays feature plays within tied to marriages that promise brave new worlds of happiness.

The Tempest, however, does not permit us the undiluted pleasure of laughing at ludicrous behavior in the name of love. The treacherous plot of Antonio and Sebastian, the revolt of Caliban, and the sorrow of Alonso over the "loss" of his son firmly remind us that we are not in the green world of ancient Athens. Oberon shares Prospero's predicament of rebellious subjects, but in Oberon's case the outcome is never in doubt. No such sympathetic divinity exists to forestall tragedy in *The Tempest*, even though we sense that Prospero, like Theseus, will not spoil a wedding celebration with a hanging. Yet Prospero's character, as father and ruler, is tested in a way in which the characters of Theseus and Oberon are not. Though his lineage is that of the fathers of the earlier comedies, Prospero is a much more complex persona — indeed, some critics have identified him with Shakespeare himself. Facing a choice between revenge and what Ariel makes him see as the "rarer action" of forgiveness, Prospero seems a Lear with a second chance. Instead of destroying his wrongers and banishing a loyal daughter, he heeds the words of his "fool" Ariel and embraces his own fallen image in the person of Caliban: "this thing of darkness I / Acknowledge mine."

In addition to fashioning a father character of greater depth than the fathers of the earlier comedies, Shakespeare devises a play within that serves the romances' purpose of exploring the relation between art and nature. The mood and tone of "Pyramus and Thisby" provide a fitting corrective to the lovers' Petrarchan excesses in *A Midsummer Night's Dream*. The lovers and Theseus see different things in the interlude — bad acting and good faith, respectively—but their reactions are consistent with characterizations and themes in early Shakespearean comedy. The entertainment follows the resolution of quarrels and confusion in the wood, so its burlesque of romantic tragedy and of love at first sight can be enjoyed in a detached and critical light by the stage audience. The theater audience, however, is invited to laugh at the lover-critics who do not make the connections between their own antics in the wood and the words and actions of these "bad actors." With the help of the mechanicals, the audience returns to a reality consistent with the aims of comedy, in which the ludicrous in human nature defeats the tragic pretensions of young enthusiasts.

The marriage masque in *The Tempest* (4.1) is a corrective of another kind. Its idealization of art and nature represents Prospero's wish for Ferdinand and Miranda's future. But Prospero's troubled state in response to Caliban's revolt affects the fabric of the play within, which is fragile, a spell in danger of being broken by any comments from the stage audience. The goddesses of the masque invite us into a pastoral paradise of plenty, free from the passions of lustful men like Antonio and Sebastian and of creatures like Caliban. And the very thought of Caliban's plot destroys the vision; quarrels and divisions must still be settled, as they were before the performance of "Pyramus and Thisby," before such entertainment can proceed (Willson 109). Prospero must decide the fates of those he has lured to the island as a prelude to the securing of his daughter's happiness. The masque contributes to the resolution of these questions by reminding Prospero of his mortality and of the baseless fabric of his magical powers. The new world he desires for Miranda can only be realized when he rejects both his magic and his desire for vengeance. He must free Ariel and embrace Caliban, gestures that symbolically mark his own regenerate faith. In the end, it is not this masque but the discovery of the "revived" Ferdinand and innocent Miranda at chess that prompts the desired response of wonder and admiration in the stage and theater audiences. Not only does Miranda symbolically embody the emotion of wonder (see Ferdinand's "Admir'd Miranda!" [30.1.37]), she also describes the "brave new world" that Shakespeare envisions as the state in which humanity has finally recovered from the Fall.

By tracing Shakespeare's use of enframing and plays within and his treatment of father-daughter relationships in early comedies and the romances, I have attempted to demonstrate the playwright's sophistication in handling these elements. From the beginning, he saw comedy as the appropriate arena to explore the question of the function of art, its dependence on imagination, and its relation to nature. Throughout he shows how imagination mends the fabric of the play and the souls of his audience. Plays are dreams, illusions, but so is life; often, in life and art, "something of great constancy" emerges (Righter 182). The marriages that mend the plots of Shakespeare's early and late comedies promise a return of paradisiacal happiness for individuals and society. While the daughters of the early comedies must overcome the opposition of blocking fathers, the daughters of the romances are the victims of more destructive forces in nature and humankind. Yet they are endowed with qualities of innocence and divinity that make them more formidable figures than their early-comedy sisters. The fathers of the romances too are more than functional or plot-determined personae. Their separations and reunitings with estranged daughters seem to mark the recovery of fallen humanity in general. Finally, in Prospero, a character whose nature subsumes the roles of father, ruler, and magus, we encounter a type of the playwright himself.

Defining the Dramaturgy of the Late Romances

Michael E. Mooney

The Tempest opens with all the sights and sounds of tragedy, and few readers who have studied the major tragedies fail to catch their echoes. "Blow till thou burst thy wind, if room enough!" (1.1.7–8), cries the Boatswain in lines worthy of King Lear's challenge to the raging storm (*King Lear*, 3.4.12; cf. *Pericles*, 3.1.44). "Be patient" (15), responds good Gonzalo, recalling the way to withstand tragic suffering that Kent and Edgar use repeatedly to console Lear and Gloucester. Indeed, the sureness of Shakespeare's hand is felt in Sebastian's reaction to this confusion, "I am out of patience" (55), with its deft characterizing touch and repetition of that basic theme. Even the stage direction, "A cry within" (35), reminiscent of that "cry within of women" in *Macbeth* (5.2), reminds us that these cataclysmic events signify loss and suffering. All stops are sounded in this tragic diapason—

> All lost! To prayers, to prayers! all lost!
> . . . .
>   *A confused noise within*: "Mercy on us!"—
> "We split, we split!"—"Farewell, my wife and children!"
> "Farewell, brother!"—"We split, we split, we split!"
> (1.1.51, 60–62)

—even to Gonzalo's scene-ending hope that, though the "wills above be done!," he would "fain die a dry death" (66–67).

These sights and sounds recall the major tragedies, *Pericles*, and also *The Winter's Tale*, where the storm similarly mocks the poor souls who "cry" to it (3.3.90). They suggest that in his final plays Shakespeare puts to new purposes previous themes and conventions, enlisting them in the service of a vision that moves beyond tragedy and loss to renewal and reconciliation. That vision is first seen in *King Lear* when, surviving just such a cataclysm, Lear awakens to find himself reunited with Cordelia and asks her forgiveness. It is recalled as well at the precise moment when, taking control of *Pericles*, Shakespeare abruptly places the spectators in the middle of a storm which so shakes Pericles's ship that he must ask "god" to "rebuke these surges / Which wash both heaven and hell" and implore those who "command" the "winds" to "bind them in brass, / Having call'd them from the deep!" (3.1.1–4). Like the Mariners and the court party at the start of *The Tempest*, Pericles and Marina seem subject to the winds of chance and providential design, and the forces that rage so violently in these plays are symbolic of those accidents and misfortunes by which, in *The Winter's Tale*, mortals are "slaves . . . Of every wind that blows" (4.4.540–41). These "oppos'd" and "sneaping" winds make people sacrifice reason to will as in Leontes's declaration, "I am a feather for each wind that blows" (1.1.30; 1.2.13; 2.3.154).

The winds of the world and the winds of human passion are aspects of those forces that drive mortals from shore to shore (Rabkin, *Problem* 119), part of that great creating nature that, through the agency of art, contains the vision of the romances. That vision, in the forms it assumes in *Pericles*, *Cymbeline*, *The Winter's Tale*, and *The Tempest*, requires not only the conversion of previous themes and conventions but also the addition of theatrical elements — dreams, multiple illusionistic planes, spectacles, music, and dance — to create illusions far different from the simulacrum of reality we associate with mimetic art. For none of the romances pretend to be real or true in any sense compatible with our understanding of realistic drama. They do not conform to our notion of theatrical representation as psychologically consistent in characterization, language, style, dramaturgy, or setting. They do not intend to. Rather, they transform conventions into something rich and strange, using a dramaturgical vocabulary so stylized, notational, and nuanced that, as in Gonzalo's plea, "be patient" (and in Leontes's jealousy, so similar and yet so different from Othello's), entire tragic sequences are evoked by words, phrases, or situations. Within their visionary, expressionistic forms (Cope 239), the romances create an illusion that increasingly resembles a dream played on the stage of the world, blurring the distinction between dream and waking, stage and world, and role and actor.

Shakespeare adds these theatrical elements to the prose narratives of his sources, integrating narrative and dramatic modes and converting "landscapes" into "scenes," descriptions into dramatizations (H. Smith, *Shakespeare's Romances* 145–74). The source of *Pericles* is the story of Apollonius of Tyre. In all its Greek, medieval, and Renaissance retellings, it is the most moldy of tales; but from it, as well as from Thomas Underdowne's *Aethiopian Historie*, Sidney's *Arcadia*, Robert Greene's *Pandosto*, and a host of other romances, Shakespeare takes his materials. The description of the shipwreck and "rotten carcass of a butt" that opens the *Arcadia* provides an obvious example (Danby 48–49), but shipwrecks and storms are common features of romance. All the conventions are present in these sources: (1) "plots that aim deliberately at the far-fetched, the astounding and the incredible"; (2) a lack of verisimilitude and "realism"; (3) "deceptive disguises and mistaken identities"; (4) "the tendency to divide . . . characters into rigid categories of black and white"; (5) "remote settings" in time or place; and (6) "happy endings" (Pettet 163–69). Not present are the dramaturgical means by which Shakespeare transforms these conventions into dramatic innovations.

The conversion of prose narrative into dramatic process occurs first in *Pericles*, which uses the author of the play's primary source, John Gower, as a presenter. Like the Chorus in *Henry V*, Gower fills in the gaps in the story, links the play's many episodes, and holds together what is otherwise a loosely connected series of scenes. Gower opens and closes the play and offers inter-act commentaries, providing a presentational framework within which the tale of Pericles unfolds. He asks the spectators to piece out the imperfections of the platform with their minds, to identify and to localize the play's scenes by transforming the bare *platea* into many different loci, and he twice asks the spectators to "use" their "imagination to hold / This stage" a "ship" (prologue, 3.1.58–59). In *The Winter's Tale*, the dramaturgical problem is more temporal than spatial, and Shakespeare uses the figure of Time as a chorus to "slide / O'er sixteen years," bring us to Bohemia and the maiden Perdita, and allow a tragedy of middle age to become a comedy of youth (4.1.5–6). In both *Pericles* and *The Winter's Tale*, overtly presentational dramaturgy helps Shakespeare reshape the narrative "landscapes" of his sources.

The Tempest has no known literary source. It draws from Virginia Company pamphlets, *commedia dell'arte scenari*, Montaigne, and previous romances to create its illusion. It begins with "A tempestuous noise of thunder and lightning" and ends with the promise of "calm seas and auspicious gales" (1.1.1; 5.1.314). In *The Tempest*, however, the force behind the storm is human, not divine; the tempest is part of Prospero's and Shakespeare's "art," not part of the benevolent providential design that "blessedly" helped Prospero and Miranda come "ashore" (1.2.63, 158). Their "seasorrow" was enacted in the "dark backward and abysm of time," but it is no less vivid for Prospero who, like Lear, still has a "tempest" beating in his mind (*Lear* 3.4.12). His kingdom usurped, Prospero was set to sea in a "rotten carcass of a butt," from which he and Miranda "cried to th' sea, that roar'd" to them (1.2.149). Now "bountiful Fortune" has brought his enemies to him, and he must accept that the "rarer action is / In virtue than in vengeance" and no longer "burthen" his "remembrances with / A heaviness that's gone" (1.2.178; 5.1.27–28, 199–200).

The storm that rages at the opening of *The Tempest* is created by Prospero. For all its echoing of previous storms, it is finally different from them. In this sense *The Tempest* is the end product of that process whereby previous themes and conventions increasingly serve new functions, with the tempests in *Pericles* and *The Winter's Tale*, like the storm in *King Lear*, becoming something else again. "It is," indeed, "as if" Shakespeare "had placed his whole tragic vision of life into one brief scene before bestowing his new vision upon us" (J. D. Wilson 13). Prospero has so "safely ordered . . . the direful spectacle" of this "wrack" that

> there is no soul —
> No, not so much perdition as an hair
> Betid to any creature in the vessel
> Which thou heardst cry, which thou saw'st sink.
> (1.2.26–32)

Indeed, such is the art of *The Tempest* that what appears to be real is in fact illusory. The tempest — that dominant symbol of suffering, chaos, and loss — here becomes a harmless "spectacle," something presented as if real but then shown to be a product of art. Emblematic of the play's dramaturgy, this storm presents and dissolves a vision. Just as in Prospero's most majestic vision, to which we, Ferdinand, and Miranda are enjoined to silence ("No tongue! all eyes! Be silent" [4.1.59]), so the storm and even the great globe itself are metamorphosed into something new. Transforming inherited conventions, self-consciously displaying the play's theatricality, *The Tempest* moves beyond tragedy, compressing into its brief first scene what constitutes the climactic third act of *King Lear* and expanding that play's fourth act into a full-blown consideration of what occurs after tragedy has spilled all nature's germains.

In *The Tempest*, residua from tragedy, comedy, prose romance, pastoral, and Shakespeare's earlier romances are reconstituted in a new form, which can be examined by considering the reverberations of Ariel's second song and the function of music in the play. Ariel's song announces the theme of transformation and regeneration and foreshadows that the characters will undergo "sea-change" and find themselves "when no man was his own" (5.1.213):

> Full fadom five thy father lies;
> Of his bones are coral made:
> Those are pearls that were his eyes:
> Nothing of him that doth fade,
> But doth suffer a sea-change
> Into something rich and strange.
> Sea-nymphs hourly ring his knell:
> *Burthen*: Ding-dong.
> (1.2.397–404)

Ariel, dressed as a "water-nymph," sings to Ferdinand. His music not only provides a sense of euphony, as opposed to the cacophony of tempestuous noise and tumult, but also bridges the world of waking reality and the world of dream. It recalls the many references to dreams that dot the romances, such as Pericles's description of the recovery of Miranda as the "rarest dream that e'er dull'd sleep / Did mock sad fools withal" (5.1.161–62) and his vision of Diana; Imogen's awakening to the sight of the decapitated Cloten and Posthumus's dream vision of his family and Jupiter, in *Cymbeline*; and Antigonus's recollection of the dream of Hermione, "so like awaking," in *The Winter's Tale* (3.3.19).

Ariel's song reminds us that in the last plays music often introduces optical illusions and dreams. The music of Ariel's first song, sung while Ferdinand sits on a bank lamenting his father's wrack, allays the fury of the "waters" and Ferdinand's "passion" with "its sweet air," making the "wild waves whist" with its sonorousness (1.2,390–94, 378). Led to Prospero and Miranda, Ferdinand finds his "spirits, as in a dream . . . all bound up" (1.2.489). Indeed, Ferdinand and all the visitors to Setebos will be subject to music's power; as in Caliban's bottomless dream, they will find themselves moving between the worlds of sleeping and waking, illusion and recognition. The same "humming . . . noise" that awakens good Gonzalo in time to save Alonzo (2.1) sounds throughout the island (312, 315). "Be not afeard," Caliban tells Stephano and Trinculo,

> the isle is full of noises,
> Sounds and sweet airs, that give delight, and hurt not.
> Sometimes a thousand twangling instruments
> Will hum about mine ears; and sometimes voices,
> That, if I then had wak'd after long sleep,
> Will make me sleep again: and then, in dreaming,
> The clouds methought would open, and show riches
> Ready to drop upon me; that, when I wak'd,
> I cried to dream again.   (3.2.135–43)

In such vaporous clouds things permanent and solid become blurred and indistinct, deliquescing, dislimning, and leaving not a trace behind. Not bedded in the oozy mire, things of substance "fade" — as in Ariel's song and Prospero's masque — becoming an "insubstantial pageant" that, like the "cloud-capp'd towers, the gorgeous palaces, / The solemn temples," and even the "great globe itself," will "leave not a rack behind." The imagery of evanescence converts matter "into air, into thin air" (4.1.150–55), and Prospero's actors participate in a "dissolving pageant of dreams" (Kermode ed., *Tempest* 104).

This pattern of projection and dissolution, the play's determining dramaturgical technique, is found in each of *The Tempest*'s spectacles as well as in the music that is heard and then "sounds no more" (1.2.389). Ariel's first and second songs enchant and lead Ferdinand. His "solemn music" lulls the courtly party to sleep — with the exception of Antonio and Sebastian, who plan their usurpation during the play's most extended dream sequence (2.1.190–310). His third song wakes Gonzalo to warn him of Antonio and Sebastian's conspiracy (300–05), and his fourth is sung as he helps to dress Prospero "as [Prospero] was sometime Milan" (5.1.86). The "zany," loutish, and drunken Stephano and Trinculo sing while Ariel "plays the tune on a tabor and pipe" (3.2.124) in a bit of *commedia dell'arte lazzi* that leads to Caliban's lyrical description of the island's "noises." "Solemn and strange music" returns to accompany Prospero's entry in 3.3 and makes Alonzo wonder, "What harmony is this?" (18). Cacophonous "Thunder and lightning" signal the storm opening the play, Ariel's reentry "like a harpy" to remove the banquet (3.2.52), and his thunderous disappearance (82). As

Alonzo acknowledges his guilt, he remembers again that the winds sang his sin to him and that the thunder, the "deep and dreadful organ-pipe" (3.3.97–99) of the storm, announced his trespass against Prospero. But it is "soft music" that ushers in the Shapes again (3.3) and that introduces the charmingly harmonious vision of Iris, Ceres, and Juno (4.1). Though this harmony is followed by that "confused noise" which disrupts the masque, it returns in the "Solemn music" that attends the entry of the court party into Prospero's charmed circle (5.1) and leads to that "conclusion of awakening which incorporates" the play's "dream action" (Frye, *Natural Perspective* 129). Even the Mariners, emerging from the dreamy state of suspension in which they have been held, are "awak'd" with "strange and several noises" (5.1.235, 232). They too have heard the island's noises, sounds, and sweet airs and have undergone a miraculous resurrection, their "garments," like those worn by the court party, "being rather new dy'd than stain'd with salt-water" (2.1.62, 64–65). "Not a hair perish'd," reports Ariel, fulfilling Prospero's promise to Miranda; "On their sustaining garments not a blemish, / But fresher than before" (1.2.217–19).

Each of the romances uses heavenly music in the interest of resurrection and renewal. The pattern is established in *King Lear*, when "Soft music" accompanies Lear's awakening to Cordelia (4.7.24). It is repeated in *Pericles*, when Thaisa, "cast," "scarcely coffin'd, in the ooze," comes ashore at Ephesus, is restored by Cerimon's music, and asks, "Where am I?," repeating Lear's very words (3.2.104; *Lear* 4.4.50). Music sounds unheard when, reunited with Marina, Pericles hears the "most heavenly music" of the spheres and falls asleep, no longer mocked as one of the world's "sad fools" in a "dream" of hope but commanded by the goddess Diana in a vision containing the promise of restoration with Thaisa (5.1.233, 162, 161). In *Cymbeline* such "Solemn music" signals the entry, "as in an apparition," of Posthumus's family; Jupiter's descent "in thunder and lightning" follows. And in *The Winter's Tale*, Hermione's statue comes to life when Paulina calls for "Music" to "awake" her (5.3.98).

Shakespeare's use of music (and dance) increases steadily from *Pericles* and *Cymbeline* (five instances each) to *The Winter's Tale* (eleven instances) and *The Tempest* (eighteen instances). Each of the romances contains at least one theophany (*Pericles, Cymbeline*, and *The Tempest*) or miracle of resurrection (*Pericles, The Winter's Tale*) that turns on musical and spectacular effects (Nosworthy 64–66). Language and imagery are elevated into music (H. Smith, *Shakespeare's Romances* 193). Music sounds most insistently in *The Tempest*, but in each of the plays it allows for a transition between the world of waking reality and the world of visionary presences and dreams (Brower 109–10; Knight, *Shakespearian Tempest* 247–66). It comforts and soothes as well as disturbs. "A solemn air" is "the best comforter / To an unsettled fancy" (5.1.58–59). In *Pericles, Cymbeline*, and *The Winter's Tale* such music serves as a prelude to moments of revelation. In

The Tempest the use of music so multiplies that it has not only thematic but structural importance. The Ferdinand-Miranda, courtly, and comic subplots each turn on a musical and "spectacular" climax; noise and music frame each episode, enclosing the action and introducing an illusionistic plane that surrounds the events. "Where should this music be? i'th'air or the earth?," asks Ferdinand (1.2.388); like him each of the visitors to the island will question their senses as they thread their way within the island's illusionistic "maze" (3.3.2; 4.1.242). They are subject to a force—Ariel—that remains "invisible" to them, a spirit who leads and lulls not only Ferdinand but also the court party and the drunken Stephano and Trinculo. They are all "tricked" by Prospero's illusions, and the charmed magic circle the court party enters in 5.1 is only the most circumscribed of the concentric illusions that, at their farthest reach, hold even the play's audience in their power.

The ability to create and dissolve an illusion is the source of theatrical power. The imagery of projection and dissolution, so dominant thematically, is also the imagery of the theater, and in this sense *The Tempest* is finally a play about the power of illusion. In *Pericles* and *The Winter's Tale*, Shakespeare needed the help of Gower and the figure of Time to create his illusion and to mark the passage of time. In *The Tempest*, those functions are performed by Prospero, presenter of and participant in the play, who comments on, describes, and summarizes the events as well as takes part in them, maintaining a dramaturgical role above and beyond his dramatis persona (Mowat, *Dramaturgy* 87–88). Like Ariel, he is at times "invisible," particularly during that central episode (3.3) when, positioned "on the top," he stage-manages the action and provides a commentary in a sequence of asides, but also when he remains "at a distance, unseen" to watch Ferdinand's courtship of Miranda (3.1), and when he and Ariel remain on stage, "invisible," while "divers Spirits in shape of dogs and hounds" drive away Stephano, Trinculo, and Caliban (4.1).

Prospero's personae as presenter and participant, along with his stage positions, draw attention to the overt theatricality of events, reminding us that we are watching a play in which the actors assume a number of different "shapes." The "several strange Shapes" who bring in and remove the banquet make Alonzo "muse" at this "living drollery" (3.3.36, 21), but these are members of the same "rabble" who create the theatrical "trick," or ingenious mechanism, that is the play's most "majestic vision" (4.1.37, 118) (Welsford 124; Kermode ed., *Tempest* 95). When they vanish into "thin air," they leave not a "rack behind"—in its double sense as a vaporous cloud and as stage framework. And when that vision abruptly dissolves, Prospero states that "These our actors . . . were all spirits," "shapes" like Ariel, who have "perform'd" "bravely" (3.3.83, 84) in the insubstantial pageants contained in the larger illusion that is *The Tempest*. Indeed, in their use of theatrically self-conscious elements, the romances stand apart, their "multiple illusionistic planes" reflecting E. M. W. Tillyard's point that "on the actual stage," Prospero's embedded masque "is executed by players pretending to be spirits, pretending to be real actors, pretending to be supposed goddesses and rustics" (*Shakespeare's Last Plays* 80). These actors *are* the stuff that dreams are made on.

The actor performing the role of Prospero "call'd forth the mutinous winds, / And 'twixt the green sea and the azur'd vault / Set roaring war" in the play's opening scene. At its end he promises "calm seas" and "auspicious gales" (5.1.42–44, 314). The play over, he acknowledges that he too has been an actor in this insubstantial pageant. His magical and musical "charms . . . all o'erthrown" (1), he is left with only his personal magic. In the epilogue the actor who plays Prospero admits that he no longer has "Spirits to enforce, art to enchant" (14). Bereft of his role, he still needs to dissolve the illusion, or he will have to remain "confin'd" on what is now the "bare island" of the stage (4, 8). To be set free like Ariel, however, he needs the spectators' help. His conventional appeal for applause, traceable to the quête of mummers' plays and disguisings, will break the illusionistic circle within which he has performed and will set him free (Brody 14–20). In this fitting conclusion, Prospero sheds his role and transfers his power to the spectators. The actor-playwright who has held his audience spellbound reveals the presented self lying just beneath his representational role as the play's mage. Indeed, as many critics note with a persistence that upholds the largely discredited allegorical approach to the play, behind the actor-playwright lurks the play's master illusionist, Shakespeare, who has sent to generations of subsequent audiences his own unmistakable farewell. *The Tempest*, like *Pericles*, *Cymbeline*, and *The Winter's Tale*, embeds illusion within illusion and turns what is "far off / And rather like a dream" into the stuff of art.

The Late Plays as Family Romance

Gary Waller

To teach the late plays in the context of what Freud called the "family romance" may get us as close to the continually decentered centers of these plays as we can get. Indeed, I confess that when reading and teaching them, I find myself, openly or shamefacedly, speaking in terms of a humanistic valorization of the "insights" and "vision" of the text that I thought had been expunged from my critical vocabulary. While that belief raises a separate issue of theory (and teaching), it is not irrelevant to the ways these plays help us understand the "tempest . . . , birth, and death" (*Pericles* 5.3.33–34) of our lives and to how Freud's concept of the family romance focuses on crucial, perhaps permanent, parts of our individual and collective lives.

These remarkable plays can produce in readers and spectators an uncanny mixture of what *The Winter's Tale* calls "joy"and "terror" (4.1.1), providing what some psychoanalysts term a "safe haven" for the acknowledgment and therapeutic release of pent-up primitive anxieties (Eagle 212). In teaching the plays, however, I do not simplistically suggest that they "reflect" some universal, dehistoricized pattern of reconciliation through suffering (although I point out how a psychoanalytic reading can fall into that trap). Rather, I explore how Freud's family romance is enacted within different historical formations (see Poster; Bennett) and, therefore, different readers' experiences of the plays.

I start by having my students read Freud's short essay "Family Romances." Like most of Freud's essays, it is surprisingly straightforward and highly suggestive and so is appropriate for an introductory Shakespeare class. With advanced classes, I introduce some recent rewritings of the Freudian reading of the family, including Margaret Mahler's study of separation and individuation and the psychological birth of the human infant, Juliet Mitchell's feminist account of the family, Gilles Deleuze and Félix Guattari's reworking of the oedipal myth, and extracts from Klaus Theweleit's *Male Fantasies*. But Freud's essay in itself gives us an uncannily powerful agenda for reading the late plays. Noting that in the process of growing up, the individual's liberation from parental authority is "one of the most necessary though one of the most painful" events of life (237–38), Freud describes a number of the family romance's characteristics. All involve the desire to change one's family circumstances — to have richer or more powerful parents, for instance, or not to have to share parental love with siblings. Other symptoms include a boy's hostility toward his father, coupled with a strong desire to bring his mother — the subject "of the most intense sexual curiosity" — into "situations of secret infidelity" with him. Connected fantasies may involve incestuous feelings for siblings, desires to return to imagined (or perhaps real) conditions of early childhood before the child was individuated from the mother, and the child's "most intense and momentous" general wish simply "to be big like his parents." In children, such daydreams emerge as wish fulfillment, as erotic and more generally ambitious aims—not only to emulate (or seduce) the parents but to be free of their control. In adults—and here we approach the relevance of Freud's essay to Shakespeare—the symptoms of the family romance reemerge in desires to establish or recapture a lost state of real or imagined autonomy. These desires may be projected, negatively or positively, on a series of love objects—lovers, spouses, or children—who thereby become incorporated into the neurotic patterns laid down early in the adult's family history.

Students today are aware, perhaps uncomfortably, of our century's major revaluations of how we understand ourselves as gendered beings, as generational subjects, and as members of that once seemingly stable institution, the family. Like the word *gender, family* is what Raymond Williams calls a "key word" in our cultural history, one that carries reverberations and contradictions far beyond its dictionary meaning: it is a verbal site of cultural struggle, where shades of meaning betray deep-rooted ideological positions. Since Freud, we have seen a marked preoccupation with the psychological dynamics of the family—with, for example, the separation and individuation of the child from the mother, the child's discovery of boundary conditions, the development of object relations, delusions of omnipotence and fears of abandonment, and the search for a lost, preoedipal, polymorphous sexual fulfillment. The psychoanalytical tradition initiated by Freud provides us with a powerful vocabulary for talking about these stages and crises of individual and familial growth. Although as many feminists rightly point out, psychoanalysis predicates the psychological narrative on the development of a male subject and although it tempts one to universalize its categories, psychoanalysis offers suggestive ways to describe the struggle for differentiation between children and parents, especially between sons and mothers and (of particular relevance to Shakespeare's late plays) daughters and fathers. Without such struggles, the plays seem to assume, there can be no viable self-identity, no later close and meaningful relations with others, no fulfilling sexual identity—not, at least, within the dominant familial and developmental patterns of postmedieval Western culture. While there are clear historical differences to account for, it appears that there are certain familial and developmental structures shared by the early modern period and our own era. Whether these are "universal" is, of course, quite another question.

Shakespeare's male characters, in particular, are engaged in continuous struggles within, and beyond, the family to form a secure gendered identity and to find (or reject) a place for women in that identity. As Coppélia Kahn shows in an essay I recommend for advanced courses and which can be summarized by the teacher for introductory classes, in *The Winter's Tale* the focus is on the self-destructive insecurities that arise from the male child's separation from the mother, an experience, whether real or imagined, represented in this play — as elsewhere in the romances and comedies and in some of the tragedies, like *Coriolanus* or *Hamlet* — by a loss of innocence or youth, which the male blames on the mother. Within the traditional patriarchal family, a boy's first object of desire is his mother, a desire produced in part by his growing awareness of his mother's otherness and therefore of his own sense of lack. The need to become what society defines as masculine is both fueled and threatened by that primary, profound (perhaps primeval) oneness with the mother. Later, as a man looks back at his childhood, he may recall, if only unconsciously, the perilous task of separation and individuation from the mother and, all too easily, project his contradictory feelings on his adult objects of desire.

I have spent time explaining this structure, as I do in class, not because Shakespeare's late plays simply reflect it. I argue, rather, that parts of the family romance surface at key moments in the plays and that reading them in the light of its characteristic patterns helps explain recurring and very powerful situations.

Let me give some examples. In the most obvious, almost literal, translation of Freud's basic family-romance pattern, all four of the romances are structured by a narrative of the foundling child discovering his or her "true" nobility. Marina, Cymbeline's sons, Perdita, and (to an extent) Miranda enact this common fantasy of upward mobility when they discover that they have a different, indeed royal, parentage despite their lowly status and surroundings. Then there are more complex variations. In *Pericles*, the motif of incest that critics have often pointed to is found not only in the crudely developed triangle of Pericles, Antiochus, and his daughter but, more profoundly, in the relational triangle of Pericles, Marina, and Thaisa. Carol Neely quotes Claude Lévi-Strauss, who writes that incest is the fantasy "that one could gain without losing, enjoy without sharing," a myth that is "eternally denied to social man, of a world in which one might *keep to oneself*" (*Broken Nuptials* 247). In *Pericles*, Neely notes, the incest motif is not merely literal but represents a desire to fix and hold the inevitably painful process of separation and individuation in changing relationships, especially within the family. The play enacts, from the man's viewpoint, a father's disinclination to acknowledge that his daughter is not a part of him but an autonomous person. Losing both Marina and her mother is, for Pericles, akin to losing an original self-unity; when he finds Marina, the temptation is to try to re-create an earlier oneness instead of acknowledging her as a grown, independent woman, one who, in her promised, though barely developed, marriage, is no longer his. Significantly, in the moving discovery scene (5.1), he envisages her as simultaneous daughter and mother ("thou that beget'st him that did thee beget"), fusing the two major roles men ask women to play in the Freudian family romance.

We can see similar idealizations and displacements of the family romance in the lost sons and the father-daughter relations of *Cymbeline* (even in aspects of Imogen and Posthumus's marriage, with its strong echoes of mother-child tensions and demands). They recur in the generational tensions, the clashes between friends and spouses, the sexual jealousy and paranoia, and the losses and returns of children and mother in *The Winter's Tale*. In the generational and familial clashes and the anger and anxieties of the patriarchal father in *The Tempest*, the pattern includes sibling rivalry, betrayed brotherly love, and battles over legacies (literal and metaphorical) from parents (also both literal and metaphorical).

Of all the late plays, *The Winter's Tale* is particularly worth considering in this context. Shakespeare's interest in the role of masculine identity in the family romance focuses on a male figure, Leontes, whose separation has been incomplete or problematic and for whom anxiety arises when, as an adult, he is called on to be a friend, a husband, and a father. As a husband, Leontes finds himself once again dependent on a woman to confirm his identity, a situation in which he may easily reenact, either positively or negatively, in displaced or disguised forms, his early crises of masculine identity. Leontes can be seen as projecting on Hermione insecurities that go far beyond their apparent cause. In his version of the family romance, bliss was in childhood, in his myth of an uncomplicated boyhood friendship with Polixenes, before the threat of otherness — represented by falling in love, marriage, and adulthood — intervened to both entice and threaten his need to differentiate. According to this reading (particularly well set out by Kahn), Hermione, marvelously serene in what many of us may be tempted (caught in a very specific ideology of the family and of gender assignment) to see as "natural" motherhood and equally serene in her roles as wife and friend, seemingly has the very self-completion that Leontes both yearns for and fears. The irrational rejection of Hermione (1.2 and 2.1) can be read as enacting such contradictions, while Leontes's objection when he believes Hermione to be dead resembles the extreme position of the child who has destroyed the person whom he most loves and yet from whom he must assert his independence. In the suspicion and persecution of his wife, Leontes can be seen as projecting on her a nostalgic fantasy of a loss of an undifferentiated world, attacking precisely what we are attracted by, her apparent serene oneness with herself. Leontes repudiates her because he is threatened by her; and in his rage, he adds to the arbitrariness of the political tyrant all the destructiveness of the patriarchally constructed male, particularly the irrationality of the child who finds that he must cut himself adrift from his mother and yet who resents having to do so. Many of us may be not unaware of our own related feelings — or, in the phrase we use in my classes, at least we know a friend who is!

These readings often prove the basis for vigorous discussion. It has been pointed out — by my students, as by feminist critics — that the Freudian model of development centers almost exclusively on the male. One response to that (it seems to me) undeniable charge is that Shakespeare appears to have had a similar obsession in these plays, focusing especially on the relations between the male child and the mother figure or function or on the adult male and his daughter. I usually get some ironical smiles—not least from the women—when the question of men's excessive idealization of their daughters is raised. The question for women readers, however, given this male-centered approach, is whether there are other places of entry for their gendered interests or whether they must read the plays as studies of male obsessions and patterns. One such point of entry may be the strong women characters: Hermione, Paulina, Imogen, even (briefly) Marina. But are such figures merely projections of the male need for strong mother figures, whom men simultaneously want to escape and be subject to? That possibility in itself often leads to as spirited a discussion for women readers as father-daughter relations does. And it leads to further questions. Why has our culture produced this recurring pattern of male loss and searching? What are the female equivalents? Are such patterns historically contingent? Or are they built into our basic biogrammar? Why are many of the mothers missing or lost for much of the plays? And, as Shirley Garner asks, why is it that, within the family romance, there is the all-too-common male fantasy "that a woman will always forgive a man no matter how much he wrongs her"? (147). *Cymbeline* and *The Winter's Tale* are particularly powerful workings out of this fantasy: are the forgiveness and reconciliation "represented" by Imogen or Hermione as noble and appropriate as traditional critics have argued? Or are these wish-fulfillment endings complex reflections of a male desire to project the all-forgiving and once always available mother on their wives and lovers? Are men in our culture to be condemned, pitied, or accepted for such desires? Are these patterns built into the basic fantasy structure of being male, or are they characteristic of a particular phase of the history of the patriarchal family and the romances it has engendered?

For those teachers or students for whom such questions sound too speculative, or who believe that meaning has to be located somehow "in" the text or in what is supposed to have been Shakespeare's own time, reading these plays as family romances can still point to useful situations. The tensions within the patriarchal and the early modern family have been much commented on by social historians and recent feminist and materialist critics. But to restrict the influence of these plays to "historical" considerations seems to me to blunt their force. Many of our students (and maybe not a few teachers), after all, are very actively caught in their own struggles of individuation and differentiation. The utterances and conflicts of all the late plays present aspects of the family romance as we enact them today—situations of generational tension, the reliance on family ties and the need to break away from them, the delusions of omnipotence and fears of abandonment that we experience as children and project on our adult relationships. Today most of us perceive such patterns as an inescapable part of childhood and as the presence of childhood in our later lives. I have learned that my students reverberate to these preoccupations and that they find the language of psychoanalysis and certain aspects of developmental psychology apt and understandable.

Such preoccupations, moreover, may help explain the remarkable popularity of the late plays in this century, not only among critics but on the stage. In 1988, between London and Stratford-upon-Avon, one could see no fewer than two productions of *Pericles* and three each of *Cymbeline*, *The Winter's Tale*, and *The Tempest*. Three of these productions traveled to the Stratford, Ontario, Shakespeare festival. The popularity of these plays — at least by contrast with their relatively modest reputation, except for *The Tempest*, in earlier centuries — has been remarked by many historians of the theater. These plays seem to have tapped into something central to the gender, sexual, and familial concerns of our age. Our society is certainly as interested in the family and its multiple romances as Shakespeare's was. Yet it is clear that the family is by no means idealized in the late plays. While many critics used to see the family as a symbol of stability in the comedies and romances, it can also be seen as yet another site of instability, a place where there is contestation between generations, where often one parent (usually the mother) is missing, and where harmonies are tentative, patched together, and founded on utopian wish rather than realistic expectation. If these plays, as so many critics assert, valorize reunited families, they do so only through great strains and, as most poignantly in *The Winter's Tale*, without restoring all that was lost. The sourness and reluctance many see in Prospero, too, is partly built on what he perceives as generational and familial betrayal. One of my women students asserted that Prospero's simultaneously opposing and favoring his daughter's relationship with Ferdinand was the behavior of "a typical father." Her comment aroused widespread grins of recognition in the class, and we felt a need to pause and probe why that should be.

The conclusion here (one seemingly thrust on many readers despite their skepticism about the inherent power of literature or art) is that when we respond to and reproduce these plays within our own histories, we are led to draw on some of our most primitive and deeply encultured memories. The continued fascination of the late plays is, I suspect, based on the ways they elicit our most primal experiences, whether we describe those as built into our basic biogrammar or (as some psychoanalysts argue) our fundamental psychological patterns, as culturally produced, or as influenced by all these. Indeed, if a combination of biopsychological and cultural layering makes up the Freudian unconscious, then the late romances are among those works drawing most deeply on what that often contentious term stands for. Indeed, we call the romances "great" not because they are somehow "universal," above the material or psychological details of our personal and collective histories, but because they are deeply embedded in those histories and have consequently been read in intriguingly different ways. The role of the teacher becomes, therefore, that of making available to students powerful and flexible languages to describe how those complex and sometimes disturbing experiences are, or might be, engaged. Seeing them in terms of the family romance is an especially compelling way.

Shakespeare's Romances and Jacobean Political Discourse

Donna B. Hamilton

In recent years, cultural-historical studies of Shakespeare have turned insistently to the question of how one might define Shakespeare's relation to his own culture. One question this interest raises is that of how Shakespeare positioned his plays in relation to the monarch. A complex issue when we are dealing with the Elizabethan plays, it is all the more keenly felt for the plays written under James I, who, at the outset of his reign, became the official patron of Shakespeare's company and renamed it the King's Men. Critics have come to understand that, despite the presence of this patronage relationship between James and the King's Men, certain plays — especially *Macbeth*, *King Lear*, and *Coriolanus* — criticize as well as compliment royal policy and that they deal with some of the most important political issues of the time, issues that concern the high politics of government under a king who was defining his power as absolute (Norbrook; Patterson 106–13; Barton).

Although critical perspectives on Shakespeare have undergone considerable change in the last decade, the romances have, to too large an extent, remained immune to the kind of criticism that has overtaken the other Jacobean plays. The use of masque conventions in the romances at the time when the masque was a popular court entertainment and the presence of beautiful and noble children in these plays written when the monarch's three children were getting a lot of attention — Prince Henry was named prince of Wales in 1610, Princess Elizabeth was betrothed and wedded in 1612 and 1613 — have encouraged the assumption that the cultural politics of the romances chiefly involves the presentation of gracious commentary on and compliment to the royal family. In other words, not only are these plays usually understood as supporting the monarch, but they are understood as works that are *safe* as well as *soft*. Or, in still different words, these plays about beautiful people doing good things in family settings have seemed to many critics not to involve the high politics found in other plays but to represent instead those values and situations that were, in many ways, uncontested.

My own approach is centered in the assumption that the romances are as deeply and importantly political as are the plays that nearly everyone would put in that category — *Richard II*, for example, or *Coriolanus*. It has been more difficult to see the political aspects of the romances because they are written in a highly metaphoric style — to which family settings and noble children are central — that is both polite and mystified, that uses uncontested values to argue contested issues. While this method of writing and arguing was a standard means of conducting social and political discussions in Shakespeare's time and was rehearsed in various rhetorical treatises (in book 3 of George Puttenham's *Arte of English Poesie*, for example), there is really nothing in such argumentation with which most of us today are not thoroughly familiar. A great deal of social and political life relies on devices for saying nicely what one wants desperately and believes in passionately. And, whether or not one is trying to sound polite, opponents in an argument regularly use metaphor and appropriate an uncontested value to argue against an opponent.

During the summer of 1990 the Iraqi president, Saddam Hussein, who had just invaded Kuwait and was holding large numbers of foreigners hostage, released a videotape in which, dressed in a Western-style business suit, he asked a young boy in the hostage group to acknowledge that there had been milk and cornflakes for breakfast. Hussein's opponents in the West responded by calling Hussein a "Hitler." These exchanges illustrate how political statement and argument rely on language that is value-driven, metaphoric, and representational. Of course, if the people listening to the news had no idea that, in the Western world, cornflakes are as deeply associated with notions of what is innocuous as with notions of nutrition and that Hitler is as deeply associated with notions of evil as with notions of power, they would not have been able to understand what was at issue in these exchanges — even if they had at that very moment been reading the biography of Hitler while eating cornflakes. As these remarks imply, if one is to read and listen with understanding — whether one's attention is on Shakespeare or the morning news — one must have knowledge of context as well as of values, idiom, and style.

In my undergraduate Shakespeare course I teach these concepts along with a good deal of history. And by the time we get to the romances (in a course that runs from *Hamlet* to the romances), my students are generally familiar with Renaissance English attitudes toward obedience and resistance, constitutionalism and absolutism. They have learned that the theater, although subject to censorship, was a medium that had the capacity to speak on controversial subjects in ways that would avoid government interference. The students also know about some of the specific issues and events that dominated national politics after 1600 and after public debate — for example, the Gunpowder Plot, the debates on the union of England and Scotland, the problems that arose over the king's financial difficulties, and the anxiety caused by James's insistent repetition of the notion that he possessed an absolute power.

Concerning Shakespeare's involvement in these issues, the attitude fostered in the classroom is that, as an intellectual, Shakespeare was engaged in the central social and political issues that occupied other intellectuals of his time. It is assumed not that he was a puppet of the king or that he was unequivocally in opposition to government policy (there are not only two choices) but that he positioned his plays rhetorically so that they provided commentary and reflection on issues of interest and concern to mixed constituencies of playgoers – the mixed constituency at court (the king and the various court factions) and also the mixed constituency at the public playhouse.

Having worked with these assumptions from the beginning of the semester, my students are not surprised when, during the second class period devoted to *The Tempest*, we turn our attention to the controversy about the king's financial settlement that dominated the Parliament of 1610. We will already have spent the first class analyzing the power relations the play displays. Asked to describe the power relations represented in the different plots in the play, students produce a lively discussion of the master-slave or master-servant relationships that Caliban and Ariel have with Prospero, of the father-child and student-teacher relationship that Prospero has with Ferdinand and Miranda, and of the repetition throughout the play of conspiracy and usurpation.

With some aspects of the structure of the play in mind, we examine the Parliament of 1610. The goal is to learn not only what the issues for this Parliament were but how the opposing sides articulated their arguments – to see not only what positions were taken but how each side structured and expressed its defense and thus tried to represent itself as right. Aware that the crisis in Kuwait produced a language that included references to cornflakes and Hitler, we want to observe what discourse was produced during this crisis between king and Parliament. How did Parliament go about telling the king that he was demanding too much power, and how did the king go about telling Parliament that the power he wanted and was using was exactly the right amount? As we figure this out, we learn of the discourse within which certain political events were enacted, and we become equipped to assess how Shakespeare encompassed and textualized these issues in *The Tempest*, a play that many people have thought is not tuned in to such important topics.

The basic information students need is that James summoned the Parliament in 1610 to secure a financial settlement appropriate for the current level of government expense. Although no one then or now would dispute that a new settlement was needed, some members of the House of Commons feared that James was interested in increasing not only his revenues but his prerogative. James had exacerbated this misgiving when he raised the customs (or impositions) on imported and exported goods without first consulting Parliament. The alarm bred by this action – that the king was inclined to overextend his power – was increased all the more by his next move, the proposal that the system for supply be changed to one of a guaranteed revenue. While most modern historians agree that this proposal, the Great Contract, was a good plan, one that would have benefited the people as much as the king, some in Parliament were wary that once the proposal was passed, the king would no longer need to summon Parliament, which would lose its voice in government. Thus, as the 1610 session proceeded, the debates focused not only on how much money might be needed, where found, and how gathered but on the relationship between king and subject. If the subjects were to supply the king, members of the House of Commons wanted to know what he would give them in return. What did each owe to each? Or, put somewhat differently, what were the limits of the king's power? Historians have provided us with narratives and analyses of the events of this Parliament (Tanner; Notestein; A. G. R. Smith), but more important for our purposes are the records of what the king and the members of the Commons actually said to each other, records that are readily available in modern editions of the speeches of James and of the speeches in Parliament (McIlwain; Foster; Gardiner).

The arguments that King James and his supporters developed focused on the idea that the king had a right to the power he was claiming for himself. Forging those arguments out of language that would define the king's power as natural and unquestionable, James compared kings to gods, to fathers, and to the head of a body: "In the Scriptures Kings are called Gods, and so their power after a certain relation compared to the Divine power. Kings are also compared to Fathers of families; for a King is trewly . . . the politique father of his people. And lastly, Kings are compared to the head of this Microcosme of the body of a man" (qtd. in McIlwain 307). Although willing to temper his rhetoric — he said that the king was not like a god who "spake by Oracles, and wrought by Miracles" (309) — James nevertheless insisted that "[t]he State of MONARCHIE is the supremest thing upon earth: For Kings are not only GODS Lieutenants upon earth, and sit upon GODS throne, but even by GOD himself they are called Gods" (307). Kings resemble gods in many ways; even as gods "create, or destroy, make or unmake," so do kings "make and unmake their subjects" and have power "of life, and of death" over them (307–08). In fact, kings can "make of their subjects like men at the Chesse" (308). In these metaphors, James was developing language that Salisbury, the Lord Treasurer, would imitate, even translate, when he referred to the king as the *"primum mobile,"* or first mover, and that Francis Bacon would use when explaining that it was the nature of the king to be the *"principale agens,"* or principal agent (qtd. in Gardiner 52, 67). James hoped, of course, that this language of agency could be translated into trust. To that end he assured the Commons that he would not abuse his power and that he had no intention of speaking one thing in public and then contradicting it in private: "Kings Actions (even in the secretest places) are as the actions of those that are set upon the Stages or on the tops of houses" (McIlwain 310).

On the specific issue of finance, James had two especially important things to say. First, he explained flatly that subjects owed him a financial settlement, or "supply," a position that, in itself, no one would deny. In exacting payments, James said, the king took only that which the subject was bound to give. His second point, the one that eventually triggered the Commons to issue a Petition of Right, was that, because supply was his right, the Commons was not to dispute the matter. On this matter, James scolded, the Commons was to be quiet, for it was "sedition in subjects, to dispute what a king may do in the height of his power. . . . I will not be content that my power be disputed upon" (McIlwain 310). Thus the reasoning rhetoric of explanation, reassurance, and definition joined the language of threat: the power of gods was not to be questioned.

As the records of the speeches given in the Commons show, the members of Parliament answered the king by developing arguments against an increased royal power, arguments that included their own characterizations both of that power and of the effect such a power would have on subjects. They answered the king's representation of his power as natural and normal by saying that the king's having increased the impositions showed "an arbitrary, irregular, unlymited, and transcendent power" that was "contrary to reason" and "beyond measur" (Gardiner 88, 76, 152). And instead of merely accepting the king's interpretation that his policies promoted a proper (and natural) king-subject relationship, they argued that an excessive royal power — manifested now in the king's demand for excessive supply — reduced the subjects to slaves. Because the money ultimately came from the people, a king who demanded too much supply deprived subjects of property and so of liberty, thereby bringing the subject into bondage.

Representative examples of how members of the Commons stated this position are available in the speeches of Nicholas Fuller and Thomas Hedley. Invoking Magna Carta, Fuller explained that his "arguments for the freedom of the subject" would show "that by the laws of England the subjects have such property in their lands and goods as that without consent the king can take no part of." Similarly, Hedley argued that "the liberty of the subject" exists principally "in matter of profit and property." Therefore, "take away the liberty of the subject" in these matters "and you make a promiscuous confusion of a freeman and a bound slave, which slavery is as repugnant to the nature of an Englishman as allegiance and due subjection is . . . proper" (qtd. in Foster 2: 152, 191, 192).

The Commons was also unwilling to accept the king's order not to dispute his policies and prerogatives. Thus, in yet another speech in the Commons, Peter Wentworth insisted, "Is not the king's prerogative disputable? Do not our books in 20 cases argue what the king may do and what not do by his prerogative. . . . Nay if we shall once say that we may not dispute the prerogative, let us be sold for slaves" (Foster 2: 82–83). Of the documents produced by the Commons during these debates, two of the most important were the Petition of Right and the Petition of Temporal Grievances, both of which were printed at the time. The Petition of Right (not to be confused with the more famous Petition of Right of 1628) was entered in parliament on 23 May 1610 and then delivered to the king. The main thrust of this petition was again the Commons' insistence that there be no infringement of "the ancient and fundamental right of the liberty of the Parliament" to debate freely the king's use of his prerogative, for only if this right to speak out was protected would it be "possible for the subject either to know or to maintain his right and property to his own lands and goods" (qtd. in Tanner 246).

The Petition of Temporal Grievances (accompanied by a Petition of Ecclesiastical Grievances) was presented to the king at Whitehall on 7 July 1610. The Privy Council and twenty members of the House of Commons attended this presentation. In this document, the Commons reminded the king that there was nothing more "precious" to them than "to be guided and governed by the certain rule of the law, which giveth both to the head and members that which of right belongeth to them" (Foster 2: 253–54, 258). Moreover, as these examples show, both the Petition of Right and this later document contain the position that the king was subject to restraint by Parliament. A notion of restraint did not mean that the king was not absolute, but it did mean that the absolute power of the king existed not in the king by himself but in the king in parliament.

The outcome of this yearlong debate was that James finally silenced Parliament by dissolving it in February 1611, before any resolution had been reached. Some historians have thought the dissolution may have been "a turning point in the financial and constitutional history of the early seventeenth century" (A. G. R. Smith 127). Moreover, having dissolved Parliament, the king would not call it again until 1614, when it would meet for only two months. I mention these details to reiterate the importance of the issues dealt with in this parliamentary session.

Once students have both sides of the argument between king and the Commons in mind, we reconsider the power relations in *The Tempest*. I ask two questions: How might we see that the play is affected by, registers, encompasses, textualizes, fictionalizes, or replicates the arguments, rhetoric, and idioms of these parliamentary debates? How might we describe the various ways in which the play encompasses the contemporary debates about the king-subject relationship and about the limits of the king's power?

We begin the discussion by reexamining the language Shakespeare uses to construct the references to and speeches of Caliban and Ariel — language the students see not only as poetic but as made up of contemporary political discourse. And we look again at how Shakespeare represents the relationships of Caliban and Ariel to Prospero as situations in which Prospero wants something from them and they want something from him. In exchange for serving Prospero and executing his plans, Ariel wants freedom. Prospero's relationship with Caliban is more complex. Originally affairs had gone smoothly between Prospero and Caliban — Caliban introduced Prospero to the island, and Prospero treated Caliban kindly — but then the relationship soured. Caliban has taken advantage of Prospero (he tried to rape Miranda, and he would like to kill Prospero), and Prospero has retaliated by exercising his transcendent, magical powers, causing Caliban to be held in bondage with cramps, pricks, and bites. Caliban now regrets that he ever served Prospero and thinks instead only of how Prospero took control of an island that Caliban regards as his property. Of course, Caliban is not the only one Prospero threatens: Prospero has warned Ariel that, in exchange for any disobedience, he will imprison and silence Ariel by putting him back in a tree — this time in an oak tree, not the softer pine tree that the former ruler of the island used. In the context of our study of the Parliament of 1610, the students come to see in these relationships a replication of the power struggle between king and the Commons and a fictional representation of the metaphoric language king and the Commons used to argue about the king-subject relationship.

When we have debated the extent to which Prospero, Caliban, and Ariel are not fulfilling their responsibilities to one another, as well as the extent to which our exercise in contextualization gives us a helpful set of terms for considering the political implications of this play, we turn our attention to Ferdinand and Miranda and to the emphasis in their relationship on chastity and discipline. In the context of the lovers in Shakespeare's other plays — Romeo and Juliet, Rosalind and Orlando, Othello and Desdemona, Antony and Cleopatra — Ferdinand and Miranda give us no excitement. If we place them in the context of the controversy over absolute power and financial responsibility, however, we can see that some of the central values of the play — such as order by way of restraint and discipline — match rather well the values that the Commons were urging James to adopt as his own.

What is especially interesting about Shakespeare's representation of these values, however, is that in the play they are the *ruler's* values. Shakespeare's ruler is the one who establishes that these are the important values when he insists that Ferdinand exist on a spare diet of seawater and withered roots, do the hard physical labor of carrying logs, and promise to remain chaste until he and Miranda are married. In these ways, the ruler himself is made to represent the value of reining in an acquisitive and appetitive nature.

When Shakespeare elects these qualities as the ones to be fostered in a young prince, we must be correct in assuming that the audience could have viewed his choice as a compliment to James for being a careful father of royal children. But to structure the compliment so that the values emphasized — restraint and discipline — could also be understood as the opposite of unlimited power, transcendent rule, and extravagant expenditure gives the play the capacity not only to compliment the king but also to side with those who thought he should temper his position.

The end is open to the same reading. When Prospero extends mercy to those who have opposed him and also gives up his magic before returning to rule, the play again depicts restraint as the most noble and heroic choice for a ruler to make. Further, Prospero's choice suggests something about

Shakespeare's own political biases. Shakespeare may not have been anti-monarchical, but he was a constitutionalist who favored a limited monarchy and who did not let the king's patronage prevent him from voicing criticism.

I have written at length elsewhere on this topic and on other aspects of *The Tempest*, including Shakespeare's use in the play of some features of Virgil's *Aeneid* (*Virgil*). If time permits, I introduce my students to the Virgilian aspects of Shakespeare's writing. When I teach *The Winter's Tale* and *Cymbeline*, I also use a contextualizing method that focuses on controversy and debate, but I present students with different contexts and so with different discourses. We contextualize *The Winter's Tale* with material from the discussions in Parliament over what would be gained or lost by union with Scotland, discovering in that discourse a set of idioms and metaphors entirely different from the one used in the debates over the king's financial settlement (see Hamilton, "*Winter's Tale*"). The language of *The Winter's Tale*, like that of Parliament's contentions over the union of England and Scotland, is filled with metaphors of kinship, strangeness, hospitality, and theft. Likewise, when we study *Cymbeline*, we look at the discourse of the controversy over the Oath of Allegiance that James instituted for his Catholic subjects following the Gunpowder Plot. The language of both sides of this argument is repeated conveniently in James's *Triplici Nodo, Triplex Cuneus, or An Apologie for the Oath of Allegiance* and *A Premonition To All Most Mighty Monarchs* (in McIlwain 71–167), where James stated his positions but also quoted extensively from his opponents' writings. And again, the discourse is distinctive to this topic, even as *Cymbeline* has a quality and a language that distinguish it from the other romances.

This method of studying the romances demonstrates what they have in common with Shakespeare's other treatments of high politics and gives students an understanding of the language of controversy that is all around them in their everyday lives. Having learned for themselves how political dialogue works and that political discourse is made up of language that answers other language, students become keener readers of the discourses that frame our own most pressing social and political issues.

SPECIFIC PLAYS

Teaching "A Thing Perplex'd": Drawing Unity from the Confusion of *Cymbeline*

Cynthia Lewis

Those of us who every now and then include *Cymbeline* on a syllabus know that doing so yields rewards even as it presents difficulties. Most of us, however, have little experience teaching the play. Given the freedom to choose, we will almost always select another, tidier work in its place. We do so even in graduate-level courses, where students might be considered more willing to entertain the play's eccentricities. But so strongly did I recently want to teach *Cymbeline* again to upper-level undergraduates that I invented a whole new senior seminar allowing me to feature *Cymbeline* in the company of three other Shakespearean plays.

As my students in that class came from their first day of discussion about *Cymbeline*, I was reminded of the intense reactions, both pro and con, that the play elicits among first-time readers. Those who instantly admire the play tend to exercise limited sway over those who are immediately put off by it, yet the disapproving group is susceptible, I have discovered, to some coaxing toward appreciating the work. Although students' reasons for disliking *Cymbeline* vary widely, their complaints fall into two general categories. Some students find the play emotionally unsatisfying: the characters, they allege, are flat and motiveless (Posthumus often excepted); the plot is so contrived and so artificially resolved as to be ridiculous; the poetry is devoid of beauty and feeling. Moreover, these students feel, Shakespeare almost seems deliberately to disappoint the audience's emotional expectations with hollow dramatic situations. Other students believe that *Cymbeline* is intellectually arid: the plot is too crowded to be followed or to be taken seriously; compared with other Shakespearean plays—in particular, *The Winter's Tale* and *The Tempest*—*Cymbeline* appears laughably disorganized and disunified, so much so that only the most charitable of disapproving students are willing to label it "experimental" at best.

Teachers, I think, will be hard pressed to defend *Cymbeline* (or any other work) on emotional grounds. But we can point students toward a great deal of intellectual satisfaction by helping them uncover the often hidden patterns that unify the play. Thus, if a play's capacity to arouse emotions depends on its ability to satisfy intellectually (as I believe it does), then we might well guide students toward a fuller emotional experience of *Cymbeline* through developing their greater understanding of the play.

I would like to suggest three broad areas in which students can enjoy rich discussion of shaping principles in *Cymbeline*: characterization, structure, and theme. I raise characterization first because some students are quick to criticize the play's characters as two-dimensional, dull, and predictable—Jachimo is an archvillain, for instance, and Imogen is an unrealistically good heroine. No sooner do my students make such charges, however, than I ask them for counterexamples.

I urge them, for starters, to compare and contrast Iago and Jachimo, and in doing so they realize how artistically sophisticated is the latter scoundrel's portrait—at least as sophisticated and profound as Iago's. Some critics, like G. Wilson Knight, even find Jachimo's scheming "far more convincing than Iago's" (*Crown* 144). Jachimo has a motive for wagering—to debunk Posthumus's pride (1.4.110–11)—and he displays ample conscience and remorse (5.2.1–10; 5.5.141–209). By contrast, Iago's pretensions to jealousy (1.1.8–33) and cuckoldry (1.3.386–88; 2.1.295–96, 307) constitute lame motives for the evil he commits. Nor does he feel any guilt, refusing at the last to repent (5.2.303–05).

Iago tries to forge an intimacy with the audience through his manipulative soliloquies, which at first glance may seem to lend him a psychological depth that Jachimo lacks, since Jachimo rarely speaks directly to us. But scrutiny of both texts reveals that Jachimo's more introverted behavior bespeaks at least as much psychological dimension as does Iago's more outgoing manner. Iago's need to influence the audience, as well as his many victims, suggests his emotional insecurity: he feels compelled to control others to achieve the self-confidence that continually escapes his grasp. But Jachimo, who urges "[b]oldness" on himself (1.6.18), needs no support from the audience; he is self-possessed and self-sufficient, uninterested in divulging his plans to impress the audience. He does not enlist other characters to execute his plans for him, as does Iago, but relies solely on himself. In short, Iago and Jachimo are complementary; that Jachimo is less open does not make him less complicated or engaging than his counterpart.

Imogen, too, exhibits a complex characterization; as Elizabeth Drew remarks, she has her own "individual 'tune'" (24–27). Granted, her unwavering faith in her misled husband can make her appear too good to be true, and yet the theme of fidelity, which Imogen's behavior conveys, should not be confused with her multifaceted personality. Not only does her treatment of Cloten in 2.3 approach a delicious nastiness, but her vulnerability to the same misconception that plagues all the other characters makes her human and thus worthy of our sympathy. In 1.6 she is momentarily duped by Jachimo; in 4.2 she mistakes Cloten's body for her spouse's, and she leaps to the conclusion that Pisanio and Cloten have murdered Posthumus. If in the last scene she springs back to go on loving the husband who has knocked her to the ground (5.5.229), it is not because she is too pure for this world but rather because she understands, as Posthumus has not understood, that human love must either endure the weaknesses of imperfect human beings or perish.

As for Posthumus, he must learn what his wife has known all along, and his moral maturation, which lies at the play's heart, lends him his own rounded, intriguing characterization. Scholars disagree on the precise point at which Posthumus changes. Homer Swander, for instance, locates the crucial turning point in 5.1 and sees the remainder of act 5 as the gradual playing out of Posthumus's promise to "fashion" himself "less without and more within" ("Religious Idea"; 5.1.33). Other readers, including many of my students, doubt that Posthumus ever essentially grows — after all, he is still abusing Imogen when he strikes Fidele in 5.5. I believe, though, that we see the final fruits of Posthumus's inner struggle very late in the play, even after he has hit Imogen, and that his characterization up to that point has been but preparation for his change and not the change itself. So I invite students to look at Posthumus's line in which he forgives Jachimo — "The pow'r that I have on you is to spare you; / The malice towards you, to forgive you" (5.5.418–19) — and I ask them to connect that speech with any other in the scene. Cymbeline, of course, offers like grace, once Posthumus has proved so generous (5.5.420–22, 458–65). But the very first character in the scene to deliver mercy is Imogen, who through the example of her own graciousness instructs her husband to treat even his enemies with generosity: "Think that you are upon a rock, and now / Throw me again" (5.5.262–63). Her injunction that Posthumus hurt her again, although teasingly ironical, provides the play's altogether serious model of forgiveness. By the end of *Cymbeline*, the entire court, including Posthumus, is emulating Imogen's willingness to turn the other cheek.

Investigating the many dimensions of such major figures as Jachimo, Imogen, and Posthumus moves students closer toward seeing the care that Shakespeare has lavished on all the characters in *Cymbeline* — characters who may, again, initially seem as shallow as those from fairy tales. For example, despite the often tiresome and clichéd speeches of Arviragus, Guiderius, and their protector Belarius, Shakespeare has taken pains to fill in the brothers' personalities by differentiating the one from the other where he might have left them indistinguishable from each other. I encourage students to go back to the text and discover passages in which the brothers' distinct characters emerge. Such instances include 4.2, where Arviragus is associated with the gentler traits of loving (20–24), of singing and playing music (48, 186–94), and of speaking in "wench-like words" that make Guiderius impatient (230); Guiderius, however, is unable to sing (240) and is characterized by more practical concerns, like his taste in food (49–51) and his physical defeat of Cloten.

Even Cloten and his nefarious mother are handled with a certain finesse. As Frank Walsh Brownlow observes, Cloten "is like many a spoiled, stupid child in the old tales," but Shakespeare complicates him so that his "crazy, sadistic design [against Posthumus and Imogen] . . . gives an alarmingly real insight into a form of criminal lunacy" (136–37). Similarly, the Queen, whose evil seems blatant to Imogen (1.1.83–85) and to Cornelius (1.5.33–44), is nevertheless trusted later on by Pisanio, who accepts her deadly potion in good faith. Pisanio is not dull; indeed, the Queen calls him "sly" (1.5.75), and the audience knows him for a clever servant who effectively aids Imogen. Thus the Queen must be capable of some subtlety to seduce one of Pisanio's discernment. She, too, is irreducible to a thoroughly predictable, two-dimensional figure. One of my students has noted how even the audience believes her to be genuinely kind in 1.1: when Imogen informs us of the Queen's dissembling nature, in line 83, we may well be surprised.

To discover the wealth of characterization in *Cymbeline* beneath the surface of apparent simplicity is also to mine one of the play's most pervasive structural patterns: the constant difference between appearance and reality. Practically all critical studies of the play mention or analyze this element; examples include those of John Scott Colley, John Dean, Bertrand Evans, Nancy K. Hayles, Knight (*Crown*), Alexander Leggatt, and Barbara Mowat (*Dramaturgy*). As we have already seen, Shakespeare often treats his audience much as he does his characters; the latter group is subject to the confusions of the play much as playgoers are misled by the confusions of life as they are rendered within the play. Repeatedly, both characters and audience are forced to interpret a cryptic appearance — "a thing perplex'd," as Imogen refers to Pisanio's inscrutable expression in 3.4.7. Often, however, Shakespeare feeds his audience correct information that he withholds from his characters. Such "discrepant awareness" (248) between characters and audience, as Evans describes it in his excellent chapter on *Cymbeline*, recurs constantly throughout the play. What's more, repeating instances of discrepant awareness becomes one of Shakespeare's most favored means of paralleling scenes and incidents and thus of tightening the play's shape. The royal brothers' ignorance of Fidele's well-being, for instance, parallels Imogen's not knowing that Posthumus lives. In another example, Cymbeline's ignorance of his wife's corruption matches Posthumus's of his wife's virtue.

The most prominent of pairings between scenes occurs when, first, Posthumus is fooled by Jachimo (2.2; 2.4) and, next, Imogen is tricked by Cloten's headless body (4.2). Each of these two episodes is elaborate enough in itself to make for excellent discussion among advanced Shakespeare students. But studying the incidents together brings both into sharper focus and points up similarities between them. To begin with, both Posthumus and Imogen are severely duped, Posthumus by what Jachimo makes him see in 2.4 and Imogen by what she sees indeed. In fact, the handling of both leading characters verges on — and perhaps amounts to — ridicule: Posthumus and Imogen misperceive in ways that can be interpreted as foolish. But just how much does Shakespeare mock these two characters for being gulled? Critics disagree acutely on this issue. Roger Warren, for instance, denies that we are meant at all to laugh at Imogen's misprision (44), and Evans asserts that audiences respond to Imogen with a mixture of "convulsive grief and raucous laughter" (274). Entertaining this question, I have learned, pushes students to review 2.2, 2.4, and 4.2 with great care. And, in my experience, the best way for students to examine the tone in all three scenes is to act them out.

I hardly need to urge such performance on my students: they seize the chance to study these crucial scenes through acting. But I pose questions for them to answer while they proceed — most especially, Can an actor playing Jachimo in 2.2 emerge from the trunk without causing the audience to laugh, or in 4.2.295–332, can Imogen deliver her lines on Cloten's headless body without having the same effect? In other words, can Jachimo and Imogen take themselves totally seriously in their scenes? Or can Posthumus when, in 2.5, he inveighs against women with so little cause? I will not pretend that my students' performances resolve all such ambiguities, yet they certainly furnish some persuasive suggestions. Most important, try as the students might to act these scenes with no trace of silliness, a sure amount of humor always asserts itself.

Jachimo's emergence from the trunk in 2.2, in addition to being unexpected, is funny for its grotesque parody of birth. (Such parodic inversions arise elsewhere throughout *Cymbeline*, as when the Queen "confesses" her evil without the slightest contrition [5.5.33–61] and when Posthumus's defense of Imogen's purity transforms into its opposite, attempted murder.) The duping of Posthumus in 2.4 is likewise made darkly humorous, in large part because in 2.2 we have watched Jachimo plot Posthumus's downfall with the precision of a comic character like Portia or Maria. We sympathize with Posthumus to an extent, but we also enjoy seeing him chastened for his pride, much as we take satisfaction in watching the revelers in *Twelfth Night* trick the arrogant Malvolio (2.5). And, although Imogen deserves no such humiliation, we are nevertheless tempted to laugh at her predicament: after all, by confusing her direst enemy with her husband, she participates in a stock comic convention — that of mistaken identity.

Furthermore, Imogen's speech about identifying the body seems undeniably designed for laughs. She first acknowledges the unreliability of conclusions based on sensory perception: "Our very eyes / Are sometimes like our judgments, blind" (4.2.301–02). Then she not only ignores her own wisdom but also convinces herself that the body must be Posthumus's because she recognizes its every feature:

> I know the shape of's leg; this is his hand,
> His foot Mercurial, his Martial thigh,
> The brawns of Hercules; but his Jovial face—
> Murther in heaven? How? 'Tis gone.
> (4.2.309–12)

Every specific feature that Imogen mentions in this litany calls attention to the folly of her erroneous judgment, and her continuing certainty about the corpse's identity although its head is missing underscores her silliness. Granted, Imogen's blindness is temporary; ultimately, she is the play's most astute seer. Moreover, if Cloten and Posthumus were originally played by the same actor, as several critics have suggested (see, e.g., Booth, "Speculations" 121–25), then Imogen has good reason to confuse them. But even if we admire and sympathize with Imogen, we still sense buffoonery in her speech. I once had a student—incidentally, a fine actress—who agreed. To make her point for our class, she performed the passage twice—once, with all the seriousness she could muster and, the next time, in the tongue-in-cheek fashion that the lines would not let her escape. Her particular way of expressing the mockery she detected was to recite Imogen's speech in the voice and accent of a dippy southern belle.

In essence, when Imogen misperceives in 4.2, Shakespeare seems deliberately to recall Posthumus's earlier misperception at Jachimo's hands. Not only is the tone in the later scene reminiscent of that in 2.2 and 2.4, where Jachimo hatches and enacts his plot, but the very language in the later episodes jogs the audience's memory of the first incident. When Lucius encounters Cloten's corpse, in 4.2, his comment forces us to connect Imogen's misprision with Posthumus's: "Soft ho, what trunk is here? / Without his top?" (353–54). The image of the play's first (and very different) "trunk" is fleetingly, but irresistibly, brought back to mind. Lucius continues to remind us unwittingly of how Jachimo has fooled Posthumus: "who was he," asks Lucius about the decapitated body, "That (otherwise than noble nature did) / Hath alter'd that good picture?" (4.2.363–65). Much as Imogen is gulled by an artificially "alter'd picture," so Posthumus has been swayed in 2.4 by Jachimo's unnatural and quite graphic manipulation of the truth about Imogen's fidelity:

> If you seek
> For further satisfying, under her breast
> (Worthy her pressing) lies a mole, right proud
> Of that most delicate lodging. By my life,
> I kiss'd it, and it gave me present hunger
> To feed again, though full.   (2.4.133–38)

Jachimo creates his own pornographic "picture" to influence Posthumus. (Notice that Iago, too, plays lewdly on the word *satisfy* as he presents his own deceptive, pornographic evidence to Othello [3.3.390–401]).

Such interplay between the action, tone, and language of scenes thus binds together a play that may seem scattered and fragmented. Add to these structural devices the unifying element of theme, and *Cymbeline* may begin to strike students as a well-made play. Thematic studies have clustered around the play's interests both in British and Roman history (see, e.g., Richmond, "Roman Trilogy"; Geller) and in religious concerns, especially the coming of Christ during Cymbeline's reign (see, e.g., Leggatt; Moffet; Swander, "Religious Idea"). But I should like at the last to return to the issue of perception—knowing appearance from reality. Perception is a theme in *Cymbeline*, as well as an action through which, as we have noticed, the play gains structure.

As I have intimated above, one of my students' most frequent—and, I think, legitimate—qualms about the reasonableness and coherence of *Cymbeline* involves Imogen's constancy: Why does she cling to a man who treats her so badly? Does Shakespeare expect us to swallow her unshakable faith as a viable option in a real world, or does he ultimately sneak away from confronting her difficult marital situation by tacking on to 5.5 a vacuous, fairy-tale ending to her troubles? Does Imogen not *see* Posthumus for who he really is? When my students raise these questions, I prod them into considering various ways of seeing, and I read them Imogen's response to Pisanio's warning that she not seek out the angry Posthumus:

PISANIO.   Madam, you're best consider.
IMOGEN.   I see before me, man; nor here, nor here,
          Nor what ensues, but have a fog in them
          That I cannot look through. Away, I prithee,
          Do as I bid thee. There's no more to say:
          Accessible is none but Milford way.
                                   (3.2.77–82)

In effect, Imogen willfully chooses blindness in her pursuit of Posthumus's love. She sees not with the eyes of reason but with those of faith, which looks past the "fog" of sensory perception and relies on the evidence of the heart rather than the mind. She follows Posthumus despite her lack of knowledge and allows herself to be guided only by this single goal. Her folly is of the very wisest kind: her failure to perceive enables her to retrieve a worthy marriage that, in the hands of a more probing woman, would have dissolved. Had Imogen once acted rationally in response to Posthumus's suspicion of her and his attempt to have her murdered, she would have shunned Posthumus completely. This refusal to behave reasonably accounts for her abiding love.

If students come to *Cymbeline* having read *All's Well That Ends Well*, as a group of mine recently did, they can profit from thinking about Imogen in connection with Helena. Like her successor, Helena fastens on the husband who scorns her, in spite of all the reasons that she should not love him. She, too, chooses grace over judgment, faith in Bertram over skepticism. Yet Helena's choice forms the knottiest problem at the close of *All's Well*. Shakespeare focuses our attention on whether Bertram will truly change under Helena's influence or whether Helena should go on loving him even if he fails to change. That issue is the source of the play's great ambiguity. In *Cymbeline*, by contrast, the stress falls not on *whether* Imogen chooses well but on our *certainty* that her faith in Posthumus is well placed. Finally, *Cymbeline* is far less a problem play — or a problem at all — than is often alleged. But its audience, like its characters, must be vigilant: to see its harmony of vision, or its structural coherence, requires some thoughtful scrutiny. Therein lies its value to capable undergraduates.

Teaching the Slandered Women of *Cymbeline* and *The Winter's Tale*

Dorothea Kehler

Like rival brothers and father-daughter pairs, sexually slandered women are a signifying constant in Shakespeare, worthy of attention in the classroom. In *The Comedy of Errors*, Antipholus of Ephesus proclaims his wife a "dissembling harlot" and vows to pluck out her eyes, to scorch and disfigure her (4.4.101–05 and 5.1.182–83). Hero, in *Much Ado about Nothing*, the first of Shakespeare's slandered women who seemingly dies, prefigures *Cymbeline*'s Imogen and *The Winter's Tale*'s Hermione. In *The Merry Wives of Windsor*, jealous Master Ford tests his wife's fidelity as Posthumus will later test Imogen's. Bertram, the would-be seducer in *All's Well That Ends Well*, slanders Diana as a "common gamester" (5.3.188), and *Measure for Measure*'s Angelo disencumbers himself of Mariana after her dowry is lost, "pretending in her discoveries of dishonor" (3.1.227). In the comedies and romances, genre dictates the survival of the slandered woman; in tragedy calumny kills, as *Othello*'s Desdemona testifies.

Notwithstanding the unhappy consequences of sexual slander, the canon teems with cuckold jokes that take women's faithlessness as axiomatic, just as the ecclesiastical courts of Tudor England teemed with defamation suits brought by those called cuckold, whore, and whoremaster (Maus 562). From the ostensibly frivolous cuckold jokes to the homicidal rages of Posthumus and Leontes, Shakespeare depicts the sorry results of such intersecting cultural phenomena as male domination, sexual guilt, and misogyny. I believe it is essential that as teachers we engage these issues, for they are inseparable from today's worldwide "crimes of gender" (see Heise, esp. 18–19).

In *Cymbeline* and *The Winter's Tale*, although the heroines are paragons of trustworthiness, Posthumus is easily imposed on, and Leontes needs no villain to induce his conviction of having been betrayed. One way of explaining the husbands' readiness to think the worst of their wives is to build a bridge for students from Renaissance literature to postmodern theory, thus encouraging them to read the romances through contemporary experience. Adapting Jean Baudrillard's concept of simulation, we can begin to understand the fictive construction of woman that plagues Shakespeare's jealous husbands. Simulation, writes Baudrillard, is "the generation by models of a real without origin or reality: a hyperreal" (253). Always already reproduced, the hyperreal looks forward as well as backward only to more reproductions, never to the thing itself. Although for Baudrillard the hyperreal is the disastrous product of a highly technological society, the construction of women from as early as the second millennium BC appears analogous to his notion of simulation in the postmodern world (on the historical basis of Baudrillard's theorizing, see Kellner). I have taken the liberty, therefore, of appropriating Baudrillard's terminology while disregarding his developmental perspective.

A simulacrum is one of the models generating the hyperreal. *Simulacrum* is not merely another name for a stereotype, which can be defined as an unfounded generalization from some limited truth; the stereotype has a referent (e.g., in *As You Like It* Jaques draws on stereotypes to describe the "seven ages of man"). A simulacrum, in contrast, is produced out of the will of its maker; lacking a referent, it is "without origin or reality," yet it passes for real. And unlike a tradition or a folk narrative, a simulacrum provides a narrative without its own genealogy. In Baudrillard's heuristic metaphor, "The territory no longer precedes the map, nor survives it. Henceforth, it is the map that precedes the territory — PRECESSION OF SIMULACRA — it is the map that engenders the territory . . ." (253). If we read the map as misogyny, the territory as woman, it follows that the "injured" husband, with or without the help of a Jachimo, sees what he expects to see, what a patriarchal culture perpetuating a myth of female infidelity has prepared him to see — a misogynous simulacrum of woman such as that which Posthumus has always known. Representation, like electronic imaging, those computer-produced photographs of what never was, generates what passes for a social "fact":

> POSTHUMUS.   for there's no motion
> That tends to vice in man, but I affirm
> It is the woman's part: be it lying, note it,
> The woman's; flattering, hers; deceiving, hers;
> Lust and rank thoughts, hers, hers; revenges, hers;
> Ambitions, covetings, change of prides, disdain,
> Nice longing, slanders, mutability,
> All faults that name, nay, that hell knows,
> Why hers, in part or all; but rather all.
>   (2.5.20–28)

Posthumus's rant might have been conceived to illustrate Baudrillard's contention that the hyperreal "no longer has to be rational. . . . It is nothing more than operational" (254).

The word *misogyny* — "hate or contempt of women" — entered the language in the seventeenth century (see the *OED*); today the practice "wears many guises, reveals itself in different forms which are dictated by class, wealth, education, race, religion, and other factors, but its chief characteristic is its pervasiveness" (J. Smith xvi–xvii). Yet few students are likely to be aware of the historical antecedents of the discourse of misogyny. For example, Merlin Stone posits that the displacement of the Great Goddess, whose worship in many personations may have lasted some twenty-five thousand years, was a primary cause of the denigration of women (xii). This displacement, with all its economic repercussions, was accomplished in part by generating a hyperreal through prototypical simulacra: Greek Pandora, "degraded from the giver of all gifts to the bringer of all evils" (Rogers 29), and Hebrew Eve, who lost us paradise by heeding a serpent — a sacred counselor in the goddess religion (M. Stone 220–21). Establishing the worship of a male deity, the Levites associated sin and shame with desire; tempted woman was herself a temptress.

Later veneration of Mary did not vitiate the earlier opprobrious simulacrum, she being "alone of all her sex" (Caelius Sedulius, qtd. in Warner xvii) by virtue of her miraculous virginity and divine motherhood. In *The Troublesome Helpmate: A History of Misogyny in Literature*, Katherine M. Rogers provides a highly readable introduction to a distressing tradition; her discussion of classical, patristic, medieval, and Renaissance writers can contextualize *Cymbeline* and *The Winter's Tale* amid successive simulacra of womankind promulgated in the course of the medieval and Renaissance *querelle des femmes*, or controversy over women.

The *querelle*'s so-called "universal slander against women" (Poisson 381) foregrounds the lecherous female. Following Plato's assertion that the womb is a *creature* ever seeking to bear children and afflicting the entire body if it does not do so (Poisson 398n12), the sixteenth-century misogynist Giovanni Della Casa expands the infinitely expandable map to include a simulacrum of woman unhinged by her sexuality:

> Do not imagine that Etna burns with more violence than the soul of woman burns with lust. And her husband is so far from being able to stop it by extinguishing it or appeasing such a fire that his labor ends by exciting it further, just as the intensity of the fire is usually increased by the addition of a small quantity of water.
>
> (trans. and qtd. in Poisson 385)

When women are unsatisfied (and when are they not?), "driven by their passion, *They lose their minds*" (trans. and qtd. in Poisson 385–86). While Shakespeare's saner view may be gauged from the juxtaposition of Imogen's and Hermione's self-possession against Posthumus's and Leontes's frenzy, the maddened husbands express no condemnation of women that could not be found in the literature of the *querelle*.

In the wake of sex as sin and woman as sex-crazed temptress slogs the jealous husband — guilt-ridden and anxious. W. D. Adamson, in an outstanding essay "The Calumny Pattern in Shakespeare," argues that despite the plays' settings, both Posthumus and Leontes suffer from Christian guilt over sex. Quoting Article Nine of the Church of England's Thirty-Nine Articles of faith, familiar to Shakespeare and his audiences — "The lust of the flesh . . . is not subject to the Law of God. . . . [T]he Apostle doth confess, that concupiscence and lust hath of itself the nature of sin" (61) — Adamson adduces the "specifically Christian origins of that infected knowledge [Shakespeare] shows driving all his men" (57).

If theology doesn't create the anxious husband, economics will. Paradoxically, although under patriarchy women may themselves be reified as property, biology confers on them the custodianship of lineage and property. Women's actions, therefore, must be circumscribed, their sexuality controlled, their potential paramours — all other men — suspected. Before his dream vision of Hermione, Antigonus disagrees with Leontes's accusation but not with the rationale behind the insistence on female chastity. If Hermione is false, then all women are false, including his three young daughters, who will "pay for't":

> I'll geld 'em all; fourteen they shall not see
> To bring false generations. They are co-heirs,
> And I had rather glib myself than they
> Should not produce fair issue.   (2.1.146–50)

And Leontes, casting out his infant daughter, echoes Antigonus: "No! I'll not rear / Another's issue" (2.3.192–93).

In classroom discussion we are tempted to neglect the slandered women for the jealous men, whose subjectivity fascinates by virtue of their conflicted psyches. In contrast, the wives are apt to seem unproblematic. Baudrillard offers a way of understanding the slandered wives' construction. They are modeled after the sanctioned simulacrum for victimized women — either Patient Griselda, suffering silently and loving long, or her Neoplatonic alter ego, Woman as Wonder:

> Love is promoted to the rank of grace and providence, and the commonplace of feigned death and burial is used as more than an example of cleverness: it is a wonder of steadfastness signifying the right human action that cooperates through love in the stability of the Unmoved Mover, who is the source of love and of the providence that controls the mutability of fortune.   (Clubb 73)

While the ennobling of the victim is preferable to her debasement, the pain of abuse seems all too easily forgotten as misery is transmuted into transcendence: "She's punish'd for her truth, and undergoes, / More goddess-like than wife-like, such assaults / As would take in some virtue" (3.2.7–9), says Pisanio of Imogen, whose reincarnation as Fidele (fidelity) heightens the simulacra of Griselda–Woman as Wonder that she enacts. Since intrinsic to these simulacra is the expectation that the offender will be forgiven, they figure a potentially dangerous male fantasy of women's unconditional love.

Forthright, impulsive, persevering in the face of grief, Imogen is reminiscent of Julia and Viola. But one of her individuating traits, for which we have Posthumus's word, is her sexual coolness—"Me of my lawful pleasure she restrain'd, / And pray'd me oft forbearance" (2.5.9–10). Such is the transformative power of misogynous simulacra, however, that Imogen's reserve paradoxically becomes proof of her promiscuity. Baudrillard explains the paradox:

> Facts no longer have any trajectory of their own, they arise at the intersection of the models; a single fact may even be engendered by all the models at once. This anticipation, this precession, this short circuit, this confusion of the fact with its model . . . is what each time allows for all the possible interpretations, even the most contradictory. . . .   (264)

For the audience, of course, Imogen suffers like Griselda, even before Posthumus's defection, vexed with "A father cruel, and a step-dame false, / A foolish suitor to a wedded lady / That hath her husband banish'd" (1.6.1–3). When she learns that Posthumus has ordered her death, she bids Pisanio "witness [her] obedience" as she offers her heart to the sword: " 'tis empty of all things but grief" (3.4.66, 69). Later she adopts Pisanio's belief that Posthumus was duped; to be near her husband she changes her identity by donning male disguise. "You must forget to be a woman" (3.4.154), says Pisanio, more wisely than he knows; for this, it seems, is the only way to escape the slander produced by misogynous simulacra. Finally, believing Posthumus dead, Imogen renounces all identity, replying to Lucius's question, "What art thou?," with "I am nothing . . ." (4.2.367).

When Imogen is restored to happiness, another woman, the murderous Queen, replaces her as a cipher: "O, she was naught" (5.5.271), says Cymbeline of his wife. A recuperative strategy may be implicit in the binarism of the virtuous princess and the evil Queen who feigned desire, who "Married your royalty, was wife to your place, / Abhorr'd your person" — a revelation that draws from Cymbeline the helpless question, "Who is't can read a woman?" (5.5.39–40, 48). Ensuring the romance's redemptive ending, the simulacrum of Woman as Dissembler is ultimately displaced, if not erased, by the play's most striking simile. As Imogen embraces Posthumus, he cries, "Hang there like fruit, my soul, / Till the tree die!" (5.5.263–64). Recalling Genesis, the image suggests not Eve the primal sinner and temptress but rather Imogen and Posthumus at last married in spirit, becoming a single uncorrupted creation—a tree in paradise.

Imogen's sufferings pale beside Hermione's. As the Queen's initial vivacity wilts before Leontes's fury, Hermione comes to embody the Woman-as-Wonder simulacrum through her spiritual acceptance of adversity and her pity for the husband who sends her to give birth in prison:

> this action I now go on
> Is for my better grace. Adieu, my lord,

I never wish'd to see you sorry, now
I trust I shall.   (2.1.121-24)

Hermione triumphs in the trial scene, where the anguished dignity with
which she delivers her moving self-defense anticipates *Henry VIII*'s Queen
Katherine. Publicly humiliated, separated from her children, Hermione,
like Imogen, nevertheless declares that, without her husband, life can be
"no commodity" (3.2.93). She speaks only once more, when, at the end of
the play, she addresses eight lines to her daughter, whom the most alert
students are likely to recognize as yet another slandered woman, defamed
by Polixenes as a witch and a harlot (4.4.422-23, 434, 437-39). Although
Hermione finds Perdita, her son is lost. Also lost are a mother's pleasure
in her daughter's childhood and sixteen years of happiness in marriage — sixteen years of living in the world.

Their identities wrenched from them first as whores, then as saints,
Imogen and Hermione nevertheless resist as well as recuperate the Griselda–
Woman as Wonder role. Each wife disregards some of the "three special
virtues, necessary to be incident in every vertuous woman . . . Namely
obedience, chastitie, and sylence" (*Penelope's Web*, qtd. in Hull 81) — though
never chastity. Imogen, Britain's heir, disobeys her father by refusing his
choice for her and eloping with the man she loves, associating herself with
"unruly" women. Shakespeare further allows Imogen anger, misjudgment,
and even a disconcerting detachment: "Your life, good master [Lucius], /
Must shuffle for itself" (5.5.104–05). By eloquently and publicly protesting
her innocence, Hermione also proves unruly. Her psychological credibility
is deepened if her sixteen-year absence is construed as a rejection of Leontes.
Resistance to simulacra may supply one answer to the question of how
Shakespeare creates a sense of the characters' inner lives. Another question
of interest to students — where Shakespeare stood with regard to gender
issues — is raised by the play's vindication of disobedient, impetuous Imogen
and verbal, aggrieved Hermione.

Students who are careful readers notice that Shakespeare extends no war-
ranty on his happy endings. Although Posthumus profoundly repents his
crime even before he learns of Imogen's fidelity, paradoxically he attacks
the code of murder *per honore* 'for honor' by insisting on women's falseness:
"If each of you [married men] should take this course, how many / Must
murder wives much better than themselves / For wrying but a little!"
(5.1.3–5). Leontes contemplates the murder of a second wife at 5.1.61–62;
and his first words to Florizel, observing the young man's resemblance to
Polixenes, are, "Your mother was most true to wedlock" (5.1.125); Hermione
says nothing to her husband and fears to look at Polixenes (5.3.147). In both
plays, Shakespeare leaves us with a recovering misogynist who lacks a
support group and who has only the memory of the great harm he did to save
him from recidivism. Women's identities remain *contingent* in a patriarchal

society. Cuckoldry is still to be feared. The social code of female chastity and male honor is still in place. Subversion of the code is ultimately frustrated in the plays and in much if not most of the modern world.

The romances *are* providential, but outside the theater our social sins exact a high price. Adamson observes that "even in his most perfunctory use of the calumny pattern, Shakespeare seems to have imagined it as a sado-masochistic outrage which the male attackers — because of inherited cultural prejudices — are really helpless to keep from perpetrating" (36).[1] As teachers, we are a significant part of a network mediating inherited prejudices, the simulacra of our culture. Let us not gloss over the sexual politics of the slandered woman. Shakespeare's incomparable richness invites many ways to read, many ideas to stress — and to challenge. We need not unwittingly reinforce an ideology that victimizes women.

NOTE

[1]Aside from the works cited in this essay, I highly recommend Coppélia Kahn's chapter on cuckoldry in *Man's Estate: Masculine Identity in Shakespeare* and Anne Parten's unpublished dissertation "Cuckoldry in Shakespeare." Useful contextualizing works include Elinor Bevan's "Revenge, Forgiveness, and the Gentleman" on the code of murder *per honore*, Ralph Hupka's anthropological study "Cultural Determinants of Jealousy," Robert Y. Turner's "Slander in *Cymbeline* and other Jacobean Tragicomedies" on the generic countermovement to satire and the attitude of detraction, and Linda Woodbridge's delightful discussion of Patient Grissel's stage incarnations in *Women and the English Renaissance*.

Teaching the Unrealistic Realism of *The Winter's Tale*

Bruce W. Young

Like most of Shakespeare's late plays, *The Winter's Tale* has elements of fantasy and romance that attract some viewers and repel others. Some consider the play light and unrealistic and all the more charming for being so; others agree that the play is unrealistic but see this quality as evidence of its lack of seriousness and worth compared with Shakespeare's other works. Such judgments are made not only by critics but by students reading the play for the first time. Here, for instance, are the responses of two of my students to *The Winter's Tale*:

> Appropriately titled a tale, I found *The Winter's Tale* to be full of coincidences and fantasy and a magical happy ending. The ending, of course, being the most fantastical of all.

> [From a response titled "On the General Stupidness of This Play"] I will admit that Shakespeare's language . . . is brilliant. Nevertheless, I didn't enjoy the play. As we watched it someone remarked that Shakespeare must have been drunk when he wrote it. I agree.

Other students — and critics — arrive at a very different conclusion and find *The Winter's Tale* as serious and, in its own way, as realistic as anything Shakespeare wrote. Though I share this opinion, the way I teach the play accommodates itself to different views on the play's realism. My approach involves bringing into the open what my students think of the play and then, while we examine the text, discussing the issues it raises in connection with my own and my students' lives. Eventually, most of us find that *The Winter's Tale* both challenges and satisfies our sense of realism.

By the time we reach *The Winter's Tale*, my students know that I expect them to consider questions that genuinely arise as they encounter the text. They also know that — despite my view that aesthetic and dramatic considerations account for many of the problems they see — I find it quite legitimate for them to question the play in terms of their own experience. Students are to bring to class a one-page interpretive response the first day we talk about the play. As discussion begins, I open the floor to concerns students have about the play: anything that bothers them, anything they don't understand, anything intriguing or unusual or problematic.

Both the question raising — we call it "brainstorming" — and the written responses always lead us to the issue of realism. Each of us, that is, at some point asks: Is *The Winter's Tale* believable? Is it so wildly unlike my own life that I can't connect the two? We start looking for answers by identifying unrealistic elements in the play. We consider the setting — long ago and far away, a pagan never-never land where the facts of geography are notable mainly for their irrelevance. We note the various coincidences (including Perdita's and Florizel's encounter), the onset of Leontes's jealousy, his quick turnaround when he learns of his son's death, Hermione's long hiding and return as a statue, Paulina's insistence on Leontes's prolonged repentance, and usually too the supernatural elements (the oracle and so forth).

We ask why these features of the play strike us as unrealistic. The setting, obviously, is unfamiliar and does not adhere to standards of strict mimetic fidelity. Yet as we consider the setting's function — the sea symbolism, for instance, and the contrast between court and country — we see that in this play, as in literary fantasy generally, an unfamiliar setting may be a kind of workshop, a provisional space, in which familiar problems and issues can be faced.

Other questions prove more difficult. Did Hermione have to remain hidden for the oracle to be fulfilled? Was she testing Leontes? Or is Shakespeare simply creating effective — but less than fully credible — theater? Some of these questions are left unresolved; often the best we can do is to open ourselves to possibilities. But usually, we find that seemingly unrealistic elements can serve realistic ends: within them may be hidden some of Shakespeare's surest insights.

It soon becomes apparent that *The Winter's Tale* deliberately raises the issue of credibility. The characters themselves question the reasonableness of what they experience. The play's frequent references to "old tales" and wildly fantastic ballads remind us of the habit we human beings have of telling beautiful — or merely entertaining — lies. But is the play saying no more than this — that we should not expect fiction to resemble real life? Many students make precisely this assumption or pick up a similar idea from introductions or critical commentary. Some agree with Philip Edwards, who emphasizes the play's "insubstantiality"and unlikelihood, the "fragility of [its] fiction" (" 'Seeing' " 91–92, 89), or with Hallett Smith, who argues, in his introduction to the play in *The Riverside Shakespeare*, that "most of the critical problems disappear if we remember the play's title and its meaning. . . . Winter's tales were not supposed to have credibility, consistency, or conciseness" (1567–68).

Believing that the play has greater depth and significance than such statements indicate, I ask my students to look carefully at the references to old tales and to consider other ways of understanding them. The following possibilities generally emerge:

First, we examine the phrases used to describe the discovery of Perdita's identity ("Such a deal of wonder is broken out within this hour that ballad-makers cannot be able to express it" and "Like an old tale still" [5.2.23–25, 61]) and Paulina's speech near the end of the final scene ("That she is living, / Were it but told you, should be hooted at / Like an old tale" [5.3.115–17]). Then we ask whether, far from emphasizing the play's unreality, these references to "old tales" paradoxically make the play seem more realistic by allowing the incredulity of the play's characters to deflect our own. In other words, the characters' response to the play's improbabilities serves as a kind of lightning rod for our difficulties believing the story.

Second, many of us see these references as going further, beyond this pragmatic function, to challenge directly our sense of what is realistic and rational. By having things happen that — except for the fact that they are happening — seem unrealistic even to the characters experiencing them, the play emphasizes the limits of human rationality, the limits set by human preconceptions and expectations, and raises the issue of faith in its many senses, including the ability to believe the apparently unbelievable.

Florizel does not see how Camillo can resolve the problems he and Perdita face — yet the problems are resolved. Paulina considers Perdita's hypothetical return to be "monstrous to our human reason" (as monstrous as a resurrection) — but within one hundred lines Perdita appears (5.1.40–44, 123). Later in the scene the messenger who announces that Polixenes has arrived starts by saying, "That which I shall report will bear no credit, / Were not the proof so nigh" (5.1.179–80). Similarly, Hermione's return would be incredible except that the characters see it happen. Credibility is not, in other words, an adequate test of truth.

One implication of this view is that literary realism is largely a matter of convention. Audiences and critics privilege certain things as realistic — consistent characters, gradual development, coherent plots, familiar settings — when in fact the lives we actually live often include inconsistencies, incoherencies, and surprises that would baffle or offend us in fiction. Fiction — at least "realistic" fiction — is often much safer than life: we are asked to accept only what is familiar and apparently rational, what we understand. Except in certain limited and conventional ways, it seems, we don't really want to be surprised — we don't want to have to stretch our view of the world beyond its comfortable boundaries. Or, at least, when we do, we don't want to have to take the stretching very seriously.

Looking at *The Winter's Tale* in this way requires us to reevaluate the coincidences and supernatural elements. We all know that coincidences are part of real life, however much we may be put off by them in fiction, and many of us believe in, or have even experienced, the supernatural. Why, then, do we reject coincidence and the supernatural as unrealistic in fiction? Coincidences, in the "unrealistic" sense, are conjunctions that are meaningful but that seem to have come about by chance; we can't explain them rationally. Likewise, the supernatural is what is beyond human power and understanding. To find the supernatural acceptable in literature, we have to enlarge our definition of what counts as real and set aside, if we can, preconceptions and biases most of us have grown up with, influenced as we are by skeptical post-Enlightenment thought.

Within the world of *The Winter's Tale*, both the coincidences and the supernatural are expressions of an overarching power — the gods, the powers above — that acts through time, through nature, to accomplish ends that humans don't entirely understand. The meeting of Florizel and Perdita is explicitly attributed to providence ("This' your son-in-law, . . . whom heavens directing / Is troth-plight to your daughter" [5.3.149–51]). Even the famous bear may be acting as part of a larger plan. As in *Hamlet*, there is more in earth and heaven than is dreamt of in our philosophy, and there is a divinity that shapes human ends, whatever rough-hewing humans do. Yet, though the supernatural in *The Winter's Tale* transcends human understanding, it is emphatically immanent in human experience. In fact, in contrast to *The Tempest*, where the supernatural element, represented visibly by magic-performing fairies, is difficult for us to view as realistic, *The Winter's Tale* presents the supernatural in strictly human, and therefore more believably realistic, terms.

But what students — as well as critics — resist in *The Winter's Tale* is not just the unusual and supernatural events. They resist, curiously enough, the happiness with which the play ends. It appears that most of us resonate to a statement by Woody Allen that I quote to my students: "In real life, people disappoint you. . . . They're cruel, and life is cruel. I think there is no win in life. Reality is a very painful, tough thing that you have to learn to cope with in some way. What we do is escape into fantasy, and it does give us moments of relief" (qtd. in Farber 80).

Does *The Winter's Tale*, despite everything we can say in its defense, finally offer an easy out, the deceptive notion that things always end happily? I argue that precisely the opposite is true. *The Winter's Tale* challenges not only the notion of the happy ending but the notion of literary closure of any kind. Despite its sometimes festive and even awe-inspiring spirit, the play does face the hard facts of life: evil, death, the potential for human misery. There are real and permanent losses: Leontes's son, Mamillius, dies, Antigonus dies, so do others; and sixteen years have been lost. This is *not* a play with an easy fairy-tale ending. Furthermore, the play reminds us that in a sense there are no endings — no closing scenes to any of our stories — except perhaps death. And in raising the issue of death, the play challenges even its right to say the last word.

The Winter's Tale is about the process of human life — birth, growth, aging, death. We are reminded in the play's final scene that, despite a strong sense of closure, this is not the end of the story. Hermione is wrinkled (as Shakespeare is careful to have us see); she and Leontes are aging; a new generation is ready to begin its own story of marriage and offspring, but meanwhile the older characters are moving toward death (5.3.28, 132). The last scene thus refuses to enter a state of static happiness, beyond time. With its emphasis on explanations yet to be given, life yet to be lived, the scene may be taken, not as a happy ending in any ultimate sense, but as a victory of happiness and love that will have to be continually renewed if the wonder and joy are to persist or reappear.

Perhaps most significantly, the play uncovers and responds to our deep suspicion of happy endings by showing this suspicion to be directly parallel to Leontes's jealousy. Both are expressions of what might be called "fear fulfillment." At root, Leontes's jealousy is an expression of insecurity. This insecurity manifests itself in his difficulty believing that Hermione actually loves him, perhaps that he is worthy of being loved, and (given his irrational assumption that she doesn't love him and therefore is not true to her vows) in his not believing her to be as good and gracious as she seems. Blinded by these failures of belief, Leontes resists and finally destroys his own happiness.

I ask my students to consider whether the play's treatment of Leontes's jealousy shows us something about ourselves. I even tell my students of some of my own experiences. I quote to them from an account of my courtship and marriage and of the difficulty I had believing in my own possible happiness:

> Bright fantasies, no matter how luminous, have never proved satisfying for long. But I have always seemed able to make my life miserable and then say to myself, "At least *this* is real." . . . [F]or some reason it seems easier to create what we fear and be done with it than to wait in awful suspense until what we fear comes of its own volition. . . . [Perhaps] we don't want to be fooled, and so we create a life or a way of viewing life that is "fool-proof" — so limited, so empty of vision, that there is nothing to be disillusioned about.
>
> (B. W. Young 269, 271)

If Leontes suffers from a similar resistance to happiness, what happens to change him? An answer, though by no means a simple one, is suggested by Paulina's statement in the closing scene: "It is requir'd / You do awake your faith" (5.3.94–95). What does she mean? Class discussion suggests various possibilities, including the view that Shakespeare is commenting on the necessity of "dramatic faith," or, as Coleridge put it, the "willing suspension of disbelief . . . which constitutes poetic faith" (7.2: 6). Most critics seem to share this view: we find happy endings only in the world of the imagination. Life is not really like this, and the only real miracle the play affirms is the dramatist's power to convince us of what we know is not real.

But if *The Winter's Tale* is more than a play about plays, if it has something to do with human life generally and the possibility and conditions of happiness, then other interpretations present themselves as well. Before Leontes's happiness can be restored to him, he must awaken his faith not only in the sense of his belief in the apparently unbelievable (the miracle of an apparent resurrection) but also in the sense of faithfulness: fidelity, trust, a willingness to believe in his wife's goodness and love — the very kind of faith whose absence destroyed his happiness and for a time destroyed his family. Closely related to this belief in his wife's love is another aspect of faith that must awaken in Leontes: a belief that he can be loved; a belief, in other words, in his own possible happiness.

But the play is more than just a feast of joy, and we have to consider what an awakening of faith could mean in a world where Mamillius (among others) dies—where all will eventually die. Many students find, as I do, that the seriousness of the play—its recognition that there are real, permanent losses; the autumnal feel of the ending; the acknowledgment of aging and death—makes its happy, even awe-inspiring ending all the more satisfying and the concept of faith emphasized as the play ends all the more powerful.

Shakespeare's treatment of death is complex, and the ways teachers approach the issue will depend on their own views and on the settings in which they teach. I take advantage of my school's religious affiliation to give the play a religious reading—though not, I would emphasize, an allegorical one. The allusions to the parable of the prodigal son and its repeated phrases, "He who was lost is found, he who was dead is alive again," invite a religious reading. Yet such a reading is made problematic by other details: the pagan setting and the fact that the apparent resurrection is only apparent. Without denying resurrection a symbolic and theatrical function, I want my students to see how the play connects the idea of such an event to the questions of realism and belief: resurrection is another of the possibilities the play identifies as "irrational," especially from a pagan viewpoint (see 5.1.40–44). As with other events that strain belief, the impossibility of even so miraculous an event as this is called into question. Of course, Hermione does not literally return to life, because she has not actually died. Yet her return to the fullness of her physical and social being—to life in a family and community—reveals the value of the very things a genuine resurrection would restore. Thus, though the play presents only a temporary "resurrection," it shows the vanquishing of death to be something worth hoping for and believing in, certainly not something to be dismissed as impossible. If Leontes's resistance to happiness is relevant to the question of death, it may, in fact, be worth asking whether the belief that death is final is yet another expression of fear fulfillment.

My emphasis in teaching *The Winter's Tale* is on problems most human beings—certainly most of my students—encounter in the mundane round of their lives. I am thinking especially of the problems involved in forming and maintaining personal relationships: whether and how it is possible to live happily with other people, the dangers of insecurity and of the desire to dominate, the terrors and blessings of trying to share one's life with others. Any play that raises such concerns as challengingly as *The Winter's Tale* does I am willing to consider eminently realistic.

But do my students find the play relevant to their "real lives"? Certainly many do, if what they tell me in class and in their writing is valid evidence. My students' class journals are especially revealing, because I tell them they can write anything there they want to as long as it relates to the class and to Shakespeare. Many use their journals to make connections—from play to play, from class to class, and from their reading of the plays to other things happening in their lives. One student in her "Last Journal Entry!" wrote:

> This is the end of the semester. It's a good feeling! . . . I think that out of all the Shakespeare plays I've enjoyed the romances the most. . . . I like happy endings even though our class seemed to think that happy endings are unrealistic. . . . I guess that many times the "Happy Ending" we're looking for doesn't always come but when I look at things on a larger scale my happiness cannot be measured.

I am moved and enlightened by this student's response. I would put things just a little differently: *The Winter's Tale* challenges our notion of what is possible, what is real, and it does so in part to help us see that the narrowing of our vision of what is possible is as responsible as anything for the misery, the destructive conflicts, that enter our lives.

By the end of the semester, my students are usually willing to grant that, in significant respects, *The Winter's Tale* is both realistic and unrealistic. It is only a fiction — an imagined, artistically shaped story — and even among fictions, it challenges belief in unusual ways and to an unusual degree. But it also raises issues we cannot avoid seeing as relevant to our lives, and it does so with characters who engage our sympathies and reveal to us truths about ourselves. In sometimes odd and disconcerting ways, the play prevents us from putting its characters and events into neat packages, comfortably subject to rational understanding. Further, the play challenges us to exercise faith, to break beyond the narrow bounds of our fears and preconceptions and dare to believe in our own and others' possibilities. *The Winter's Tale* can help us see our lives anew; it can help us keep our lives open to new realities, beyond the usual and the plausible, especially as we move forward on the edge of possibility, as we always do.

Negotiating the Paradoxes of Art and Nature in *The Winter's Tale*

Charles R. Forker

Like all the romances of Shakespeare, *The Winter's Tale* is a subtle compound of the fantastic and the verisimilar, the improbable and the credible, the ideal and the real, the mythic and the naturalistic. In my experience, undergraduate and, on occasion, even graduate students often need some help in accepting a theatrically mixed mode that invokes the narrative traditions of the folktale (with its implications of strangeness, artificiality, and distancing from ordinary experience) but that nevertheless insists on a high degree of dramatic engagement; that, treating potentially tragic characters and situations, represents intense psychological states and embodies serious moral, aesthetic, and philosophical ideas.

Shakespeare stresses one side of this opposition not only in his title but in details of the dialogue — in Mamillius's reference, for example, to stories of "sprites and goblins" (2.1.26) and in the Second Gentleman's allusion to tales the "verity" of which would be "in strong suspicion" (5.2.29–30); these references have the effect of italicizing the romance conventions and miraculous vicissitudes in which the plot abounds. The apparently "broken-backed" structure of the play, with its three acts of pain and disaster followed by two in which new characters are introduced and in which the former misery is transmuted into present joy — the contrasting sections being joined somewhat perfunctorily by the chorus Time, who in a single speech leaps blithely over a gap of sixteen years — also reinforces the sense of a play that is consciously anachronistic, "antique" or "storied" in dramaturgy and deliberately antinaturalistic in appeal. Yet the volcanic eruption of Leontes's jealousy, the powerful episode in which Hermione publicly defends her innocence, and the action in which Paulina reveals the statue and presides over its quasi-mystical vivification have the very opposite effect; for these scenes engage audience emotions strongly and directly, leaving little leisure for fanciful detachment, and they depend on characters whose inner being is not only imagined in depth but rivetingly actualized in stage performance. Merely noticing this mixture of modes can help focus students'attention on some of the play's more absorbing interpretive problems — problems that, when more fully investigated and discussed, can sometimes convince the less sophisticated that what they may have perceived initially as a loose collection of naive, confused, or absurd elements on closer inspection composes a richly complex web of actions, characters, and symbols possessing coherence and even profundity.

An obvious way of overcoming resistance to the apparently diffuse or desultory aspects of the plot is to have students consider the matrix of thematic and symbolic contrasts that the play clearly projects — age and youth, winter and summer, court and country, aristocracy and peasantry, death and resurrection, sin and redemption, decay and growth, innocence and guilt, suspicion and trust, tyranny and freedom, love and friendship, sadness and joy, time and eternity, life and art — and then to suggest how these mesh and overlap, often through simultaneous opposition and parallel. In its two halves, for instance, the drama clearly shifts its emphasis from the older generation to the younger, yet children are already present in the early segment just as adults figure in the concluding one; and although progeny are certainly meant to be associated with continuity and life (as in the case of Perdita and Florizel), the death of Mamillius and the "resurrection" of Hermione show us that biological age is too simple and inadequate a means of symbolizing the tension between fruitfulness and mortality. Moreover, Shakespeare appears to invite very different responses to death: the wasting away of Leontes's son in the early action evokes tragic emotions and seems to connote irreparable loss, not only of the boy himself but of all that is morally and psychologically healthful, whereas the predatory devouring of Antigonus later on, while equally irreparable, is filtered semicomically through the narrative of the clown, who describes the event as a grotesque meal at which "the bear half din'd on the gentleman" (3.3.102–03). Much of the comedy of the play, as in the example just cited, depends on traditional contrasts between the humbly and the nobly born, but nobility and peasantry obviously intersect in the country royalty of Perdita, who is both a "queen of curds and cream" (4.4.161) and the future consort of a monarch.

The thematic polarities of the play, like the early and late phases of its action, tend to contain each other in embryo or in retrospect, one term already implying or helping to define its counterpart, in the same way that Milton's "L'Allegro" and "Il Penseroso" must be properly understood as conceptually related poems rather than as discrete works. Shakespeare's pervasive dualities suggest the complementarity and indivisibility of experience rather than its fission into mutually exclusive units, and some discussion of these cross-relations can bring the structural and intellectual subtleties of the play into clearer focus.

An opening pedagogical gambit I find useful is to pursue the question of how audiences are intended to receive the abruptness of Leontes's jealousy in the first act and its almost equally abrupt abandonment in the third. It is usual of course to say with F. R. Leavis (and many others) that we should neither look for nor expect in a fairy tale the "psychological interest" (177) found in *Othello*, that in generic romance, such fits of irrationality are "notoriously unmotivated" (Bethell 48) and can descend and evaporate as arbitrarily as supernatural spells or diabolic possession. Yet it is possible (with Wilbur Sanders) to analyze the triangular relationship of Leontes, Polixenes, and Hermione as hinting at complex patterns of suppressed tension, insecurity, and discomfort such as one might find in a novel by

Henry James. Polixenes, for instance, finds it awkward to extend his stay in the court of a boyhood friend whom he has only recently come to know as an adult, whose grown-up reality may cause him to exaggerate nostalgi-cally—even sentimentally—the innocence of their youthful attachment, and whose attractive wife and son remind him of his own pressing obligations of family and state at home. For his part, Leontes reveals a perverse tendency to associate every human failing with sexuality, so that almost any evil, however hypothetical, takes on a repellent lubricity in his prurient imagina-tion. Whether or not one accepts all the psychological subtleties Sanders describes, he at least makes a good case for regarding the scenes of jealousy as symptomatic of the play's mixed mode: certainly "we can make out the mythic triumph of wickedness, the paradigm of fairy tale. But," Sanders continues, "this co-exists with, and is empowered by, a psychological natu-ralism of quite amazing depth and resourcefulness" (30). We may there-fore add to the thematic and structural contrasts that encourage bifocal responses to *The Winter's Tale* a certain doubleness in the characterization — a means of presenting the central figures so as to give the illusion of fully rounded personality without sacrificing any of their larger symbolic or archetypal functions.

At the very heart of the dramaturgical and conceptual dividedness to which I have been pointing is of course the pastoral tradition in which *The Winter's Tale*, like *Cymbeline* and *The Tempest*, is deeply rooted; for most of the contrasts or polarities mentioned above involve the question of nature versus art. This concern, deriving ultimately from Theocritus and Virgil, pervades almost all versions of Renaissance pastoral (as Frank Kermode has illustrated in *English Pastoral Poetry*) and, apart from its adaptation to the English stage in plays by Greene, Shakespeare, Fletcher, and others, is central to works as influential as Castiglione's *Courtier*, Sidney's *Arcadia*, and Spenser's *Faerie Queene* (esp. book 6), not to mention its later manifes-tation in the poetry of Milton and Marvell. It can be illuminating to students, therefore, to expatiate a little on the aesthetic and intellectual assumptions of pastoral literature with a view to showing how vital these are to Shake-speare's conception of nature and to the larger universe of which nature, in at least one of its many senses, was seen as a simulacrum.

Pastoral traditionally concerns itself with the antithesis between the cultivated and the primitive and between the spoiled and the unspoiled in nature, but sophisticated pastoral is rarely content merely to idealize bucolic simplicity out of escapist motives or for its own sake. Rural or shepherd life may be the standard image employed, but as George Puttenham observes in his *Arte of English Poesie*, poets have the warrant of classical precedent for "glaunc[ing] at greater matters" in their "counterfait[ing]" of "the rusticall manner" and in their writing "vnder the vaile of homely persons" (38). Puttenham alludes here to the pastoral tendency to allegorize, to comment on political, religious, or social issues under the thin guise of humble speakers in remote country settings but his principle applies equally to the consideration of philosophical and aesthetic questions. William Empson points out how pastoral characteristically reconfigures the complex in terms of the simple (23), so that it becomes a medium, to quote Kermode, in which "the cultivated, in their artificial way, reflect upon and describe, for their own ends, the natural life" (*English Pastoral Poetry* 12). The confrontation between nature and art so endemic to pastoral can hardly be regarded, then, as a simple antithesis.

At one level, to be sure, such literature contrasts city or court life with life in the country at the expense of the former: here the Arcadian setting with its attendant rusticities of attitude and behavior is taken to epitomize human innocence before it was corrupted by the artificial distortions and accretions of immoral human institutions such as class, property, finance, and government. As such, the so-called green world was inevitably associated or identified with the Golden Age of classical myth and suggestive of the original Eden before Adam and Eve (through their fall and expulsion from the garden) prepared the way for the redemption of humankind by that ultimate incarnation of divine love, Christ the Good Shepherd. But on another plane, nature in its raw state could be regarded as savage, wild, and inhospitable to humanistic ideas of virtue and so could symbolize a state in which humankind remained as yet uncivilized by art or learning, in which conscience had yet to be informed by right reason, and in which the soul might even be deprived of grace. Caliban, the subhuman character of *The Tempest*, represents Shakespeare's most extreme embodiment of "natural man" in the pejorative sense. In reaction to this conception of untutored or bestial wildness, an idealization of true naturalness (nature with a human face) would imply an alliance between the world of rural simplicity and the advantages of nurture. And, indeed, as Ernst Robert Curtius notices (187), the shepherd's world has been conventionally linked to the making of both love and poetry, the erotic and the lyric being obviously related arts. In an alternative view, then, nature could be thought of as reflecting or encapsulating art (particularly if we imagine God as the supreme Artist) as well as standing in opposition to it. Applying the analogy of the divine Creator, civilized human beings might legitimately "complete," "improve," or (to use Polixenes's term) "mend" nature by refining and reshaping it in the pursuit of a more harmonious concord between the landscape and its inhabitants, both of which could be seen Neoplatonically as aspiring to the condition of Christian perfection — the Arcadia of Heaven, so to say.

The Winter's Tale inherits this matrix of philosophical and literary patterns and actively invokes them, not merely decoratively for effects of atmosphere and setting but as part of the structural and intellectual substance of the play. Nor does Shakespeare confine his pastoralism to the fourth act, in which we actually see shepherds and shepherdesses onstage. Polixenes, for instance, projects what we might call the "soft" image of pastoral in his slightly prettified account of his childhood frolicking with Leontes:

> We were as twinn'd lambs that did frisk i' th' sun,
> And bleat the one at th' other. What we chang'd
> Was innocence for innocence; we knew not
> The doctrine of ill-doing, nor dream'd
> That any did. Had we pursu'd that life,
> And our weak spirits ne'er been higher rear'd
> With stronger blood, we should have answer'd heaven
> Boldly "not guilty," the imposition clear'd
> Hereditary ours.   (1.2.67–75)

Here pastoral imagery is used to call up a nostalgic concept of boyhood guiltlessness that the speaker associates with pristine nature — nature of an almost unfallen purity — that nevertheless belongs more to the world of art than to that of actuality. The aestheticizing of nature in this passage helps to point up the contrast between the gildings of memory and ordinary perception in the here and now, between an idealized past and a relatively sullied present, between childish freedom and adult constraints, between innocence and experience; and of course it also establishes a vision of moral perfection against which Leontes's insane outburst of suspicion, which occurs only moments later, seems all the more terrible. Students find it interesting to debate the function and placement of this speech, to notice how it offers a glimpse of summer, both seasonally and morally, in a context of winter and to see it, in part, as an artful prolepsis of the sheepshearing scenes that are to follow. But Peter Lindenbaum argues, with a certain cogency, that Polixenes's words also set up an escapist image of pastoral bliss that the actual pastoral setting of the play partly contradicts: Shakespeare's Bohemia after all has a "storm-ridden seacoast" and "man-eating bears" (119); according to Antigonus, it is more like a desert than a *locus amoenus*, and it is far from innocent, serving, as it does, as a venue for the thieving Autolycus, whose name derives from a word meaning wolf. Viewed in this manner, the visiting king's poetical daydream erects a pastoral cliché that may then be critiqued and challenged by the more complex and realistic treatment of pastoralism that dominates the fourth act.

Shakespeare highlights the pastoral tension between nature and art most explicitly in Perdita and Polixenes's charming debate on the grafting of flowers. The youthful princess defends the naive view of natural process, rejecting the "streak'd gillyvors, / Which some call nature's bastards" because they are produced by crossbreeding, "an art" that usurps a power proper only to "great creating nature" (4.4.82–88). Her older and more sophisticated interlocutor counters with the argument that whatever agency the gardener may employ to improve upon nature is itself an *aspect* of nature.

> nature is made better by no mean
> But nature makes that mean. So, over that art

Which you say adds to nature, is an art
That nature makes. You see, sweet maid, we marry
A gentler scion to the wildest stock,
And make conceive a bark of baser kind
By bud of nobler race. This is an art
Which does mend nature, change it rather, but
The art itself is nature.   (4.4.89–97)

Discussion of this passage in the classroom can yield instructive ironies, for Polixenes's view of nature at this point, although still idealistic, is rather more closely related to genuine experience than was his earlier fantasy of boys as "twinn'd lambs." But of more central importance is the dramatic irony that his justification of horticultural cross-breeding runs precisely counter to his views on marriage, for we know that his purpose in attending the sheepshearing (in disguise of course) is to prevent his royal heir from allying himself ignobly to a "scion" of "the wildest stock" — to a girl of humble birth such as Perdita, however refined, fresh, and desirable she may appear. An even deeper irony lies in the circumstance that the alluring shepherdess is truly royal in the genealogical as well as the moral and aesthetic senses, a point that her ceremonial role as "mistress of the feast" (4.3.40) and her festive costume as the goddess Flora help to symbolize. Nor is Perdita as unsophisticated generally as her attitude toward grafting might suggest, for the beautiful speech that accompanies her distribution of flowers draws equally from nature and from art. Her several references to classical deities and particularly to the myth of Proserpina forge an alliance between literacy and the landscape, and her passage of sustained lyricism distinguishing the flowers appropriate symbolically to their various recipients depends not only on actual stage props (the flowers in season at the time of the action) but on those blossoms that she must evoke imaginatively through the verbal resources of imagery and rhythm.

A useful writing assignment for students of *The Winter's Tale* is to analyze Perdita's much excerpted floral aria in 4.4 as a kind of inset lyric, or even as a detachable play within the play, that possesses a completeness and coherence of its own while nevertheless relating in complex and symbolic ways to what precedes and follows it — first, in terms of the long and varied act in which it is embedded, and second, within the drama as a whole. This exercise can uncover many linkages between the natural and the artificial and explore their most fruitful resonances. A close reading of the floral speech, for instance, can suggest connections to Leontes's unnatural illusion of Hermione's transgression, for it glances at both chastity and sexual desire. In retrospect it is equally possible to regard the king's diseased mental construct as a manifestation of bastard art, art of the kind that bears no mimetic relation to the truth and that interferes (as Perdita thinks hybridizing may do) with the sanctity of "great creating nature."

Perdita's elaborate verbal bouquet (through her emphasis on seasonal change) relates also to the idea of time and its triumph, a central theme of the play; but her breathtaking description of the "Daffodils, / That come before the swallow dares, and take / The winds of March with beauty" (4.4.118–20) not only recalls Autolycus's rollicking song, "When daffodils begin to peer, / With heigh, the doxy over the dale!" (4.3.1–2), but suggests as well the chill that lurks in the unrecognized presence of Florizel's father, who intends to nip romance in the bud. The formal celebration of fertility in this scene clearly looks forward to the reunion of the separated kings, one of whom will greet the other with the lines, "Welcome hither, / As is the spring to th' earth" (5.1.151–52). Most of Perdita's flowers and herbs bear an iconographic significance — not unlike Ophelia's in the comparable scene from *Hamlet*; J. H. P. Pafford's commentary on this scene in his New Arden edition of *The Winter's Tale* (including his extended note in app. 1, 169–72) is a useful aid to an investigation of iconography. Indeed I have suggested elsewhere (*Fancy's Images* 113–25) that the entire floral episode explores the complex relation of nature to art by serving as a microcosm of the drama as a totality and by calling attention to itself as a self-contained expression of literary-theatrical artifice while simultaneously offering its audience the experience of natural spontaneity and unspoiled freshness. The distribution of flowers by a shepherd-princess enacting the role of Flora, "Most goddess-like prank'd up" (4.4.10), obviously participates in the traditions of the court masque, the most elaborately artificial species of entertainment that Jacobeans knew; and the dance of shepherds and shepherdesses, balanced by its antimasque, the dance of satyrs, reinforces the notion of pastoral simplicity self-consciously presented through the cultivated adornments of poetry, music, and ballet.

Nowhere is the art-nature motif more movingly dramatized in *The Winter's Tale* than in its final climactic episode, the statue scene. Whereas the floral ceremony had rendered nature in terms of art, the scene of Hermione's disclosure and revival reverses the rhythm, letting nature emerge from and transcend artifice. Once more, students may be encouraged to examine both the dramaturgy and the language of this action, noting especially the quasi-liturgical tone and the symbolic importance of music, which accompanies the mysterious transition from the illusion of painted stone to the reality of living flesh. Again a certain self-conscious theatricality is evident, for the inert figure of Hermione is revealed by the drawing of a curtain (as in the "discovery scenes" of many earlier plays), and there is considerable emphasis on Paulina's "gallery," to which the stage audience has already been introduced and which contains "many singularities" (5.3.10–12) worth appreciating in their own right. Julio Romano's masterpiece, the "dead likeness" (5.3.14) of the putatively deceased queen, has been reserved for the final and supreme aesthetic experience, since "that rare Italian master" is famed for such skill that he "would beguile Nature of her custom, so perfectly he is her ape" (5.2.98–101). Here obviously Shakespeare dwells on the affinity between nature and art, an affinity that in the greatest examples makes the sculpture difficult to distinguish from the living figure it depicts. Both Perdita and her father are so moved by the sight of the likeness that they are impelled to kiss it and can be restrained only because, in doing so, they might mar the colors as yet not finally set. Leontes notices the wrinkles of age — a change from the youthful queen he had imprisoned — but is informed that the "carver's excellence" (5.3.30) has imaginatively made allowance for the intervening years. When Hermione finally descends from her pedestal, her incredulous husband believes at first that he is experiencing "magic," an "art" of dubious legitimacy but one, under present circumstances, that he would suddenly legalize (5.3.110). Here indeed we have Sidney's poetic principle of the "speaking picture" (*Defence of Poesie* 80) actually staged.

As I argue in another place (*Fancy's Images* 43–53), the last plays of Shakespeare, especially *The Winter's Tale* and *The Tempest*, offer a fresh perspective on the value of theatrical artifice and, in consequence, of the reality it usually seeks to imitate. The reflexiveness and self-referentiality that characterize so much of Shakespeare's dramaturgy in earlier plays tend to betoken a certain confidence in the value of mimesis, in the capacity of art to imitate nature powerfully and meaningfully. That same faith in the way art may serve nature by representing it forcefully is obviously exemplified by the genius of Julio Romano in our play. But Shakespeare also seems to suggest through the symbolic modulation from inert statuary to human movement, from silent stone to speaking and feeling personality, that however ingenious or convincing the artist's skill may be, aesthetic imagination can provide no true or final substitute for reality. As important as art may be, then, as an index of the human cultivation of nature — and indeed (following Polixenes's reasoning) as a *part* of that nature — a statue, when it is compared to a living woman, must translate, in another sense, as a metaphor for death. Paulina's term "dead likeness" would seem to refer not only to the image of the dead but also to the deadness (or fixity) of art in comparison with the fluidity of life. One thinks of Keats's Grecian urn with its artistically perfect but nevertheless "cold" pastoral. Through a moving expansion of context, Shakespeare's scene seems to conduct us outward and upward from art to life, from the relinquishing of the beautiful but factitious illusion to the higher joy of reawakened faith and shared love.

Students may be encouraged to note the theatrical means by which the dramatist enforces this shift from one plane of reality to another. They might compare it with the similar moment in *The Tempest* when the charming artifice of the wedding masque is suddenly dissolved in midcourse, allowing Prospero to tell his amazed onlookers that "We are such stuff / As dreams are made on" (4.1.156–57). The figure of Hermione is at first a kind of "show" — a thing "lonely" and "apart" (5.3.18) — before she steps forward to reenter the life stream of those who at first had been her audience. But, as in a court masque (which typically concludes with the actors joining the spectators), the art of the performance merges into the social fabric of those for whom it was designed and from whom it originated.

There is no mistaking the religious implications of this symbolism, for the miracle of transformation takes place in a "chapel" (5.3.86). Perdita has kneeled to the statue of her mother as one might to the image of a saint, and Paulina's speech (her name would seem to contain overtones of Saint Paul) is incantatory, ritualistic, almost priestly, in vocabulary and tone:

> Music, awake her; strike! [*Music.*]
> 'Tis time; descend; be stone no more; approach;
> Strike all that look upon with marvel. Come,
> I'll fill your grave up. Sir, nay, come away,
> Bequeath to death your numbness, for from him
> Dear life redeems you. You perceive she stirs.
> > [*Hermione comes down.*]
> Start not; her actions shall be holy as
> You hear my spell is lawful.   (5.3.98–105)

Our response must be "a reverential wonder," to quote G. Wilson Knight, "at knowledge of Life where Death was throned" (*Crown* 127). Shakespeare finally absorbs the paradoxical relation of art and nature into a more expansive and metaphysical context, suggesting an ultimately transcendental continuum from the lesser to the greater — from the artifice of human agency to the artifice of eternity, or the redemptive work of God. For students who are receptive or sympathetic to Christian theological ideas, it may not be out of place to mention the overtones of the Incarnation and the Resurrection that surface here, for Hermione's descent may be regarded symbolically as both a mystical enfleshment of undeserved (and unexpected) grace and a triumph over mortality.

I do not suggest that even a detailed consideration of the relation between art and nature exhausts the richness of this infinitely rewarding text. I believe, nevertheless, that the theme is too much a part of the action, characterization, language, dramaturgy, and structure of *The Winter's Tale* to be safely ignored. My experience, in fact, has been that when students raise questions about this play in respect either to its specific details or to its larger concerns, the discourse almost always (and usually sooner than later) drifts back to the pastoral mode, which is to say, in effect, to considerations of the nature of artifice and its complement, the artifice of nature.

Trusting Shakespeare's *Winter's Tale*: Metafiction in the Late Plays

William W. E. Slights

> Never trust the artist. Trust the tale.
> — D. H. Lawrence

Those of us who have the chance to teach Shakespeare's late plays can benefit from, rather than just grumble about, the predominance of prose fiction in academic curricula across North America. The peculiarly self-reflexive, tale-telling quality of the late plays presents an excellent opportunity to explore an aspect of Shakespeare's art and of postmodern fiction that many of our students are intrigued by and may well have already studied, namely, metafictional narrative. Forging links between the intensely self-conscious narrativity of a play like *The Winter's Tale* and metafictional works by such writers as John Barth, Donald Barthelme, and John Fowles helps correct the too common notion that Shakespeare's modes of representation are dated, stagy, and unbelievable. The entire matter of believability has been opened to a fascinating process of renegotiation in the broad wake of poststructuralist literary theory and postmodernist fiction. Shakespeare's plays, particularly the late ones, have a great deal to say about the question, Can we really trust either the teller *or* the tale anymore?

In my undergraduate Shakespeare course I generally explore Shakespeare's mature dramatic technique in *The Winter's Tale* under four headings, one for each of the seventy-five-minute classes I allocate to the play: Storytelling and the Sources of Suspense; Theories of Metafiction and the Drama; Dramatic Deceit and the Narrated Self; and Frozen Actors and Speaking Statues.

Storytelling and the Sources of Suspense

In the first class I focus on the storytelling methods of Robert Greene's *Pandosto: The Triumph of Time* (1595), Shakespeare's main source for *The Winter's Tale*. The antithesis of metafiction, Greene's technique assumes and repeatedly asserts a stable relation between fiction and reality that is never opened to question. The resulting text is highly determined, first, by the author's thesis (that jealousy "is such a heavy enemy to that holy estate of matrimony . . . [that] there oft ensueth bloody revenge, as this ensuing history manifestly proveth" [Greene 184]) and, second, by the reified force of Fortune ("Fortune, who all this while had shewed a friendly face, began now to turn her back and to shew a louring countenance . . ." [202]). Jealousy, a given in the character of Pandosto, prompts his alienation from his chaste queen, Bellaria, and Fortune disposes the fates of his family and friends until he is reunited with his long-lost daughter, Fawnia, for whom, true to his "unnatural" character, he conceives an incestuous but unfulfilled passion. The relation of psychological and supernatural agencies is never questioned, the second being presented as a simple reaction to the first.

To get the class to see that Shakespeare's recasting of Greene's story is altogether a different matter and to anticipate comparisons to postmodern fiction, I have students prepare brief accounts of how *The Winter's Tale* story must look to selected characters: the Second Gentleman, Polixenes, and Paulina. The idea behind this exercise is that point of view limits the characters' interpretations of what is said and done in the play and also an audience's shifting perspectives on what it is watching. For example, students of mine have argued heatedly about what Polixenes and Hermione should actually be doing while Leontes describes what he "sees" them doing: "paddling palms and . . . / Kissing with inside lip" (1.2.115, 286). The question is, Who exactly is creating this text and this performance? One possible answer is that the "author" of this tale is certainly not Greene's self-projected moralist or the all-powerful figure of Fortune but, more likely, the viewer, under the powerful scripting influence of Paulina, one of Shakespeare's notable additions to Greene's cast of characters. Under Paulina's direction, the play, especially its ending, might well be called, not the Triumph of Time, but the Triumph of Good Women.

Theories of Metafiction and the Drama

In the second class on *The Winter's Tale* I provide students with some of the introductory material from Patricia Waugh's *Metafiction: The Theory and Practice of Self-Conscious Fiction*, including the following definition:

> *Metafiction* is a term given to fictional writing which self-consciously and systematically draws attention to its status as an artefact in order to pose questions about the relationship between fiction and reality. (2)

Choosing a novel that a few of the students know—such as Thomas Pynchon's *Crying of Lot 49*, Barth's *Lost in the Funhouse*, or Fowles's *French Lieutenant's Woman*—I introduce two topics that enable the discussion of metafiction and Shakespeare's late plays to proceed: *self-reflexivity*, a prominent concern of semiotic theoreticians such as Mikhail Bakhtin and psychoanalytic ones such as Jacques Lacan; and *framebreaking* (Goffman), an element of storytelling that has been greatly enriched in recent years by the fragmentation of the unitary self, experiments with temporal discontinuity in fiction, and movements among various levels of reality within the fiction and without. Armed with these basic concepts, which are already familiar to some of the students, we are ready to consider Shakespeare's exploration of similar attitudes toward storytelling in *The Winter's Tale*.

A good place in the text to start is Leontes's semiotically destabilizing and theatrically self-reflexive dismissal of his young son in the midst of his jealous fit:

Go play, boy, play. Thy mother plays, and I
Play too, but so disgrac'd a part, whose issue
Will hiss me to my grave: contempt and clamor
Will be my knell. Go play, boy, play.

(1.2.187–90)

It is not just foreplay or stage play or child's play that is Shakespeare's subject
here but his own wordplay as well. Such semantic playfulness starts a notice-
able wobble in the expository framework of royal history established in 1.1
by the expository characters, Camillo and Archidamus, a wobble accen-
tuated by Mamillius's starting to tell his own winter's tale:

HERMIONE.   Pray you sit by us,
            And tell's a tale.
MAMILLIUS.   Merry, or sad, shall't be?
HERMIONE.   As merry as you will.
MAMILLIUS.   A sad tale's best for winter. I have one
            Of sprites and Goblins.
HERMIONE.   Let's have that, good sir.
            Come on, sit down, come on, and do your best
            To fright me with your sprites; you're pow'rful at it.
MAMILLIUS.   There was a man —
HERMIONE.   Nay, come sit down; then on.
MAMILLIUS.   Dwelt by a churchyard. I will tell it softly,
            Yond crickets shall not hear it.
HERMIONE.   Come on then,
            And give't me in mine ear.   (2.1.22–32)

Both the storyteller and his audience are included within the frame of
Mamillius's whispered incipit, and the man who dwells by the churchyard
for sixteen years may well be the boy's penitent father, Leontes, whose interrupted story continues in the very next line.

The time frame of Leontes's generically dislocated tragicomic plot is interrupted once again when at the start of act 4 Shakespeare introduces the
blatantly allegorical figure of Time to transform a winter's tale into a spring-
time fantasy. Time's opportune intervention makes clear how risky it is for
an audience to identify with this author of whimsical deceptions: Time
"makes and unfolds error" (4.1.2), not truth, with a turn of his glass, and
it is *as if* we "had but slept between" (4.1.7) the scenes. The unreliability
of narrators, the uncertainty of dream states, the unknowability even of
the reader's "self" — these are all elements of Shakespeare's play and also,
for example, of Italo Calvino's ontologically subjective and perpetually
recommencing work *If on a Winter's Night a Traveler*. Here is part of
Calvino's caveat emptor:

> But a situation that takes place at the opening of a novel always refers
> you to something else that has happened or is about to happen, and
> it is this something else that makes it risky to identify with me, risky
> for you the reader and for him the author; and the more gray and
> ordinary and undistinguished and commonplace the beginning of this
> novel is, the more you and the author feel a hint of danger looming
> over that fraction of "I" that you have heedlessly invested in the "I"
> of a character whose inner history you know nothing about, as you
> know nothing about the contents of that suitcase he is so anxious to
> be rid of.   (15)

There is both risk and excitement involved whenever we "identify" with
those unreliable sorts who are given to telling lies. The point of "danger
looming over that fraction of 'I' . . . invested in the 'I' of a character" is
precisely the hook that can catch for Shakespeare's late plays the imagina-
tions of a generation of students schooled, or at least self-taught, in the world
of the new, self-conscious, frame-breaking novels, films, and television
shows. While I refer students to such related critical works as Lionel Abel's
Metatheatre and James Calderwood's *Shakespearean Metadrama* and *Metadrama in Shakespeare's Henriad*, they seem best able to grasp the Shake-
speare-metafiction connection when dealing with the primary texts, for
instance, with *The Tempest* and Fowles's *Magus*.

Dramatic Deceit and the Narrated Self

In this class I use video clips from Jane Howell's BBC production of *The
Winter's Tale* to place before my students such metafictional moments as
Autolycus's brilliantly deceptive self-narration at 4.3.50–123. I stop the video
frequently to discuss ways that relying on impromptu narrative both creates
and foils dramatic expectations. Having turned his rather handsome coat
ragged- and seamy-side out, Autolycus crawls toward the Clown and tells
him of being beaten and robbed by a man who, like himself, was "once
a servant of the Prince [Florizel]" and who

> hath been since an ape-bearer, then a process-server, a bailiff, then
> he compass'd a motion of the Prodigal Son, and married a tinker's wife
> within a mile where my land and living lies; and, having flown over
> many knavish professions, he settled only in rogue. Some call him
> Autolycus.   (4.3.87–100)

With these words, the present rogue, having picked the Clown's pocket,
places another, implied Autolycus far from the scene of the crime. This
carries the stage convention of the impenetrable disguise to new, metaphysical heights and often instigates among students explicit concerns with

matters of truth-value and playfulness in relation to the constructed self, whether fictional (e.g., Nabokov's Kinbote-Botkin, from *Pale Fire*, sometime putative King of Zembia, who writes academic glosses on his own poetic biography) or real (e.g., the president who constructs himself as champion of liberty by starting wars). Unlike a play such as *As You Like It*, *The Winter's Tale* not only includes but is also *about* the possibility of such incredible actions. By "systematically draw[ing] attention to its status as an artefact in order to pose questions about the relationship between fiction and reality," the play becomes genuinely metafictional. This is nowhere more evident than in the elaborate "resurrection" of Hermione's statue that Shakespeare invented to round off — or to blow apart — Greene's story of jealousy, separation, and death.

Frozen Actors and Speaking Statues

In this, the final class on the play, I address the problem of credibility in the romance form (Second Gentleman: "This news, which is call'd true, is so like an old tale, that the verity of it is in strong suspicion" [5.2.27–29]) by having my students use the acting techniques of improvisation. Working from Keith Johnstone's observations and exercises in *Impro: Improvisation and the Theatre* (33–75), I set up modern parallels to sequences from *The Winter's Tale* for students to act for the rest of the class (e.g., Florizel and Perdita's first date; a suburban father forbidding his son from seeing a girl from the inner city). Initially, student audiences demand naturalistic performances, but often the more improbable scenarios and bizarre dialogue produce the best impromptu performances. Having raised the issue of credibility that is central to Shakespeare's ending, I then use the improv technique of "freeze-frames" (directing the students to stop moving and to hold a position at a prearranged signal) to demonstrate what the actor's body can do, with and without motion. We then consider the coup de theatre of the moving, speaking statue in 5.3.

No other action in the play so radically dislocates the audience's perspective on what has "really" been happening as this scene does, once again posing questions about the relation between fiction and reality. Hermione's transformation from stone to flesh effectively collapses the distinction between the artificial and the real. It stands at the head of a substantial list of parallels between *The Winter's Tale* and twentieth-century metafiction: placing self-reflexive stories within stories (such as Mamillius's winter's tale within Shakespeare's), presenting characters in the act of reading themselves (as with Autolycus's impersonating his own nonexistent victim), confusing ontological levels (as in Leontes's *tremor cordis*, a form of hallucination, or the dream of Time), disrupting expected temporal sequence (as Jonson berated Shakespeare for doing), and relying on reduplicating narrative (as Shakespeare does with his mirror-image structure). Certainly, to demystify standard notions of character, creator, and entertainer, as Shakespeare does with his arch-deceiver, Autolycus, is to adumbrate recent developments in self-conscious prose fiction. And when Paulina requires all present to "awake your [their/our] faith" (5.3.95) and Hermione steps down off her pedestal, the mimetic magic of stage illusion is astoundingly reinvoked to balance the harsh realities of personal loss against the benefits of art. Questions that can engage students with the text at this point include Did Hermione really die and come back to life through the power of faith? Did Paulina (as one student put it) "smuggle table scraps out to the garden shed for sixteen years to keep Hermione alive?" Has Paulina tricked everyone into seeing what they want to believe? The fascinating thing about *The Winter's Tale* is that it so often has it both ways: the play brutally deconstructs the conventions of narrative and drama before our very eyes and at the same time insists that if we clap our hands, the fairies will be there for us. Disconcerting though it is to be so lost in the fifth acts of Shakespeare's late plays, we are at least still in the funhouse.

The teaching methods I have evolved to deal with the special problems of *The Winter's Tale* and the other late plays are especially directed at counteracting the idea that Shakespeare's dramatic conventions are somehow fixed far apart from vital developments in recent literature. There are, of course, differences as well as similarities between the fictional discourses of Shakespeare and of postmodernist literature, and I try to suggest those differences to my students as well. No one is likely to confuse Prospero with Kurt Vonnegut's Kilgore Trout, however similar their authorial and metaphysical dilemmas may be. I use a combination of classroom techniques — comparing parallel dramatic and nondramatic texts in class, conducting theoretical discussions, using video clips, and getting students to do improvs — in an attempt to recommend some nontraditional conclusions about Shakespearean dramaturgy through nontraditional classroom experiences. Instead of trying to deny the massive presence of prose fiction in the current curriculum, I have transferred the critical methods of metafiction to the study of texts of another age and genre. In the process I have found that Shakespeare's late plays both take from and give to contemporary writing reasons to proceed with the creative and interpretive enterprise.

Making the Statue Move: Teaching Performance

Kathleen Campbell

Ever since Ben Jonson lamented dramatists' use of those "moldy tales" that "make nature afraid," critics have complained about the implausible stories that Shakespeare chose as sources for the late plays. Filled with magic, supernatural intervention, and, except for *The Tempest*, overflowing the bounds of space and time revered by Renaissance theorists, these romances often disturb modern readers too, even students exposed to films like the Star Wars trilogy. Shakespeare himself is evidently aware of the improbability of his material, which the Second Gentleman in *The Winter's Tale* describes as "so like an old tale that the verity of it is in strong suspicion" (5.2.28–29). At the same time, however, Shakespeare repeatedly indicates a way to make such events credible. In that often criticized scene in *The Winter's Tale* (5.2), in which the gentlemen of the court report the reunion of Leontes and Polixenes and the discovery of Perdita's identity, characters speak repeatedly of the inability of their account to convey the actual experience and of the superiority of that experience over narration: "I make a broken delivery of the business" (9); "[S]uch a deal of wonder is broken out within this hour, that ballad-makers cannot be able to express it" (23–25); "Then you have lost a sight which was to be seen, cannot be spoken of" (43–44); "I never heard of such another encounter, which lames report to follow it, and undoes description to do it" (57–59); "Like an old tale still, which will have matter to rehearse, though credit be asleep and not an ear open" (62–64).

The characters are suggesting that such stories of loss and recovery, of repentance and restoration, must be experienced to be believed. A tale is always an account of the past, of events completed; as such, to be believable it is dependent on our trust in the narrator. A drama, by contrast, unfolds for its audience in a perpetual present; what happens is, through the theatrical art, happening before us — we accept it, as the gentlemen in *The Winter's Tale* do, because we see it, we experience it. Traditional criticism, which freezes a play and analyzes it as a unified whole, may provide valuable insights into the play's meaning but lose contact with the direct experience of the work. When Charles Frey, for example, describes the opening scene of *The Winter's Tale*, he interprets its language from the perspective of the final scene: "[T]he Bohemian Archidamus and the Sicilian Camillo represent not only two countries but two climates and two sets of attitudes that similarly intersect. . . . The Sicilian court, the art context, stands now in winter, and, as we soon see, a kind of dream. . . . Winter and dream equal nature and art or nature as art" (116). This understanding is unavailable to the audience in the theater, who will have to wait several hours to discover, if they do at all, that "Shakespeare makes this emblematic preview cover the whole range of the play's degeneration in aging friendships and regeneration in the 'promise' of youth (1.1.36)" (117). And for students readings of this sort do precisely what Frey warns against; they tend "to veil the experience even as they reveal its meanings" (311).

To become aware of the import of these late plays, to appreciate them as theater, students must experience how they work as dramatic action unfolding in time before an audience responding to that action as it is revealed. In other words, students need to see productions and perform scenes themselves, but they are often ill-prepared for these activities. Without theater training, students tend to evaluate performances much as they would a written text, paying scant attention to the theatrical problems of a script, and class performances are often limited to reading scenes or reciting lines. Students need to learn to approach a script as theatrical artists do. Introducing simple acting exercises and vocabulary helps students see more clearly the relation between script, performer, and audience. These exercises draw students' attention to the performance problems of character and action and provide tools with which to analyze plays from a theatrical rather than a literary perspective.

For the theatrical artist, the script is the blueprint for the realization of a concept of human action. Aristotle insists on this idea in his discussion of tragedy: "For tragedy is an imitation, not of men, but of an action and of life, and life consists in action, and its end is a mode of action, not a quality" (Butcher 27). But in the actual presentation of a play, the sense of action is much more complicated, for several levels of action occur at the same time. Michael Goldman distinguishes three levels of action in a theatrical performance. Using terminology adapted from Aristotle, Goldman explores the relation between *praxis*, the actions the characters perform, "the action" of a play; *poiesis*, the action of the actors in creating, sustaining, and projecting their roles; and *theoria*, the action of the audience "in responding to and trying to possess the events it watches" (*Acting* 12). To understand the theatrical life of a dramatic work, students need to be aware of the contribution of performances to the meaning of the event—they need to see that the continual movement between engagement and detachment, between being drawn into the world of a play and stepping back from it and trying to make sense of it, strongly shapes an audience's experience.

A beginning step is to separate the action of the play from the language of the script. For the literary reader, the text is often everything: the language is the play. But it is a truism in the theater that a script is like an iceberg: the recorded words are merely the tip above the water's surface; the play, the praxis, is the invisible mass underneath the waves that supports the visible shape. Actors create an illusion through physical activity—gestures, movements, facial expressions, inflections, pauses—that reveals the underlying dramatic action resulting in particular words being spoken.

Contentless scenes, brief sequences of dialogue that can carry many different relationships and actions, can be used to demonstrate the importance

of the actor's creation of illusion in establishing action. Here is an example
from Robert Cohen's *Acting Power*:

A. Hi!
B. Hello.
A. What'd you do last night?
B. Oh, not much. How about you?
A. Oh, watched a little T.V.
B. Anything good?
A. Well, no. Not really.
B. See you later.
A. OK.   (55)

As acting exercises, such scenes illustrate the playing of relationships and
provide a simple way to show how actors create meaning by fleshing out
the bare bones of a script. Students, working in pairs, are given a specific
relationship to play, using only the dialogue provided; they can improvise
any business — physical activity — they desire, but they can use no other
words. Examples of relationships are a boy and a girl whom the boy wants
to ask for a date, a mother and a daughter at breakfast after the daughter
has been out late, lab partners who don't like each other. (After a few of
these scenes have been played, students usually begin to generate their own
ideas for relationships.) The students who are watching the scene are not
told the situation but asked to figure it out. Even with inexperienced performers, students have little trouble recognizing the relationships portrayed,
and they see that their perception of the action, the praxis, comes from the
acting, the poiesis, rather than from the language of the scene.

Because the dramatic structure of a scene is entirely independent of the
words of the script, contentless scenes illustrate what an actor may call
subtext. Most scripts, of course, provide clear connections between text and
subtext; the relationships are set by the author, not established at the whim
of the dramatic artists. That at least is what we say, but in fact many scenes
require almost as much invention on the part of the actors as do contentless
scenes. The first scene of *The Winter's Tale* is a good example. Camillo and
Archidamus talk, first about friendship and hospitality, then about the young
Mamillius. We learn that they are from different countries; that the circumstance of their meeting has been a visit of one king to another; that
Archidamus, at least, perceives Bohemia to be less magnificent than Sicilia,
where they now are. No indication is given of the specific setting or occasion
of this particular conversation. Camillo appears in other scenes that tell us
about his character, but after exiting Archidamus disappears from the play
entirely. What kind of relationship exists between these two courtiers? Have
they become close friends during this extended visit? Are they acting politely
with each other but really feeling ready to part company (much like Leontes

and Polixenes)? Is there a slight competition here over who can be more hospitable? Is Archidamus perhaps drunk, or at least a bit tipsy, and Camillo tolerant, or a bit irritated? Is Camillo trying tactfully to get away from Archidamus's overflowery compliments? The text supports each of these relationships, and each provides a distinctive structure for the scene and a somewhat different introduction for the crucial scene that follows. Although the content of the language introduces thematic material that will become increasingly important — hospitality, expectancy, birth, children — our perception of the play and our introduction to the dramatic action comes largely through the choices made by the actors rather than from the words of the script.

Shaping the actor's choices, in each scene and in the play as a whole, is the actor's sense of a character's objective. An objective is simply what the character wants to accomplish, wants to do at any given moment. Actors build a character by working from objective to objective, each in line with a superobjective, the overarching desire that drives the character's actions. In the above scene, for example, Camillo's objective might be simply to be polite to a guest; this intention would be in line with the larger objective, to serve Leontes, which motivates him throughout the play. Discussion of objectives, which are always expressed by a verb form, undermines the tendency to talk about characters exclusively in terms of descriptions and corrects the conception that acting is a matter of pretense or imposture. The actor William Hurt emphasizes the difference: "Acting is about actions. . . . It's not pretending. Acting is not *looking like* you're doing, it's *doing*. The problem begins when you get adjectives into acting. Acting is not about adjectives. It's about verbs and adverbs" (Hinson 10).

The relation between objectives and dramatic action can be illustrated effectively through another simple exercise often used in beginning acting classes. Two students are asked to improvise a brief scene. One student invents an objective that requires the assistance of the other person. The objective should be specific and somewhat urgent, and there should be a limited time frame in which it must be accomplished: one student could ask the other to pick up food and No-Doz to help her get through an all-night study session; the other could resist but eventually agree. To accomplish an objective, the character may be teasing, angry, sweet, or upset, changing strategies as needed to move the other person to action; how the person behaves is a function of what he or she wants to accomplish. Playing these scenes reveals how intentions shape behavior and illustrates how expressions, gestures, and physical relations function along with language to help a character achieve an objective.

Objectives link the actor's poiesis to the praxis of the play, for understanding the sequence of objectives in a scene often reveals elements of the dramatic action. The action of a scene can be broken down into smaller action units, or beats. A relatively simple scene such as 2.2 in *The Winter's Tale* illustrates the process. There are four large movements in the scene: Paulina's entrance, her conversation with the Gaoler, her conversation with Emilia, and the intervention of the Gaoler as they exit. Smaller units suggest the interplay of objectives: lines 1–2, Paulina enters and calls for the Gaoler; 2–4, Paulina worries about Hermione; 4–11, Paulina unsuccessfully tries to see Hermione; 11–16, Paulina successfully asks to see Emilia; 16–18, the Gaoler states rules of meeting; 19–20, Paulina complains; 20–29, Paulina receives news of the child's birth; 29–35, Paulina decides to take the child to Leontes; 35–55, Paulina instructs Emilia; 56–66, the Gaoler intervenes. The objective that drives the scene is Paulina's desire to help Hermione. That intention remains constant as Paulina attempts various immediate objectives (to see Hermione, to see Emilia, etc.) that, blocked or advanced by the Gaoler, determine the beats of the scene. The analysis points to other significant elements of structure and character in the scene: the two large sections that each end with an intervention from the Gaoler concerning an impending action; the increase in Paulina's frustration, which leads to her decision to act boldly to help Hermione; the domination of the scene by Paulina despite the Gaoler's presence and authority (which immediately tells the audience something about Paulina).

Such a detailed analysis reveals the forces and counterforces, represented here by the Gaoler and Paulina, at work in the play. The playwright William Gibson, in *Shakespeare's Game*, refers to these thrusts and counterthrusts as move and object: in each scene a character has the possibility for a move against an impending object; after a move is completed, the next move is up to the other player. Act 2, scene 1 has ended with Leontes's move against Hermione — her imprisonment. The next move is Hermione's, but it is taken by her surrogate, Paulina (a character who does not appear in the play until Hermione is unable to act for herself). The scene consists of a series of moves and countermoves between Paulina and the Gaoler that result in the determination of the next move against Leontes, which Paulina will complete in the following scene.

Through this analysis of move and object, thrust and counterthrust, students can begin to see that the plot of *The Winter's Tale*, once the onset of Leontes's jealousy disrupts the more or less stable world of the Sicilian and Bohemian courts, comprises a series of moves between Leontes and Hermione or their surrogates. Several elements confuse the pattern: the number and kind of Hermione's surrogates (including Camillo, Paulina, Antigonus, the Old Shepherd, and Autolycus), who often do not seem to know that they are acting in her behalf; the switching of surrogates from one side to the other; and the seeming intervention of supernatural forces or uncanny good luck in the action. Antigonus, for example, makes a move for Hermione by saving Perdita from death, but he then acts as an agent for Leontes's move against the queen, the exposure of Perdita, until the courtier's dream of Hermione transforms Leontes's move into Hermione's; next the Old Shepherd unknowingly completes the move by taking up the abandoned baby. In the trial scene, Hermione places herself in the hands of Apollo, whose oracle proclaims her innocence and who, at least in the judgment of Leontes, makes the final move against the king, the striking down of Mamillius. The use of these surrogates reveals the central comic action of this play — the gathering of a community that supports and protects Leontes and eventually brings about his restoration. Beginning with an exploration of an element of poiesis, the use of an objective, students come to an understanding of the praxis of the play as it is revealed through the shifting involvement of characters in the plot.

Further exploration of problems of performance in *The Winter's Tale* suggests a complicated relation between praxis, poiesis, and theoria, the action of the actors and of the audience providing an analogous experience to that developed by the praxis of the drama. For example, the suddenness of Leontes's jealousy is a problem for both actor and character, who must each create a motivation for its existence out of more or less whole cloth. Leontes has no sinful or domineering mother as Hamlet or Coriolanus has, no Iago or Don John to trick him as Othello or Claudio has; the actor creates his nightmare vision, as Leontes does, out of his own imagination, his dreams: praxis and poiesis are identical. Similarly, whatever motivation the actor creates, the eruption of this dark suspicion amid the play's pastoral vision of familial bonds and hospitality takes the audience by surprise. Like the characters onstage, the spectators must suddenly sit up and take notice; they seek to understand the origins of the king's "diseas'd opinion" (1.2.297) at the same time that they question its validity. Even before Camillo voices the dilemma, the audience is caught by the conflicting claims the play lays before the Sicilian court: the unwavering dignity and grace of Hermione and the undeniable reality of Leontes's feelings. The objective in praxis and theoria becomes identical: to understand the cause of Leontes's loss of faith. Through an awareness of the play as acted, the audience participates in an experience comparable to that which the play sets forward. Spectators do not just hear a story of jealousy; like the characters, they experience confusion and distress.

This doubling of praxis and theoria keeps audience and characters similarly off-balance as the play progresses. New strategies for countering Leontes are proposed, tried, and defeated or abandoned; new characters (Antigonus, Paulina) are introduced and familiar ones (Polixenes, Camillo, and, later, Antigonus) drop from sight. Potential plots and subplots spin off in several directions, and neither characters nor spectators know which ones will bear fruit. Camillo saves Polixenes, but not Hermione; the innocent child is placed before Leontes, who is called on publicly to acknowledge the truth of her lineage, which her features image forth — but the plan backfires, placing the baby in immediate danger; the attempt by Antigonus to pawn his life for Perdita's merely reduces her intended fate from burning to exposure: "a present death," Antigonus laments, "would have been more merciful" (2.3.183–84). Characters and spectators alike alternate between hope and despair, between the exhilaration of possible solutions and the disappointment of their defeat, between the expectation of supernatural intervention and the inadequacies of human efforts.

If in the first half of the play poiesis and theoria parallel the confusion of the dramatic action, in the final scene they mirror the play's effort at overcoming the impossible. As with the revelation of Leontes's jealousy, the full effect of the statue scene depends on the audience's awareness of the acting, particularly that of the actor playing Hermione. Shakespeare, maintaining the doubling of on- and offstage experiences, carefully keeps the fact of Hermione's preservation from both characters and audience. Students can imagine sharing the feelings of the characters, who gradually begin to consider the possibility that the statue may come to life. The deep emotion of the scene engages the audience, which also grows increasingly curious: Is the statue really Hermione? Will it move? Are there any visible signs of life? Just as spectators watch for signs of breathing in an actor mimicking death, they look for signs of movement in the actor playing Hermione during the long preawakening dialogue. And for the actor, the problem of maintaining stillness for an extended period and then gracefully moving is perfectly analogous to Hermione's experience of returning to the world after her prolonged absence. Also part of the event is the spectators' enjoyment of the other actor-characters' reactions, particularly Leontes's, whose responses to the developing possibility of life mirror their own. Even the most elemental staging of this scene can give students a sense of what the experience is like for both actors and spectators and of the way in which the interweaving of praxis, poiesis, and theoria build the feelings of surprise and wonder that culminate in the restoration of Hermione, allowing the audience to understand *The Winter's Tale* in a particularly profound and moving way.

Approaching plays from a theatrical perspective emphasizes the participation of actor and audience in creating the dramatic action. Instead of seeing a play as a fixed entity with a clear thematic meaning, a theatrical approach emphasizes what Northrop Frye identifies as the precritical phase of literary criticism: "As long as we are reading a novel or listening to a play on the stage, we are following a movement in time, and our mental attitude is a participating one" (*Natural* 9). Teaching approaches that ignore the precritical experience of the romances risk stripping the plays of their dramatic life, often making them sound like sermons rather than dramatic events. At the same time, more than experience is necessary if we are to help students grasp these complex works. A performance-oriented approach encourages students both to participate in the theatrical experience and to be aware of how and why their involvement and understanding are shaped by the relation of poiesis and praxis. Attention to the unfolding experience of the play for characters, actors, and audience allows students to share something of the awe and mystery, the sense of magic, through which these plays work toward their miraculous conclusions.

Using Film and Television to Teach
The Winter's Tale and *The Tempest*

Herbert R. Coursen

Most of the BBC-TV productions of Shakespeare plays are video versions of Classic Comics that confirm the worst clichés about Shakespeare. But if we energize the passive medium, we can accomplish something for our students and for the ongoing phenomenon known as Shakespeare. My approach is to show several versions of the same scene or sequence, thus hinting at the myriad decisions that actors and directors must make at every instant of any production. Unfortunately, we have little that is good in available video or film productions of *The Winter's Tale* or *The Tempest*. The question we must ask is—why? I offer some tentative responses.

Where only one version of a script exists, we cannot compare the choices that other directors and actors have made. Jane Howell's BBC-TV *Winter's Tale* strikes me as pallid, although it was well-received when it first appeared (Hedrick; Bulman and Coursen 276) and has been studied since then (Blum; Cook, "Manipulation"; Dunbar [2 works]; Westlund [2 works]). It may be, however, that this script is difficult to translate to television. The inverted ice-cream cones, the Maginot Line ramp, the tree, the contrast between icy Sicilia and golden-red Bohemia, and the use of close-up asides and soliloquies for Leontes, Camillo, and Autolycus seem to try to share inner thoughts with us and to create a zone for "romance," a "stage" for television viewers, "a mysterious world in which illusions yield to higher realities" (Westlund, "Sets" 3). But the fantasy that the set invites and the psychology on which the close-ups insist are uneasy together here. We are invited into one space, possibly an interesting site for the unusual and unexpected, even as our own space is invaded by heads only inches from the camera. This production forever reminds us of the infinite wash of "studio land" behind everything. That impression may be intentional, suggesting that "we leave Shakespeare's play and return to some no man's land outside it" (Westlund, "Sets" 4). Howell herself says that she wanted to "change the set into something that was much more fluid, but [she] left it too late" (qtd. in Willems 84).

It is possible, however, to contrast two approaches to the notorious statue scene (5.3). In the BBC production, the statue is seen only briefly, usually in the same frame as Leontes, Camillo, Paulina, and Perdita. It is finally alone when Paulina's incantation ends. Its hand reaches toward Leontes. He takes it, says "she's warm!" and pulls a living Hermione toward a two-shot embrace. But "the focus on individuals denies us the sense of simultaneous involvement, the thrill of ritual participation as the stone is made flesh. The approach is intelligent and honest, the acting accomplished, but the medium has reduced the message" (Wells, "'Goes out'" 197). What Howell does communicate is "intimate awareness of reunion by interconnected individuals in a small group" (Blum) and "moment by moment nuances of each distinct movement towards restoration" (Dunbar, "Statue" 1).

A brief version of the scene appears in the splendid "Passion and Coolness" segment of the Royal Shakespeare Company's consistently illuminating "Playing Shakespeare" series, with John Barton and actors from the RSC. Here we have a three-person scene: Lisa Harrow as Hermione, Patrick Stewart as Leontes, and Sheila Hancock as Paulina. Hermione is in the frame between Leontes and Paulina. Stewart speaks across the statue to Paulina, as if discussing a work of art. Once the positions are set, the camera cuts back and forth from Leontes to Paulina, as her warnings excite his interest. Hancock's speech to the statue suggests that language is capable of infusing warmth into stone but that it is a taxing process. At the phrase "dear life redeems you," Hermione stirs, almost imperceptibly. Stewart exhales when he realizes "she's warm!" The camera closes up for a tight two-shot that features a tear coming from Hermione's left eye.

The statue of the BBC version is part of a grouping that includes the "living." The RSC version has Hermione on a pedestal above Leontes and Paulina. Sheldon Zitner reminds us of the importance of placement and camera angle:

> When Tintoretto or Veronese places the eye of the observer below a noble banquet or a deposition, he employs the vantage of respect and adoration. . . . [T]he BBC *Winter's Tale* . . . gave us Hermione now from slightly above, now almost level. The angles were chosen presumably to include the noble spectators[,] but their positions were cramped and awkward so that they would not fit in the frame. Farce may romp in a closet, but miracles can't be crowded.   (8)

Thus the less-crowded RSC version, with its elevated Hermione, may work better than the BBC scene. RSC also edits the script down to three voices. While the play does demand its Perdita, the relatively complete text of the BBC productions can clutter the limited space of the tube.

Here, of course, is a chance for the question — How is the scene staged? The question may call for a perusal of John Cranford Adams, Robert Speaight, Arthur Colby Sprague, and others, the Shakespeare in Performance series edition of *The Winter's Tale*, and production reviews in periodicals. If a student's interest is piqued by this scene, one can assign that troublesome "research paper."

Three television versions of *The Tempest* exist: the Maurice Evans production of 1960, directed by George Schaefer; the 1983 Bard version, directed by William Woodman; and the BBC production of 1980, directed by John Gorrie. None of the "complete" versions is particularly successful. The reasons lie not only within the productions, of course, but perhaps more deeply in the nature of the medium. Television seems not to be a good vehicle for this script.

The Schaefer production is pleasant but lightweight. Jack Gould accurately notes that the play "poses a severe traffic problem" for the small screen and that close-ups are not helpful in a play that "requires reporting that is fanciful, not factual" (qtd. in Bulman and Coursen 241). In other words, television lacks the magnitude for the play's larger effects, even as its capacity for intimacy proves no advantage. Close-ups tend to invite "psychological interpretations" that are, perhaps, less appropriate for this script than they are for others.

The farcical byplay among Caliban, Stephano, and Trinculo, abetted here by an Ariel voluntarily concealed in a tree, is nicely framed for television in this production, as is the wine-induced descent into the stereotypes of paranoia, megalomania, and compulsiveness. Tom Poston's vulnerable Trinculo, Ronald Radd's queasy and cowardly Stephano, and Richard Burton's sonorous Caliban—replete with finlike ears, armadillo shoulders, and a brush of tail—work well together. All are "obviously having a good time" (V. Vaughan 9).

The play is shaped, shortened, and simplified for commercial television and its presumed audience. The opening storm is unconvincing, brief (one minute), and narrated. We are introduced to characters who rock and roll "near a mysterious and uninhabited island." But Prospero and Ariel are there! Their discussion is placed before Miranda's plea and Prospero's story, perhaps to keep the action boiling. Prospero's narrative is accompanied by a crystal ball in which the disembodied characters swim. The Caliban-Stephano-Trinculo meeting precedes the Antonio-Sebastian conspiracy, a transposition intended to permit Burton and the other actors to hold the audience. Antonio is a potbellied villain, while Sebastian is a fop in peach, pink, and pearl. Claribel is eliminated. Sebastian doesn't realize that he is heir of Naples until Antonio points it out to him. The "living drollery" are squat and dancing rocks. No banquet appears or disappears. Ariel does appear, and he gets one of his harpylike wings tangled in a bush. The wedding masque is miniaturized and lasts for one minute. Prospero's "No more!" expresses disapproval, not merely dismissal.

Maurice Evans's Prospero is of the crinkly, "father knows best" model. The role suits the actor's tendency toward recitation. Roddy McDowell's Ariel has stiff, sticklike spangles gleaming from his head, as if he has just emerged from the frost-baked earth. Ariel admires Lee Remick's dewy Miranda and wishes he *were* human. Having an experiential sense of what punishment is, he pities Caliban. McDowell makes one hilarious entrance, from above, to Trinculo and Stephano. Released too soon, he seems lucky to escape a broken leg. Another moment such as one misses in today's productions "in the can" occurs in the last scene, when Alonso's ornate collar brushes a camera lens.

The production ends, à la Margaret Webster, with the "Revels" speech. Evans moves forward as the camera dollies back. The rest of the characters become indistinct on a diminishing promontory. This is a good production for 1960, but except for the Caliban underplot and a few moments in the Antonio-Sebastian conspiracy, the effect is bland.

The Bard production begins as Prospero's head dreams up the storm. Or — are we to take the entire play as Prospero's dream? The production is set on a Globe-like stage, with Tudor facades on the sides, a long balcony between, and a long inner stage below the balcony. The ship is on the balcony, a placement that gives the storm a strangely linear quality. Two long blue streamers, pulled up and down by spirits, simulate wave and wind. The problems with having Prospero in command from the outset are that the storm lacks even a theatrical sense of danger and that his subsequent calming of Miranda is irrelevantly ex post facto.

Efrem Zimbalist, Jr., who plays Prospero, is a naturalistic television actor, magus of a different island. Toward the play's end, his mild ingratiation finally begins to work, but it is an attitude that should, by then, represent modulation. Here it is bland consistency. J. E. Taylor's Miranda is not helped by having her hair pulled back to emphasize her severe bone structure. Prospero's luxuriant mane would have looked better on Taylor. William Hootkins plays Caliban with sullen rejection and understated precision. The scene between Caliban, Stephano, Trinculo, and the hidden Ariel is, as usual on television, very good. A lithe dancer, Duane Black, as Ariel, would have been excellent in live performance.

The Tudor facade in the Bard production is too often in the background. It forces us to unsuspend whatever disbelief the stagelike setting and the consistently front-on camera might have encouraged. And its very presence begs the question of the nature-nurture, savage-civilized tension. Woodman keeps the same lights on all the time, although they brighten as the conspirators awaken on "All torment." For this set and the lack-of-lighting technique to work, the production would need a live audience, like that of the opening of Laurence Olivier's *Henry V* film. The lack of contrasting tonalities makes the production duller than it needs to be.

One effective technique of Woodman's is to have events occur off camera. The banquet is replaced by skulls, but we do not witness the substitution. While the camera concentrates on Prospero, the table disappears, as (blessedly!) does the masque later on. Thus, "staging problems" are no problem here.

The BBC version has merit in spite of critics' hostile reception: "Everything goes wrong here" (Charney 290); "Horrendous . . . a lead-footed production" (Cecil Smith, qtd. in Bulman and Coursen 263); "Stiff. Aimed at the archives, and one can certainly see it gathering a lot of dust there in the years to come" (Stanley Reynolds, qtd. in Bulman and Coursen 263). Certainly the critics have something to complain about. The opening scene is filmed, not done with stage effects, yet it presents no sense of emergency. Masts and sheets appear under the opening credits, while the rain falls straight down, as if the king's ship were safely moored in a windless harbor. Film, if carefully scaled, works on television. BBC wastes four minutes and forty seconds of film on this sequence.

This production tends to fall between stage, which can incorporate long speeches, and film, which demands visual equivalents for the language. Even in a basically oral medium like television, Michael Hordern's expositions are tedious, though Pippa Guard does what she can as listener and delivers the "Abhorred slave" speech, one that surprises and frightens Prospero. Having seen Hordern in Clifford Williams's tame 1978 RSC production, I thought that the muted Prospero might work well on TV, a medium that can reward underplaying. But Hordern pulls his performance further back for television. "What has been very interesting," Hordern says, "is that, instead of trying to reach the back of the gallery with your most innermost thoughts, you have only to cover the distance between you and the camera, which may be only eighteen inches away" (qtd. in Fenwick 26). The result is the irascible-schoolmaster model, a "droningly grandfatherish" Mr. Badger (Charney 290), only warmed by the mild affection he feels for his daughter.

Caliban's is the complaint of the aborigine, who, having instructed the colonist on the local environment, is consigned to its slums. None of the *Tempest* productions touch on the ideological implications that recent historicist and materialist critics discern in the script (Barker and Hulme; Breight). This Caliban is a potbellied bum awaiting introduction to his first six-pack. Warren Clarke's shaggy Caliban contrasts with David Dixon's frail, androgynous Ariel, with his boy-soprano voice. Each, of course, contrasts with Christopher Guard's tall, dark, and virile Ferdinand.

Gorrie's concentration on body types runs into disaster with the group of virtually naked men who, prancing to the lascivious pleasings of a pipe, form the "living drollery" (3.3.21) of the banquet scene. It is, as Cecil Smith notes, "quite embarrassing in a professional production" (qtd. in Bulman and Coursen 263). Almost as embarrassing is the masque, meant to resemble an English Morris dance (Fenwick 22). It is all remarkably awkward. Spirits step on the other spirits' lines. Spirits cast heavy shadows, and those naked boys return as pale sicklemen bent on having an orgy with nymphs peeled from a Victorian mural.

For all the lapses in taste that make students laugh and teachers cringe, the production is effective at times. Its "staging" is often good. As Miranda and Ferdinand exchange the sight of first love, Prospero, downstage left, tells us that he must prevent "too light winning" (1.2.451). Antonio and Sebastian plot downstage, framing Alonso and party. Trinculo's lines about Caliban (2.2.144–73) are delivered as sour asides. This technique grants the jester surprising "interiority." The main-plot and the subplot conspiracies are splendidly orchestrated. Nigel Hawthorne's Stephano is particularly good as he attempts to press his concentration on Caliban through the former's stupor. Clarke's "Be not afeard" is fine, as Caliban expresses a sense of selfhood symbiotically interfused with his island. Since the banquet disappears beneath Ariel's enclosing wings, Prospero's "A grace it had devouring" has a visual antecedent. At the end, Miranda's "how beauteous mankind is" is directed at Antonio. It is a wonderfully ironic instant, and it makes the intratextual point that television can make so well.

While television productions of Shakespeare can incorporate splendid "spots of time," the good moments tend to be unintegrated. Unlike stage, television cannot give us an incorporating frame, a sense of the total space within which the large and the small, the spectacle and the soliloquy will occur. Something else that television cannot do, and something essential to this script as electronic vehicle, are special effects. The Bard version, a stillborn stage version, suffers from its director's unwillingness to vary his lighting. The same set can be remarkably protean through lighting alone, as Howell shows in her *2 Henry VI*, and, for that matter, as Bard shows in its *Othello*. Schaefer's special effects are better than those for his 1954 *Macbeth*, but they are silly, particularly for the latter-day audience who knows that television doesn't try to do such things. At one point, Prospero attempts to help Ariel waft from the former's arm. But the timing is off. Ariel leaves too late, and Prospero seems to be fending off a clever and irritating insect. Gorrie tends to eschew special effects. "We felt," says his producer, Cedric Messina, "it wasn't fair to the play to do too much. If you make an electronic night's dream, you are asking for trouble." A wise decision, but it leaves Gorrie with his heavy Doré set and the blank wash of studio land, not "a real place where magic things happen" (qtd. in Fenwick 17).

"Magic" on television is, to borrow a phrase from Robert Frost, a "diminished thing," where Kirk and Scotty "beam up" amid a squiggle. Television is a "fourth wall" medium that asks nothing from us. Film forces us to believe in the twisters tugging at Dorothy as she struggles with the storm door, in the flames behind Rhett and Scarlett as they flee Atlanta, and in the biplanes buzzing around King Kong as he straddles a pretelevision Empire State Building. Film has the width and depth within which to create its effects. Television denies the possibility of anything larger than the person (Dessen). Its scale diminishes the image and erases any opportunity for depth. Special effects on television become "questionable, even laughable" (Dessen 8). Thus directors of those Shakespearean scripts that incorporate the supernatural are likely to be defeated as they try to calibrate the material to television. So far, they have been.

The Tempest has produced two interesting filmic offshoots: *Forbidden Planet* (dir. Wilcox) and *Tempest* (dir. Mazursky). Each production offers a different inscription of the story that Shakespeare tells. While Pauline Kael calls *Forbidden Planet* "the best of the science fiction interstellar productions of the '50s" (qtd. in videocassette cover), the film amuses most students today.

The special effects, however, are the product of Arnold Gillespie, who provided them for *The Wizard of Oz*. In *Planet*, Altaira (Anne Francis), the Miranda counterpart, loses her virginity symbolically. Her symbiotic relationship with her environment fades as her contact with the space visitors grows. Francis here is a function of the "male gaze" (Mulvey 57). Perhaps the film's most interesting theme is its suggestion that the person who attempts to control nature represses *in* nature powerful and destructive forces, here known as "Id." The extension of Freudian or, for that matter, Jungian psychodynamics from individual-psychic to planetary dimensions gives the film an unexpectedly strong and convincingly apocalyptic ending.

Paul Mazursky's *Tempest* is a slow and underwritten contrast between the world of Manhattan upper-crust careers and a sexless Aegean island, which does have some horny inhabitants. It has its king, duke, jester, islander, mariners, prince, and princess, the last luminously played by Molly Ringwald in her film debut. Students respond to Ringwald's line "We're studying *Macbeth* in school. It's unbelievably boring!" Also of interest are allusions to the source, such as "It's a paradise here! You're learning things here you'd never learn anywhere else" (John Cassavetes—"Prospero"—to Ringwald); "I was boss here before you showed up" (Raul Julia—Kalibanos—to Cassavetes); "I'm a monkey just like you" (Cassavetes to Julia); "Anyway, I'm a virgin" (Ringwald to Freddie ["Ferdinand"]—Sam Robards). We are asked to believe that Cassavetes achieves magical powers through celibacy, which, in turn, is the product of a mild and unconvincing midlife crisis out of Gail Sheehy's *Passages*. Lucianne Buchanan is wonderful as Dolores, who seems an afterthought of the scriptwriter, and the film ends with a song from the superb vocalist, the late Dinah Washington.

Neither film, obviously, is in a class with Akira Kurosawa's Shakespearean adaptations, *Throne of Blood* and *Ran*, but each chases the student back to Shakespeare's script, and each, however marginally, argues Shakespeare's power to generate further imaginative efforts. *Planet* invites futuristic conceptions of other scripts, which can be a good assignment for a student or group.

To involve students in the issues of translating Shakespeare to television and film is to get them to ask good questions: What are the difficulties of *this* script as film? as television show? To what extent do one's expectations of a light-sensitive or of a magnetic medium condition what can occur there? How does zeitgeist affect the work and one's response to it? This question has become controversial with the advent of a new *Henry V*, directed by and starring Kenneth Branagh. At the risk of sounding like T. S. Eliot, I suggest that each new production alters our perception of all prior productions. And since a filmic or televisual version is "fixed" in its time, we learn about that time as it treats Shakespeare and about our own time as we respond to an artifact from the past. We thus move out of the biased formulations, either positive or pejorative, that are likely to produce a too immediate reaction and into the zone where we can create contexts for evaluation.

Perhaps the major contribution of film and video to learning is to get the student to notice details. If the student selects a short segment from three *Tempests*, for example, she or he is forced into a detailed analysis. Perhaps we contribute most to a student's growth when we move the person from the vague blandness of generalities into the friction of specifics. To teach these plays may also be to teach the student who, someday soon, will bring either or both brilliantly to film or television.

Teaching *The Tempest* and the Late Plays by Performance

Hugh M. Richmond

From Shakespeare's time on, the later plays have received mixed reviews, beginning with Ben Jonson's characterization of *Pericles* as a "mouldy tale" (*Literary Criticism* 194). Almost two centuries later, Samuel Johnson viewed any effort to comment on *Cymbeline* as "to waste criticism upon unresisting imbecility," despite the play's "many just sentiments, some natural dialogues, and some pleasing scenes" (183). G. B. Shaw partly confirmed Johnson's view when he rewrote *Cymbeline*'s "cobbled-up" original conclusion; Shakespeare's ending might delight "the more childish spectators," Shaw thought, but he could not "share these infantile joys" (62–64). Adverse critics have explained some of the supposed defects of *Henry VIII* and *The Two Noble Kinsmen* as resulting from the limitations of dual authorship. Even the more popular plays, *The Winter's Tale* and *The Tempest*, are seen to present difficulties from their very beginnings, as in Leontes's unexplained jealousy and Prospero's labored exposition, which puts the adoring Miranda to sleep. It is helpful for teachers to face such negative views at once rather than gloss over problems, for students can be challenged to find valid grounds for discounting the criticisms. One effective method shows why the plays have often found sympathetic audiences in the theater, if not always in the study.

For several years I have experimented with performance approaches to teaching the late plays, which have provided a dynamic and convincing demonstration of the dramatic effectiveness of the mature Shakespeare. Such staging experience can be readily applied to heighten appreciation of *The Tempest*. The late plays differ from the others, not simply in genre, plots, characters, structure, or thought but — most significant theatrically — in "tone." This elusive characteristic is hard to identify on the printed page; it is better understood by direct experience of the power of the human voice and the resulting audience affect. This is why late plays such as *Pericles* and *The Two Noble Kinsmen*, which had received mixed evaluations from literary critics, began their modern recovery of critical favor through theatrical revivals.

My experience with some of the least admired of the last plays corroborated this observation. The plays offered a tempting field of pedagogic experiment because their neglect guaranteed an audience out of sheer curiosity. Our production of *The Two Noble Kinsmen* in 1978 was the first ever in California, and our television film of it probably remains not only the first but the only recording made anywhere. In producing this play, along with *Pericles* and *Henry VIII*, my students and assistants often expressed anxiety about the outcome, which made the success of the play the more heartening and impressive. As one performer exclaimed after our performance of *Kinsmen*, "Damn it all, it works!" Until one sees the audience's favorable reactions to the spoken lines, the play's unique effect cannot be anticipated or defined even by the performers themselves.

Let us begin with a problem raised by Prospero's interminable exposition of his biography in 1.2. All the late plays make laborious use of this kind of narrative: it recurs in the chorus in *Pericles* and in *Kinsmen*, as well as in the opening dialogue of *Cymbeline*. *Henry VIII* seems more an expository chronicle than a play, as confirmed by its prosaic alternative title: *All Is True*. Yet a part of *Henry VIII* (4.2) won Samuel Johnson's praise as "above any other part of Shakespeare's tragedies, and perhaps above any other scene of any other poet, tender and pathetick, without gods or furies, or poisons, or precipices, without the help of romantic circumstances, without improbable sallies of poetical lamentations, and without any throes of tumultuous misery" (151). Among the few devices left for heightening a script are the natural tones of the actors. History amply confirms Johnson's view of the quality of *Henry VIII*, for he convinced Sarah Siddons to play the role of Queen Katherine, which she did with irresistible conviction. A contemporary spectator of the resulting production, James Boaden, observed that from her first challenge to Wolsey it was "obvious that she would here excel any level of speaking that she had ever delivered on the stage"; he added, "I can hardly bring myself to think [her] Lady Macbeth a greater effort" (2: 261). In 1.2 Mrs. Siddons's intensity so overwhelmed the actor playing the wicked surveyor opposite her that he refused to play against her ever again (Clark 214–15).

If students read silently to themselves, the latent power of such scenes is almost imperceptible. The style is plain to the point of prosiness: the script of the famous scene of Katherine's divorce trial (2.4) follows the court records closely. Yet these scenes have often caused disruptively strong audience reactions, as Thomas Davis records:

> [W]hen the play was acted before George I at Hampton Court, about the year 1717, Wolsey's filching from his royal master the honour of extending pardon to those who resisted payment of the "exactions" appeared so gross and impudent a contrivance that the courtiers laughed loudly at such an example of ministerial craft. His majesty, who was imperfectly acquainted with the English language, asked the Lord Chamberlain the meaning of this mirth, and upon being informed of it joined in a hearty laugh of approbation.   (qtd. in Clark 210)

Our production often evoked this unexpected intensity of audience reaction to verbal nuances: Wolsey's other low-key asides provoked wry laughter. When Cardinal Campeius censures Wolsey's replacement of the king's secretary by his own appointee, Gardiner, after driving the previous secretary mad with despair, Wolsey coolly replies, "Heav'n's peace be with him! / That's care enough" (2.2.129–30). The cynical cardinal's too perfunctory regret always elicited amusement.

The late plays are written in a minor key, so that the least shift in tone should be vastly suggestive. The BBC series' staff found *Henry VIII* adapted well to close-up in television shots: the prose cadences allowed the actors full use of modern nuanced acting (BBC ed. 21). Similarly, in our production, when Anne Bullen, learning of her new titles from King Henry, flinches and whispers, "it faints me / To think what follows," our audience also flinched, surely thinking of her later execution, as Shakespeare intended. The expository dialogue between two courtiers that opens the BBC *Cymbeline* proves a virtuoso exercise in vocal irony perfectly accommodated by a close-up television shot. After the brief, melodramatic violence of the storm scene that opens *The Tempest*, the play modulates permanently to this intensely intimate emotional range, in a scene that is almost entirely retrospective. We now react not to major events but to Miranda's tender responses to Prospero's calculated reminiscences of long ago. Theatrically the point is less what is told than how it is told. If we take the scene literally, as telling us important facts, it is boring, and this is the way it reads initially on the page. But in the 1989 New York production of *The Tempest* by the Roundabout Theatre Company, the emphasis was on the paternalistic nuances of Prospero's overconcern for Miranda rather than on the subject of the exposition. As played by Frank Langella and Angella Sherrill, the scene became an exquisite study in parent-child tensions and moods, full of ironies and of discrepancies between Miranda's innocent empathy and Prospero's tender authority and wry expertise in manipulating feelings.

This performance revealed the play's subtlest level of interest, which is delicately subjective, despite the efforts of the new historicism to coarsen it, in grimly Marxist terms, into a didactic treatise on European colonialism. Even that fashionable interpretation derives inspiration from Jonathan Miller's notorious production of *The Tempest* in 1970 at the Mermaid Theatre, which was a study in white-settler domination of native factions, as outlined by program notes from Octave Mannoni's *Prospero and Caliban: The Psychology of Colonization*. This perspective may well be one plausible way to make the script "relevant" to our modern preoccupation with ethnic priorities (Orgel finds such ideas "are fully implicit in the text or valid extensions of it" [Orgel ed., *Tempest* 83]). Still, ideological polemic risks drowning out the unique tone of the last plays, which repudiate the authoritative assertion of human volition and invalidate any ratiocinative solution to human dilemmas. Perhaps this attitude is why the romances were unfashionable in the Age of Reason and irritated Victorian rationalists like Shaw. It was because Prospero was once more intellectually inclined to bookishness than sensitive to nuances of behavior that he proved politically incompetent and was expelled from the Dukedom of Milan — then forced to recover such sensibility in the seclusion of his island. In his earlier phases Prospero somewhat resembled the bookish King of Navarre in *Love's Labour's Lost*. Unlike that ruler, by the start of *The Tempest* Prospero has been resensitized to human feelings and can temper his own reactions — talents that he needs as an effective magistrate. (Of his 1973 Old Vic production, Peter Hall says, "Prospero is a man who is contained and careful" [qtd. in Orgel ed., *Tempest* 86]). His magic exploits the emotional conditioning of his associates by a mastery of impressions, but the potency of his manipulative process itself assumes the evanescence and malleability of all human motivations, hence the importance of the speech "We are such stuff / As dreams are made on" (4.1.155–56). From this gently skeptical perspective it is not possible to treat any human motivations more seriously than we do those of Stephano and Trinculo.

Equally, therefore, Prospero himself must finally surrender the right to any dictatorial role based on confident affirmation of his own feelings and resentments: "Let us not burthen our remembrances with / A heaviness that's gone" (5.1.199–200). His patriarchal authority must also be repudiated, like the "rough magic" (5.1.50) that expressed it. Any delight in human power is invalidated, even that resulting from Prospero's restored dukedom, which is only reluctantly resumed. Pursuit of power is too crude a theme for the mature Shakespeare: the art of surrendering it gracefully is a more rewarding study. This is perhaps the "message" of all the late plays, if our students insist on one (as they regrettably will), for it is made explicit in many other late roles — Wolsey, Cymbeline, and even Augustus Caesar, whose army is vanquished in *Cymbeline* in a typically ironic sequel to the end of *Antony and Cleopatra*. The delicate texture of the romances is incompatible with either bold personal confidence or public affirmation of values, which might invite broad comedy or fierce tragedy — both alien to the romances.

For example, when Posthumus denounces women's promiscuity (2.5) after believing Jachimo's misreport of Imogen's adultery, his situation approximates that of Othello, yet audiences remain as distanced from his feelings as he is from Imogen — a measure of how emotional effect is denied him. In performance, instead of arousing horror, his excessive misogyny provokes amused if pitying laughter. Our confidence in this detachment derives from the play's relentless neutralization of all its previous moments of crisis (such as Dr. Cornelius's substitution of a benign drug for the poison that the wicked Queen gives to Pisanio). We sense that by the time Posthumus has journeyed from Rome to Britain, his feelings will cool by inevitable exposure to other vicissitudes, which the claustrophobic situation in the last acts of *Othello* denies its hero and audience. Alerted by our knowledge of the earlier plays, we accept and understand the feelings of the late plays' characters but do not identify ourselves with them compulsively, as the tragedies require of us.

This sense of the late Shakespearean vision as one of godlike pity for human vicissitude was confirmed during our productions of *Pericles* and *The Two Noble Kinsmen* by the audiences' discreetly subdued laughter, which, we then realized, these improbable situations were designed to elicit. In each play the oscillation of human fortunes approaches the ridiculous: accident, fate, magic, or providence consistently invalidates human intentionality. No sooner do the imprisoned kinsmen swear eternal friendship than they glimpse Emilia and fall to quarreling over which of them shall possess her — assuming that they ever escape from prison! The competition for Emilia leads each man to determine to kill the other, whom he has just declared to be his best and only friend. In *Pericles*, Marina escapes her murderer by falling into the hands of pirates, who preserve her virginity to sell her for a higher price to a brothel keeper, only for her to convert that establishment's whole clientele to chastity, including the previously promiscuous head of state, who forthwith marries her with the assistance of her newly recovered mother and father. This kind of plot makes that of *The Perils of Pauline* look like plain sailing. However, we found that, after their initial bewilderment at such vicissitudes, our appreciative audiences began to savor the humorous pathos of the characters' belief that they had any meaningful choices in such unpredictable and frustrating situations. The spectators adopted the role assigned to the gods by Theseus at the end of *Kinsmen*:

> O you heavenly charmers,
> What things you make of us! For what we lack
> We laugh, for what we have are sorry, still
> Are children in some kind. Let us be thankful
> For that which is, and with you leave dispute
> That are above our question.   (5.4.131–36)

All our audiences responded to the last plays with detached, amused sympathy for the characters — a feeling that could not be predicted or evoked without performance and that indeed was often the reversal of sympathies derived from reading. The kinsmen may seem offensively supercilious, egotistical, and aggressive in print, but observed onstage they present themselves as sympathetic if incompetent adolescents who arouse both laughter and pity. The same mood is induced by the role of the Jailer's (mad) Daughter, which we found pivotal to our production and which epitomizes the effect of the last plays. She is so compulsively in love with one kinsman that she helps him escape from her father's jail, without realizing that her beloved wants to escape only to pursue his passion for Emilia. She thus risks death and ruin for herself and her family to no purpose, as she ruefully discovers, and as a result she loses her mind. The Daughter is a blend of the pathos of Ophelia and the bizarre humor of Helena in *A Midsummer*

Night's Dream (to which Glynne Wickham sees *Kinsmen* as a wry sequel ["*Two Noble Kinsmen*"]).

We also found that onstage the extravagant affection and pathetic frustrations of the Daughter prove irresistible to audiences (Richmond, "Performance" 163–85). Her abrupt rejection of her rustic suitor in favor of the courtly Palamon is amusing, plausible, yet ominous: one laughs with and at her, identifying instantly the hopelessness of her aspirations. Our audience's early responses to this single character determined the successful outcome of the whole production, for they shared her feelings yet at once perceived her grotesque self-delusions. The subtle mood proved as seductive in our production as when King Charles II saw the part played in 1662 by Mary Davis and awarded her his ultimate accolade: "She performed so charmingly, that not long after it raised her . . . to a bed royal" (Richmond, "Performance" 165). Three hundred years later, in 1979, the Los Angeles Globe Theatre production earned Suzanna Peters the more sober award of the Los Angeles Drama Critics for a performance they too found "charming" and "moving." When the Royal Shakespeare Company opened the Swan Theatre with this play, the role of the Jailer's Daughter won celebrity for Imogen Stubbs because of its blend of pathos and humor.

Such sympathetic amusement is also elicited when Prospero manipulates the love of Ferdinand and Miranda, which they judge to be spontaneous and autonomous, even while we perceive it as involuntary and predetermined:

> They are both in either's pow'rs, but this swift business
> I must uneasy make, lest too light winning
> Make the prize light.   (1.2.451–53)

The audience registers the manipulative power of Prospero, while it happily admits and gently savors the humorous pathos of young lovers, who falsely believe in their own freedom of choice. As Prospero says,

> So glad of this as they I cannot be,
> Who are surpris'd withal; but my rejoicing
> At nothing can be more.   (3.1.92–94)

Humor lies in a sense of discrepancy, and the divergence of will and situation here constitutes a muted aesthetic pleasure for the audience. But it is not simply pleasure in contrivance: Prospero himself has been taught a similar lesson in humility by his expulsion from Milan, which is why he now excels.

The perspective induced in the audience is one of experienced maturity that no longer feels the compulsions and confidence of youth but has not forgotten them and seeks as best it can to avert the heavy penalties meted out in *Romeo and Juliet*. These late plays display a detachment from conventional human motivation similar to that seen in the last plays of other dramatists, such as the *Amphitryo* of Plautus (the classical prototype of Shakespeare's late plays). This mature perspective challenges young students, who tend to take their emotions so seriously that perhaps they need to see them humorously reframed in the distanced youthful relationships of the late plays, instead of through their customary uncritical empathy with Romeo and Juliet (Richmond, "Peter Quince" 224–26).

Indeed, there is in the later plots a strong sense not simply of a detached view but of an explicitly divine and even providential perspective. If anything, the ritual and the musical choreography of the late Shakespeare make the presence of the transcendental more visible, if less intelligible, than ever before. While these performance elements may reflect the fashionable masquing at the Stuart court, it is intrinsic to the texture of all the late plays that meaning tends to sublimate itself into music and dance, such as the pastoral festival of *The Winter's Tale* or the Morris dance of *The Two Noble Kinsmen*. True, dance is present in Shakespeare's earlier works: Wolsey's ball, where Henry first courts Anne, matches the Capulets' ball in *Romeo and Juliet*. But it is harder to find in the earlier plays precedents for the direct expression of the will of the gods (or providence), as seen in the balletic visions of Posthumus and Queen Katherine. Their transcendental stylization matches the masque of Ceres in *The Tempest*, which is also not just a picturesque distraction but an expression of the cosmic forces governing human behavior.

The late plays thus effectively combine prosaic vocal precision and a musical, even mystical, stylization. A fully professional performance may readily achieve this blend, as the Roundabout production did by adding the talents of B. D. Wong's Ariel to the tones of Frank Langella's Prospero. True, the BBC's clumsy *Tempest* fails even to attempt exploration of the balletic dimensions of the script, which have been a persistent feature of the play's stage history (Orgel ed., *Tempest* 64–87) and which were exquisitely illustrated in Michael Smuin's choreography for the San Francisco Ballet's *Tempest* (PBS, 1 April 1981). Yet *Cymbeline*, in the same BBC series, displays well the range of naturalistic elements in the script within a salon setting, with Claire Bloom deftly underplaying the wicked Queen and Helen Mirren delicately exploiting Imogen's charming plaintiveness. Their conventional tones match the close-up camera work perfectly in the play's most intimate scenes. Such understatement is dexterously offset by a stylish background of Stuart refinement, displayed in Vermeer-like settings.

However, because the late plays are so low-key, there are dynamic alternatives to recordings of professional productions. Students may perform scenes themselves (a possible substitution for minor tests). The characters' muted and unrhetorical personalities suit modest acting talents, as Shaw observed in unkindly reviewing Henry Irving's production of *Cymbeline* (with Ellen Terry as Imogen): "It can be done delightfully in a village schoolroom, and can't be done at the Lyceum at all, on any terms" (44).

In my class I recently saw a successful undergraduate version of Jachimo's invasion of Imogen's bedchamber (played solo, with the aid only of a passive Imogen recruited on the spot), which fixated the audience while provoking much nervous laughter. I also saw unrehearsed high school students effectively perform the confrontation scene between Cloten and Imogen. Another sure student hit is the discovery of Caliban, hidden under his cloak, by Trinculo and Stephano (a high point in the Roundabout *Tempest*).

Thus the conversational texture and light tone of the late plays ideally suit the modest resources of student performers. Although the balletic choreography may seem more daunting for students, our Berkeley programs have successfully incorporated dancing. The rustic and court dances of the period are well documented, and the relevant music has been frequently and well recorded by groups such as that of David Munrow. The ritual function of traditional dancing is itself a rewarding and attractive subject for students, and dancing is central to the Shakespearean tradition of courtship and social symbolism generally. Overall, then, I am convinced that teachers seeking to communicate a full and accurate impression of the unique flavor of the late plays of Shakespeare should make substantial use of student performance, reinforced by professional productions—whose availability is one happy result of our electronic age.

A Metacritical and Historical Approach to *The Winter's Tale* and *The Tempest*

William Morse

I usually teach Shakespeare in a survey course for upper-division nonmajors, and for several years I have taught the course metacritically, that is, by emphasizing the plays' multiple strategies for foregrounding the synthesizing imagination and the human construction of all perception. The self-reflexivity of Shakespearean dramatic art, its constant articulation of human activity in terms drawn from the stage itself, provides both a powerful thematic perspective and an open invitation to pursue the relation of structure and content, especially when we end the course with *The Winter's Tale* and *The Tempest*. Recent new-historicist approaches to the canon, however, raise questions about the ahistorical presuppositions of the metacritical perspective. Not only does concentrating on the individual as the author of his or her own worldview devalue the role of culture in shaping individual perception, but teaching the coherence of any one critical reading of a text obscures the actual play of significance within it, with its openness and surplus of meanings. Metacriticism may thus misrepresent not only the historical contingency of the given play itself but the relation of art to culture as well. Thus I have been faced with the need to reconceive Shakespeare's metacritical art and, in particular, challenged to "open" it to some of its historical contexts.

However, a dialogue between the two approaches becomes possible if we focus on the historical emergence, in Shakespeare's day, of modern discourse, which responds to a Renaissance epistemological crisis by positing the objective independence of discursive reason from the world it observes in order to valorize the reasoning individual mind as the source of knowledge. The pervasive cognitive reflexivity of Shakespearean drama, with its progressive construction of self out of the encounter with the otherness of a reality discovered beyond social convention, is revealed as both implicated in this historical development and struggling to articulate a critique of its most dangerous presuppositions. The work of Timothy Reiss, particularly his *Discourse of Modernism*, which carefully traces the rise of our modern "analytico-referential" discourse through the sixteenth and seventeenth centuries, demonstrates that self-reflexive art, in the context of the rise of this new discourse, is inherently political.

Thus it becomes possible to retain the powerful pedagogical strengths of a thematic approach to the canon — and the metacritical approach is effective in the classroom exactly because it encourages students' questions about identity and social roles, even as it challenges their assumptions about human nature — and at the same time to provide a more historical articulation of the skepticism, openness, and overdetermination of the texts. Of course, the challenges of introducing such a perspective are obvious: how to present such a second critical pole clearly and succinctly; how to ensure that it complements rather than compromises the metacritical approach that is still the essence of the course; and, regarding the romances, how to maintain their pedagogical value as the most metacritical plays in the canon while also utilizing their potential for revealing historical contingency. But while I still want nonmajors to focus on the texts themselves rather than critical perspectives on the plays, it is well worth the effort to raise these important questions about the nature of literature and its place in society.

In my survey, with a syllabus of ten plays, I now devote about a quarter of the course, or ten classes, to *The Winter's Tale* and *The Tempest* so that I can explicitly introduce a new-historicist perspective. While trying throughout the semester quietly to nurture the students' historical sensibility, only with the romances do I address at length the issue of culture and the cultural circulation of all meaning. The place of the two plays at the conclusion of the traditional syllabus is felicitous, because the first is the most self-consciously metacritical in the canon and thus marks a natural culmination of this line of inquiry in the course, while the latter is historical in ways quite accessible to students.

The metacritical richness of *The Winter's Tale* well repays several classes, and we unfold this complexity by responding to the "artfulness" of all the play's human activity. The romance genre, to which I introduce the students by means of the opening chapter of Howard Felperin's *Shakespearean Romance*, makes natural the play's references to oracles, defenses, dreams, reports, ballads, old tales, and plays but can't explain the careful development Shakespeare gives to their appearances. Following Mamillius's naive tale in the second act (which, presumably, gives the play its name), the tale immediately comes to life in a carefully orchestrated elaboration of the many types of human narration, the stories that, in all their forms, we tell about ourselves and the world. To speak metacritically of *The Winter's Tale* means to recognize the large claims that the play makes for narrativity, in particular for the dramatic enterprise, for this is a play "self-reflexive" not about drama per se but about the dramatic, the artful, in all human endeavor. The play is filled with references to narrative forms because narrative best represents the quintessential cognitive form-imposing activity that distinguishes the species.

In opposition to the parodic or dysfunctional world-creating narrative of Leontes, a narrative perverted by emerging analytic practices revealed as only pseudobjective, stands the artful "making" (5.3.63, 71), by both Camillo and Paulina, of stories that affirm relation and the possibility of humanly constituted orders resonant of "great creating nature" (4.4.88). Camillo's intervention in the action of act 4, presented in the terminology of the stage, reveals all the attributes of a playwright; Paulina, not "Julio

Romano," is the presiding artist of the final scene. If Leontes's self-destruction exemplifies the rationalist alienation of the incipient modern culture from communal and psychic roots of meaning, then the play is clearly shaped to draw on this self-destruction, foregrounding an alternative mode of being centered in imaginative identification with the world. Paulina's creation of a reconciliation scene so thoroughly interpenetrated with "art" and "reality" depends on her conceiving of the human within the cyclical rhythms of creating nature itself. Far from being presented as "like" a statue, Hermione is both statue *and* human precisely because human reality, as cognitively constructed, *is* artful, that is, imaginatively devised.

Once we have established a metacritical reading of the play, I find that the most immediate approach to the historicity of *The Winter's Tale* is through a rereading that monitors the play's striking relation to its audience. The romances are marked particularly, as David P. Young makes clear, by their manipulation of detachment and engagement: detachment is a primary concomitant of Shakespeare's sophisticated move to the primitive romance form itself, and the plays carefully distance their audience in many scenes. As Franco Moretti's discussion of "the birth of (the audience from the structure of) tragedy" implies (19), this detachment recognizes and addresses the development, over the course of Shakespeare's own career, of a sophisticated audience associated with the emergence of modern rational discourse; because we are a product of this discourse, the students can easily be led to catalog points in the drama where they feel "alienated" from the action. But this detachment proves ultimately ironic (much as was Theseus's reason in *A Midsummer Night's Dream*), established to make all the more compelling the final peripety, the discovery of Hermione in the statue scene. As we consider this issue in the dual context of the students' reading of the play and a lecture on Reiss's cultural premises, we discover that audience detachment has important parallels to the new seventeenth-century emphasis on objective reason and that, conversely, Shakespeare uses audience engagement in close alliance with imaginative dramatic constructions to actively question the assumptions of this new focus. If the students have for our fourth class explored detachment, then the final class can examine the way theme, action, and spectacle work in the fourth and fifth acts to undermine this detachment. The omnipresent theme of narrativity and art itself, while at first apparently related to the sophisticated evocation of a "primitive" dramatic form, works progressively, and, finally, insistently, on the audience's half-reluctant engagement to replicate in their own theatrical experience the imaginative, world-constituting activities of the dramatic action. The apparent meaning of the statue scene follows on a *dramatic* experience of the inadequacy of any rational understanding of the communal moment. Such a consideration of the relation of the play to its audience provides the first step in setting aside the students' habitual assumption that the play, as a species of "art," is to be taken (objectively) as isolated artifact.

Thus we move in our understanding of the play from the metacritical to an awareness of the dialectic between the play and its historical audience, and I end with a lecture on this context and the ways in which it has both shaped and been shaped by the production of this play.

Having broached the question of the cultural contextuality of art, we turn to *The Tempest* to address the issue directly. Again, though, we begin with a class devoted to an initial reading and a discussion of the play from our usual perspective, as the first of opposed interpretations that demand choices of the students. How does it reticulate the dialectic of "art and nature"? What is the import of Prospero's project, and what is the nature of the "sea-change" associated with it?

After this cursory first reading, Montaigne's *Of Cannibals* and excerpts from Sir Walter Raleigh's *Discovery of Guiana* (the first part of his summary of the value of following up his expedition with colonization [388–91]) can be used to provide a particular historical context. We are interested in these texts not as relevant (from the old historical perspective) "explanatory" agents that fix a meaning assumed to be inherent in the text but rather as contemporaneous manifestations of the culture's discourse that help alert the students to the overdetermined play of meaning represented by the text. This perspective reflects the new pedagogical goal in teaching this last play: if the students have thus far succeeded in learning some of the critical skills necessary for their independent work with a literary text, they now need to discover that every text represents a surplus of meaning and that for *The Tempest* there is no one determinate reading. For at least once in the course they must recognize the constructedness of rival readings and thus of meaning itself.

Montaigne's straightforward use of the nature-culture topos leads the students to work on the metacritical aspect of the play, especially Prospero's "art." But beyond this Montaigne's perception of European ethnocentrism — an ethnocentrism vividly exemplified in Raleigh's comments — raises two questions that complicate the students' first reading of the play. Most obviously, both Montaigne's ennobling and Raleigh's exploitation of the native challenge the students' usual identification with the Europeans at the expense of Caliban. Montaigne's idealization of the primitive is intimately connected with a critique of the European sociopolitical as well as moral "civilization" that Raleigh represents. Students may be asked in what ways Montaigne's criticisms resonate against the behavior not only of such characters as Antonio, Sebastian, and Stephano but against Prospero and even Miranda, even as the behavior of these positive characters reveals contiguities with Raleigh. This complexity takes a further turn when we consider Gonzalo's allusion to Montaigne's essay when he evokes an edenic commonwealth in 2.1. The discovery that Gonzalo's views are those of Montaigne tends to stimulate a revaluation of Gonzalo's position in the economy of the play. The class might consider what Shakespeare's purpose is in alluding to Montaigne's argument and, more generally, what we are to make of the presence of the Europeans on "Caliban's island."

Raleigh's text is productive in a second way, for it brings into the open a driving motivation of early modern European culture, the desire for power over nature as a species of society's material acquisitiveness, its greed. Motivation is a crucial question in *The Tempest*, as it has been in all the other plays we've studied. Shakespeare is preoccupied with human will, especially "rude will" (*Romeo and Juliet* 2.3.28); though Prospero's silence is sometimes overlooked in critical studies, it troubles students throughout the first few acts, which concern his own precise goals. Even the first reading reveals Antonio's manifest motives, and students draw on them to construct the basic oppositions in the play, but Prospero's silence undermines this dichotomizing. And although students recognize in Raleigh a stance akin to Antonio's toward the objective world, Raleigh's more immediate parallel to Prospero as a colonizer now further complicates their assumption that they "ought" to identify with him. This complication crystallizes the class's heretofore peripheralized unease with Prospero's imperiousness and focuses attention on his unarticulated motivation through the early acts, thus tending to produce a subversive counterreading. (Though generally beyond the limits of a survey for nonmajors, the bearing on the play of recent feminist and psychoanalytic criticism should be noted; see, e.g., Kahn; Williamson; Sundelson [2 works]; Orgel, "Prospero's Wife".)

How do these sociopolitical perspectives relate to the metacritical approach to the plays that students have been prepared by the course to take? Here the class needs to be given some means of relating these specific forms of economic motivation to those more universal forms of will that they have seen Shakespeare address. Thus for the session following Montaigne and Raleigh I ask them to read the peroration (129) of Francis Bacon's *Novum Organum* (537–39). Here they find a claim for the power of European culture's emergent model of rational, objective knowledge to which, as Bacon's heirs, they assent unquestioningly. But as we read Bacon's text more closely and consider it in conjunction with Raleigh's particular "discovery," this founding celebration of science and invention seems shot through with a vocabulary of power, empire, and ambition so metaphorically charged that it decenters the speaker's claim to disinterestedness. In noting that the basis of Prospero's power is his knowledge — his "books" — and the commandment over nature that they give him; that it is Prospero's books that hold Caliban in awe; and that these books must in some profound sense be disavowed before Prospero can complete his reconciliation, students begin to discover a means of interrogating the species of will represented in the play, particularly that motive of Prospero's so conspicuously absent from his early self-presentation. To recognize in Prospero a type of the culture's emerging analytic individual is to discover the play's deep involvement in our culture's most insistent discursive structures. Thus students can begin to ask the true price that the scholar's study, his pursuit of power, has exacted in terms of social and spiritual alienation; they can begin to recognize the deeper significations of that "state" to which his search for knowledge had made him stranger. In short, triangulating Bacon with *The Tempest* and the other works clarifies the presence within the text of a central issue of the culture: its incipient adoption of a new ground of discursive practice in the assumption of an implicitly idealized human rationality.

The secondary readings help to undermine, as we return our attention to the dramatic text, the habitual modern dichotomy between "art" and "reality" that students take for granted. To what extent do Raleigh's excursions presume the learning that Bacon fosters? To what extent is Bacon's pursuit of "pure" knowledge implicated in the less abstract motives of Prospero and Raleigh? To what extent does Prospero finally recognize and renounce such motives as the price of his reconciliation?

By this time, then, we have been through a preliminary dialectic, having complicated an original assumption of Prospero as a beneficent mage with a second perception preoccupied with his darker and more self-serving side. For the last two classes we pursue the complexity of Prospero's characterization, and especially the implications of his ultimate reconciliation, in the new context of plural interpretations demanding choices and critical debate. The epilogue bears on these concerns, for there we discover once again that strategy of audience engagement already observed in *The Winter's Tale*. Prospero's address to his audience is too complex to abide simplification for long, and whether a student focuses on its thematic import or dramatic presentation, she or he is now capable of addressing its significance in complex, critical terms. Whether the speech is approached thematically as a Neoplatonic fusion of mage and dramatist or as a renunciation of power that critiques the conception of knowledge as power; whether it is approached dramatically as ironic affirmation or as direct subversion of the emerging objectivity of the Renaissance audience, the course ends with every student challenged to begin to face the openness, the contingency of meaning in Shakespeare, in literature, in the world. If we have begun to understand the meanings of *The Tempest* in terms that follow from the practices of the culture and if we have equally been returned to culture with a perception altered by the practices of the play, then we have begun to appreciate the material and historical implications of Shakespeare's metacritical art.

The Utopias of *The Tempest*

Douglas L. Peterson

Utopia is both a fiction and a concept, an imaginary region where an ideal social order is imaginatively represented. As a place — whether it be the Land of Cockayne of the Middle Ages or the Big Rock Candy Mountain of the Great Depression of the 1930s in America, the country discovered by Thomas More's Raphael Hythloday or one of the several countries visited by Jonathan Swift's Gulliver on his travels — utopia is always geographically remote from where we live. It may also be at considerable remove from the social world we know; but however great the distance between the ideal social order it represents and the real social order of the world in which we live, the freedom, justice, and equity it manifests are conceived to be at least in some measure attainable. In this respect utopias are optimistic, visionary dreams of, or blueprints for, a reformed society (Elliot).

The Tempest presents four utopias, two of which are envisioned by characters. The first is Gonzalo's (2.1.148–65). The betrothal entertainment (4.1.60–138), in which Prospero imagines a winterless world of timeless "increase," is another. A third is contained in Caliban's brief, fragmentary descriptions of the beauties of the island to which, years earlier, Caliban had introduced the newcomer Prospero (1.2.332–37; 2.2.167–72; 3.2.135–43). These descriptions contain exotic details that hint of contemporary accounts of voyages to newly discovered islands in remote tropical seas, like the Bermudas and the New World. Such connections with the discovery of new places, and, conceivably, even real utopias, offer intriguing opportunities for teachers and students to investigate the extent to which Shakespeare has fashioned the play out of the discourses of travel, exploration, and colonization (Cartelli; Barker and Hulme). Fourth, the island itself, which is now under Prospero's governance, is both stage ("this bare island" [epilogue 8]) and setting for Shakespeare's own utopian vision, *The Tempest* itself.

In what sense is *The Tempest* utopian? And what purposes are served by the two utopian visions it includes? We may begin to answer the first question by addressing the second. Gonzalo's "commonwealth" is mistaken by Alonzo, Sebastian, and Antonio, and commonly by playhouse audiences too, as the foolish ramblings of an aging councilor. In actuality it is an entertainment, a "recreation" conceived to cure Gonzalo's companions of the gloom with which they regard their situation (on recreational theory, see Olson; Peterson, "Lyly"). Gonzalo begins by urging the king to take heart:

Beseech you sir, be merry; you have cause
(So have we all) of joy; for our escape
Is much beyond our loss . . . .

> . . . Then wisely, good sir, weigh
> Our sorrow with our comfort.
> (2.1.1–9)

When his counseling falls on deaf ears, Gonzalo exchanges his role as councilor for that of fool, creating the fiction of an ideal commonweal without laws, magistrates, or governor, but of which he would be king. When his audience laughs derisively at him, mistaking the folly of his fiction for his own, Gonzalo has achieved his purpose. As he observes when responding to Alonzo's request to be silent (2.1.171), he has "ministered" to an occasion calling for a recreation that will revive fallen spirits:

> I do well believe your Highness, and did it to minister occasion to these gentlemen, who are of such sensible and nimble lungs that they always used to laugh at nothing. (2.1.172–75)

Reason failing, he has turned to "merry fooling," all the while enjoying his own private sport:

> ANTONIO.   'Twas you we laugh'd at.
> GONZALO.   Who, in this kind of merry fooling, am nothing to you;
> so you may continue, and laugh at nothing still.
> ANTONIO.   What a blow was there given!
> SEBASTIAN.   And it had not fall'n flat-long.
> GONZALO.   You are gentlemen of brave mettle; you would lift
> the moon out of her sphere, if she would continue in it five
> weeks without changing. (2.1.176–84)

Besides presenting Gonzalo to the audience as a sagacious, if misunderstood, councilor, who is alert to what the immediate occasion requires, the episode foregrounds metatheatrically not only the idea of utopia itself but also what proves to be the limited efficacy of one form of conceptualized recreational play. Once the audience has been introduced to one version of utopia, conceived to cure discontent by distracting from their present plight the survivors of a shipwreck who are stranded on the desolate shore of an unknown island, it should be prepared to recognize the two other utopias presented as entertainments by *The Tempest* — Shakespeare's as well as Prospero's — and to appraise the relative value of each utopia as recreation. By the end of the play, it is evident, for example, that neither Alonzo's distress over having lost a son nor the bitter discontent of his unpleasant attendants, Antonio and Sebastian, is going to be permanently cured by Gonzalo's fooling. Both unhappy states of mind will require, in addition to Prospero's own resolve to forgive, that the sufferers come to see their present situations as consequences of crimes committed years earlier. As they are informed by Ariel following the disappearing banquet, only "heart's sorrow" and "a clear life ensuing" (3.3.81–82) will guarantee their re-creation.

But what of the utopian vision presented by Prospero to celebrate Miranda's betrothal to Ferdinand? While appropriate as an entertainment for a festive occasion, it proves a deceptively alluring distraction to both its conceiver and director as well as to its onstage audience. A product of Prospero's imaginings — performed, as he explains to Ferdinand, by "Spirits, which by mine art / I have from their confines call'd to enact / My present fancies" (4.1.120–22) — it is an aging father's wish-fulfilling dream for the future of a much beloved daughter. Whereas Gonzalo's utopia contains echoes of the Land of Cockayne, Prospero's is Arcadian, a mythical and timeless terrestrial Eden in which there is no winter. Ferdinand is overcome by wonder, mistaking the vision for the island itself:

> Let me live here ever;
> So rare and wond'red father and a wise
> Makes this place Paradise.
> (4.1.122–24)

That Prospero's utopia is as conceptually flawed as Gonzalo's is becomes apparent when Prospero suddenly remembers the "foul conspiracy" of "Caliban and his confederates" (4.1.139–40), just at that moment when "the sunburn'd sicklemen, of August weary" join the "fresh nymphs" of spring in a dance celebrating a "Spring" that has come "in the very end of harvest" (4.1.114–15). The vision is shattered. Time, as well as malice, is in Arcadia (see Berger; McNamara). Distracted by his hopeful imagining of his daughter's future, Prospero is again very nearly victimized by inclinations of the kind that, years earlier, had made him vulnerable to the conspiracy in Milan. Such are the dangers latent in utopian wish-fulfilling fancies, which, at best, offer only temporary escape from the claims of the seamy present rather than authentic hope for personal and social reform.

Prospero's shattered vision is followed by another vision (4.1.148–58), an "antiutopian" envisioning of the whole of human history as inconsequential. Like Gonzalo's utopia, this vision, too, has commonly been misconstrued as Shakespeare's. A vision of life and "the great globe itself" as no more substantial than the "insubstantial pageant" it succeeds, it is expressive of a momentary cynicism and despair; and Prospero apologizes for it:

> Sir, I am vex'd;
> Bear with my weakness, my old brain is troubled.
> Be not disturb'd with my infirmity.   (4.1.158–60)

What cure is there for a despair born of the recognition that mortality and evil are irradicably conditions of the world in which we live? The answer is to be found in the final utopia, the "recreation" that Shakespeare and his company present on the "bare island"of the Globe playhouse's stage.

All Shakespeare's romances are utopian (Peterson, "Ideal Comedy"), as in fact are all but two of his comedies (*The Taming of the Shrew* and *The Merry Wives of Windsor*), because they articulate and celebrate ideal, or exemplary, modes of conduct that, however improbable, are nonetheless ethically possible. Acknowledging things as they are, they envision what can and ought to be, offering ideal solutions to real problems. Earlier plays, like *As You Like It* and *Cymbeline*, represent adumbrated versions of an ideal social order — *As You Like It* in the Arden community formed by the banished Duke Senior in Arden, *Cymbeline* in the model community established by Belarius in the uplands of Wales, into which Imogen/Fidele is welcomed as a brother (Peterson, *Time, Tide* 125–29). Shakespeare, in returning to the notion of a perfect social order in *The Tempest*, formulates the ideal requisites of civil authority. In earlier models such authority, abused or misused, is simply a given. Duke Senior and Belarius each demonstrate that they are exemplary wielders of power. Vincentio, too, in *Measure for Measure*, through the ludic action he initiates in his effort to reform a Viennese community that under his lax rule has fallen into sensual excess, proves he is finally capable of responsible government. But it is in the figure of Prospero that Shakespeare articulates most fully the exemplary governor — a duke, father, brother, friend, and human being who, in each of these roles, shows that he has learned the meaning of prudence.

It is in the depiction of Prospero as exemplar of prudence that *The Tempest* as utopian romance discloses most clearly its grounding in the humanists' secular version of salvational history. Since time in humanist ideology is at once cyclical and linear, it is incumbent on individuals, especially those who are governors and magistrates in the hierarchical society of Renaissance England, to know the past in order to make choices in the present that guarantee the future health of the self and the body politic. The past through its recursivity provides abundant examples of actions to emulate as well as to avoid. The prudent governor from an awareness of the past knows how and when to act in the present to ensure the country's future as well as his or her own, whereas those who imprudently neglect time find eventually that time wastes them (Peterson, *Time, Tide* 16–17, 222–44).

Indeed, prudence is represented and defined in humanist ideology in exactly these temporal terms. Peter de la Primaudaye, citing Cicero, writes:

> Moral Philosophers attributed three Eies to this vertue of Prudence, namely, Memory, Understanding, and Providence. . . . [A] prudent and wise man, by the consideration of things past, and of that which hath followed since, judgeth of that, which in the like case may fall out in the time following. And after long deliberation, he inspecteth the times, weigheth the dangers, and knoweth the occasions: and then,

yeelding now and then to the times, but alwaies to necessity, so it be not against duty, he boldly setteth his hand to the works.   (43)

Thomas Wilson, defining prudence in *The Arte of Rhetorique* (1560), employs essentially the same terms:

> The memorie, calleth to accompt those things that were done here-tofore, and by a former remembraunce getteth an after wit, and learneth to auoyde deceit.
>
> Vnderstanding, seeth thinges presently done, and perceiveth what is in them, weighing and debating them, vntill his minde be fully contented.
>
> Foresight, is a gathering by coniectures, what shall happen, and an euident perceiuing of things to come, before they doe come.
>
> (31–32)

The prudent person knows when as well as how to act.

As a metaphorical configuration of providence, time is also "forgiving" or "merciful," offering through its cyclicity the hope that those who have neglected or used it imprudently may have a second chance to redeem themselves. George Wither, in an emblem devoted to "occasions past," makes this point: "Occasions-past are sought in vaine, / But oft, they wheele-about again" (qtd. in Peterson, *Time, Tide* 33–34). The truth of Wither's emblem is borne out in *The Tempest*. Prospero recognizes, as he explains to Miranda (1.2.177–84), that time has provided him with just such an occasion. Thanks to "accident most strange" (1.2.178), he now has the opportunity to recover all that his neglect of office years earlier had cost him. Should he fail a second time, his "fortunes / Will ever after droop" (1.2.183–84).

His success depends not only on what but on how he remembers. The play itself distinguishes early in the action among several ways of remembering. Sebastian and Antonio, recalling their success years earlier as conspirators, see in their present situation a chance to murder Alonzo and seize his crown (2.1). Caliban, when reminded of his attempt to rape Miranda, shows no remorse:

> O ho, O ho, would't had been done!
> Thou didst prevent me; I had peopled else
> This island with Calibans.   (1.2.349–51)

Miranda, not remembering the events leading to her father's deposition and exile, asks her father to reconstruct them so that, "not rememb'ring how [she] cried out then, / Will cry it o'er again" (1.2.133–34). Ariel, accused by Prospero of having forgotten how Prospero had freed him from the pine tree in which Sycorax had imprisoned him, insists that he does indeed remember (1.2.250–67). In this instance, Ariel serves as a foil to Miranda. Being a spirit, and therefore without feelings, Ariel is incapable of gratitude or compassion. It is also possible to remember and experience sorrow for what evils one has done in the past—in short, to remember, as Ariel informs Alonzo and his attendants, in order to experience "heart's sorrow" (3.3.81). Finally, one may remember to gain satisfaction through vengeance, exacting retributive justice—an eye for an eye and a tooth for a tooth.

How, finally, will Prospero remember? After very nearly repeating the mistake he had made years earlier by allowing himself almost to forget the present while indulging in the practice of his magical art, he confronts, in the play's final action, a critical moment when the choice of how he remembers the past determines closure. His enemies are completely in his power and in so pitiable a state that even Ariel is moved. "Your charm so strongly works 'em," the spirit reports, "That if you now beheld them, your affections / Would become tender."

> PROSPERO.   Dost thou think so, spirit?
> ARIEL.   Mine would, sir, were I human.
>   (5.1.17–20)

Prospero's decision to forgive—"the rarer action" dictated by "nobler reason" (5.1.26–27), even though, as he confesses, "with their high wrongs [he is] strook to th'quick" (5.1.25)—is exemplary, a utopian vision for governors in the world of the here and now to emulate.

Vengeance, too, is reasonable, but forgiveness is "nobler" because it is proof of the benevolence, beneficence, and liberality that, for the humanists, distinguish *humanitas*, or human*kind* (Elyot 120–21). As an exemplary act within a utopian social model, forgiving, which is not to be mistaken for forgetting, distinguishes Shakespeare's utopian model from Gonzalo's and Prospero's by recognizing that the realization of "perfect patterns" is contingent on the fallibility of those who govern as well as of those who are governed.

Prospero's decision to forgive even those he suspects of being uncontrite is the utopian action of a governor who, having given up the powers that have enabled him physically to control all who are on the island, rejoins the human community and reassumes the specific responsibilities within it that are required of him as father, brother, friend, and duke. He knows full well that the future of that "brave new world" (5.1.184) remarked by Miranda depends precariously on the freedom he has restored to its members to use time as they choose, foolishly or prudently—and always to use it with an awareness, as Prospero reminds the audience in the epilogue, that even in utopia all humans stand in need of mercy and forgiveness:

Now I want
Spirits to enforce, art to enchant,
And my ending is despair,
Unless I be reliev'd by prayer,
Which pierces so, that it assaults
Mercy itself, and frees all faults.
    As you from crimes would pardon'd be,
    Let your indulgence set me free.
                    (13–20)

In these last lines a final and definitive characteristic of the play as a utopian "recreation" grounded in the ideology of English humanism emerges, namely, the particular kind of emotional involvement *The Tempest* is conceived to elicit from its Jacobean audiences. As with all Tudor utopian comedy from its inception throughout its several stages of development in Shakespeare's dramatic oeuvres, the play endeavors initially to arouse wonder and admiration in its audience. These emotions ought, in turn, ideally to inspire spectators to emulate the "rare" and "wonderful" actions they have seen figured forth in the play's utopian fiction. Thus the play awakens or reaffirms their faith in the beliefs from which the exemplars within that fiction have drawn strength.

Such an awakening or reaffirmation of faith is "re-creational" in its most profound sense, collectively and individually. Audience members are not only inspired to emulate "perfect patterns" but also united communally as an audience and as members of a body politic grounded in a body of shared beliefs. Admiring the exemplary acts of forgiveness and prudence in *The Tempest* and embracing the beliefs that have inspired them, spectators are reminded in the epilogue, when the actor who has played Prospero steps out of his fictional role to address them directly (first as a player who has endeavored to entertain them and finally as a human being whose vocation is playing), that players and audience are separated only temporarily by the perimeters of illusion. All, players and audience, are members of a common community whose well-being and perpetuity depend on the prudence and forgiveness that have been celebrated in the play's utopian fiction.

"An Odd Angle of the Isle": Teaching the Courtly Art of *The Tempest*

Kristiaan P. Aercke

In my seventeenth-century comparative drama class, we study about a dozen plays, emphasizing the baroque sensibility of the golden age and technical aspects of seventeenth-century play production and stage architecture. We begin with *The Tempest* and pay particular attention to the transformation of English courtly art in the 1610s. I highlight the importation of baroque aesthetic models, which James I stimulated to modernize English court art and to affirm himself as a cosmopolitan monarch, and I show Rubens's illusionistic *Apotheosis of James I* (assembled on the ceiling of Inigo Jones's Banqueting Hall) to introduce the courtly-baroque aesthetic. A comparison of Rubens's work with Elizabeth's ideologically very different *Rainbow Portrait* in the style of Marcus Gheeraerts is helpful. Of the five class sessions available for *The Tempest* I use about three to help students discover how Shakespeare addressed the changes within the theater as an institution under James and experimented with Continental models on the private rather than the public stage. This essay focuses on that section of the class and suggests or formulates a few questions of the sort that come up in discussion. Not all these questions require a formal solution in the present context.

We set out looking at Prospero's island itself. We quickly dismiss geography as futile ("Could it be Isola Ustica, halfway between Tunis and Naples?") and turn to a discussion of baroque private or courtly theaters and of the era's histrionic self-consciousness. Early in the seventeenth century, private theater and stage architecture were modeled after Italian designs that promoted, above all, illusionism. We introduce the island as an explicit metaphor for such a stage (confirmed in the epilogue). Whereas the earlier theatrical forms in the West grouped the audience *around* a central stage by daylight, the baroque theater places the audience in a dark rectangular auditorium *in front of* an elevated stage (a "magic box," an illusionistic cube), which facilitates the escape into the effects of the entertainment. This aesthetic of illusion implies an invisible "fourth wall" that isolates the play area and turns it into an "enchanted island" where magician-playwrights orchestrate events and where characters act in a state of hallucination — a form of collective madness: "Not a soul / But felt a fever of the mad, and played / Some tricks of desperation" (1.2.208–10; Rousset). Students note that Prospero's island-stage is vaguely located but perfectly circumscribed, inaccessible from profane reality except by some magic act. They reflect on the function of the unusually detailed stage directions of *The Tempest*, many of which emphasize representational artifice and "acting." Why is the tempest actually staged (1.1) rather than narrated? Note that the Mariners enter "wet" (1.1.49). What are the financial and ideological consequences of such a catchy play-opener on an indoor stage? Ariel's report of his activities (1.2.195–237) alerts us to the mechanical possibilities available to the private or courtly baroque stage.

Such considerations lead to a discussion of Prospero's role as director of events, or "playwright" of his own play, a function he shares with many protagonists in seventeenth-century drama. Students find that Prospero often draws attention to artifice and the techniques of art and illusion. He is not so much a gifted artist as a dilettantish amateur who cannot resist an occasion to amaze an audience — as when he "discovers" to the courtiers Ferdinand and Miranda at chess (5.1.171). Although he claims that his soul "prompts" him (1.2.421), he is incapable of perceiving his own human or artistic defects. His long speech to Miranda (1.2) is useful as exposition — but, interminable as it is, this speech (and not his "magical" gesture) charms Miranda into dozing off. So much for expositions — but for the island-stage to become a "magic cube," for us to be lulled into its illusion, we do need such a charm. Ariel's crucial role in the context of courtly theatricality is emphasized. He is not only the ideal courtier (1.2.247–49) but also a stagehand (1.2.194) who responds promptly on cue (4.1.34) and whose changes in costume indicate his different functions (1.2.303). Students note the great number of references to time; accurate timekeeping is on characters' minds (1.2.239; 5.1). Prospero frets incessantly about "finishing on time." His concern with minutes (1.2.37) is interesting, given the fact that clocks in the 1610s did not have minute hands. The stage action ("played time"), we hear repeatedly, lasts three hours and thus equals the "playing time." In other words, together with the play-plot, the island-stage will cease to exist at the end of this period.

Prospero knows that the finale of a baroque spectacle often implies the destruction of the stage (the site of the illusion), as scenic action, fire, or water devours the scenic milieu. Do the vanishing banquet (3.3) and the interrupted masque (5.1) provide encapsulated examples of this convention? Prospero's "cloud-capped towers" speech (4.1.148–58) testifies to his melancholy, which increases during the course of the play. He expresses a basic baroque fear of dissolution into nothingness, a sceptical pessimism, an anxiety regarding the futility of human action.

This specific concern with apocalyptic time is the first of several courtly-baroque themes that we study in *The Tempest*. The play shares the courtly-baroque and pagan view of time as an annihilating, utterly negative force. By contrast, the Christian, anticourtly attitude appreciated time as the great vindicator, exposing and laying to ruin the vanity of people (Metzger and Metzger). Given a penchant for the former, near-tragic notion of time, seventeenth-century court life was deliberately crowded with complex incidents — feasts, entertainments, pleasure gardens, very long novels, lengthy rhetoric — designed to stop time or the realization of its passing and to delay the unavoidable dissolution. Of course, the conclusion of such events increased the agony of the time awareness. Is *The Tempest*, as a play, a time-obliterating event? Do the reminders of Prospero and others that time flies contradict this idea? What about the fact that several time-obliterating courtly incidents contained within the play—the clowning scenes, the banquet mirage, the masque—are incomplete and interrupted?

Prospero's characterization brings to mind the attitude of seventeenth-century courtly art toward the absolute ruler—who is the ultimate focus of such art and the subject of elaborate analogies with a divine being. Whereas anticourtly baroque art sees God and ruler as benevolent father figures, inviting close relationships with individual worshipers through meditation or prayer, Rubens's *Apotheosis of James I* typifies the courtly equivalent. Rubens shows an unbelievably vigorous James ascending to heaven, where angels welcome him with music. Clearly analogous to God, James is implied to be an omnipotent and omniscient manipulator of art and nature. His God-like will, indifferent to the joys and sufferings of mortals, is inscrutable (Metzger and Metzger). Prospero, the absolute ruler of the island-stage, is similarly drawn, as students easily see. He is a creator (1.2.82–83) who manipulates nature, art, and people (1.2.461–65). His will is inscrutable (1.2.16; 5.1.128–29). Caliban has fallen from his grace (1.2.347–48). Untouched by the pain and sorrow of the shipwrecked, Prospero wreaks revenge (4.1.259–62; 5.1.7–19) but will ultimately provide some sort of justice and mercy (1.2.251; 5.1.67–80) with a generosity that borders on arrogance (*sprezzatura*). In the light of the "tempest" that has been performed, Gonzalo's remark that a God-like ruler determines the weather for all his courtiers (2.1.143–44) acquires additional meaning.

The erotic relationship of Ferdinand and Miranda is developed in terms of dynastic regeneration—another courtly-baroque theme, one very prominent throughout the play (Schmidgall). In this context, erotic attraction must be politically constructive before it is tolerated and celebrated with mythopoeic fertility masques in aristocratic settings (Metzger and Metzger; Schmidgall). The political relevance of Eros explains the definition of the relationship as a struggle for domination (symbolically present in the chess game [5.1.172]), and it encourages metaphors of chivalric servitude (lovers "enslave"each other [3.1]) as well as the interpretation of the female as a purchased object or a precious prize (expressed in similes of precious things [3.1; 4.1.7–14; 5.1.189]). The anticourtly view of Eros, in contrast, is more spiritual and emphasizes partnership, Christian agape, and constancy.

The involuntary movement of the characters toward a central space on the island-stage (Prospero's cave) and their simultaneous quest for self-knowledge are our final subjects for discussion. Not only does each act end with an invitation to come, follow, or go somewhere, but the play as a whole *is* mainly movement. Antonio suggests correctly that the incidents constitute a play in the making (2.1.256–58), in which plot development, topography, and knowledge are closely connected. The quest for knowledge about oneself and the world is typical of the romance mode to which *The Tempest* belongs; in this case, it is unsuccessful, for the characters (and readers) are left with too many unanswered questions when Prospero's center is reached. One discovers in *The Tempest* various involuntary attempts by characters to move from the coast of the island to the interior and, correspondingly, from a state of confusion and unclarity to greater knowledge. Is there in the interior a fixed center that will provide final knowledge? The initial confusion is caused, and metaphorically represented, by the tempest. It is in confusion that Ferdinand (and all the others) "sighs / In an odd angle of the isle" (1.2.223). Are there any but odd angles to this island-stage? The confusion is sustained by topographical reality as the characters (and we with them) are led in groups through a setting that appears to them "unclear," though less so to Ferdinand and Gonzalo than to the "evil" courtiers or the clowns. Prospero's realm is indeed difficult to maneuver in. Gonzalo (3.3.2) and Alonso (5.1.242) justifiably call it a "maze." The maze is another major metaphor of unclarity; of all time-obliterating diversions available to seventeenth-century courtiers, it was — practically speaking — the most useless. How does the maze metaphor express the fundamental nature of the island-stage and Prospero's role? What has one learned on reaching the center of a maze — in this case, Prospero's magic cave? Are any unequivocal explanations to be found at the heart of the maze that is *The Tempest*? We will now argue that the answer to this question is a resounding no.

For their entire stay in this maze, *The Tempest* provides its characters with many fragmented, apparently unrelated events and motives that they question and handle quite ineffectively. *The Tempest* and its setting thus resemble very closely the form and ideology of a typical baroque play. In Renaissance plays, discrete interrelated scenes usually move linearly along a clearly outlined, ultimately closed principal plot. Baroque plays, by contrast, often sustain a certain openness or "unclarity" in the movement of their design and content, playing with what is hidden, avoiding any hint that forms or motives might be resolved or exhausted. In some plays many not clearly related short scenes define the unities of place, time, action, and tone; other plays have several plots or foci, of which the principal is not readily identifiable, or surprise endings, digressions, puzzling masques, unresolved questions, and so forth.

The Tempest is replete with motives of confusion and unclarity, which symbolize or contribute to the ultimate failure of the characters to acquire the knowledge they seek. Among these motives, my students usually recognize the following:

1. Metamorphoses, suggested by implied references to Proteus and Circe (1.2.191–92; 4.1.171–81).
2. The relativity of interpretation: What about the unresolved contradictions regarding the sweetness or harshness of the island, the cleansing

power of seawater, Prospero's popularity in Milan, the plagues that Prospero unleashes against Caliban . . . ?

3. The symbolic value of sleep or sleeplessness: What *if* life is a dream? Caliban's speech (3.2.136–44) can be fruitfully compared with Segismundo's ravings in the first act of Calderón's *Life Is a Dream*. Of related interest is the decay of memory and forgetfulness (4.1.139, 159).

4. The unreliability of sensory perception: Since Ariel deceives sight and hearing, one does not know whether to trust one's eyes and ears.

5. The question of what constitutes distractions of the mind or what leads to insanity (as in 3.3.106–08).

6. The fragmentation or partial distribution of knowledge: Since not all Prospero's commands to Ariel are presented onstage, we (with the characters) are left in the dark and only later find out why certain things happened (or we do not find out). This secrecy is in line with Prospero's tendency as dilettantish director to keep something up his sleeve at all times (1.2.220, 318, 496–501). Similarly, character groups say, hear, or see things that others do not perceive, or they indulge in puns, irony, and ambiguity to the same purpose. The implication is that we as audience also miss many things that matter as we stumble through the play.

7. The function of alcohol as a depriment rather than a stimulant: Besides Stephano, Trinculo, and Caliban, the boatsman in 1.1 drinks too. Baroque art, including *The Tempest*, tends to represent "reality" from the point of view of the drunk, which is important for the appearance-versus-reality theme. Naturalism and realism, by contrast, approach drunkenness from the point of view of sober society, thus emphasizing social-moral themes.

8. The multisignificance of abstract notions (freedom, hope, the natural, confidence, and so on), which, in the wake of Montaigne, lead to a consideration of the stunning powers of the mind (best expressed by Ferdinand).

9. The function of mirror episodes, such as the three conspiracies or the banishments of the pregnant "black magician" Sycorax and the "white magician" Prospero with his infant daughter. Equally relevant are the false mirror episodes: for example, being human, Prospero is innately superior to Caliban (1.2.313–14), but the courtiers are not so to the sailors (1.1).

10. Mistaken trust and confidence.

In addition to discussing these motives, students find it instructive and entertaining to look for confusing elements or questions that are indirectly built into the fabric of the text. For example, why did Prospero "often" begin but never finish the story of his exile to Miranda? Surely, he has had time enough. Has Miranda never inquired about her mother? Isn't Milan rather far from the sea? How could Gonzalo have given Prospero all those supplies and books? Would the conspirators have left Prospero his rapier? Why does Prospero say that he will release Ariel "after two days" (1.2.298–99)? What is the reason for the presence of the clowns? Would Prospero know if Ferdinand did indeed "give dalliance too much the rein" (4.1.50–51)? What about the fact that Ferdinand has loved before or that Claribel was married off to the king of Tunis against her will? Why does Prospero tolerate living next to a stinking pool, or, being a magician, why does he need Caliban's labor? Why does he not denounce the courtiers for their attempted murder of Alonso?

Among courtly-baroque plays, *The Tempest* is remarkable because these confusions and questions remain unsolved by the play's end. Contrary to our expectations, the island's center, the cave of the God-like ruler and magician, is not the comforting source of clarification that defines order. Rephrased in the terminology of the baroque self-consciously theatrical aesthetic, this center does not provide the focal point at which the scattered incidents come together in a meaningful whole. For it is essential in much courtly-baroque art (ceiling painting as well as plays and stage architecture) that a participant or spectator (these two roles are undistinguishable in such art) discover the visual angle from which the fragmented essentials and accidents form a pattern, a unified whole. Thus, courtly stage architecture and scenic design favor a selected place in the auditorium from which the perspective illusion makes most sense: the royal box, the fixed point of reference. The closer one sits to the ruler, the more one shares the privileged, God-like view. In terms of design (of a play, a decor, a facade, the *Apotheosis of James I*), individual motives are like dynamic particles whose gyrating motion toward a center of gravity becomes meaningful only for an observer with such a "correct" angle of approach (adapted from Wölfflin). Clearly, Prospero's magic cave does not provide such a center of gravity, because Prospero does not give the information that solves the problems posed in and by the play and its events.

Why he does not is the crowning question of the entire movement of the play and usually forms the end of our discussion of *The Tempest*. Relevant to consider is the possibility that Prospero is not only a second-rate magician but also an obvious failure as "absolute ruler" (of Milan, of the island-stage) and thus undeserving or incapable of representing the "fixed point of reference" that courtly-baroque art attributes to the prince. His double flaw, as director-magician and as ruler, is most painfully obvious in the curiously interrupted masque (4.1), a poetic model on mythic scale of the lawful relationship of Ferdinand and Miranda and a symbolic representation of how divine sanction of the dynastic betrothal may conquer time after all. This masque is Prospero's present for the betrothal and, theoretically, the play's most courtly diversion. Masques were a favorite English courtly-aesthetic method of presenting special effects, the equivalent of ballets in France and opera in the German states. Thus it is all the more significant that the masque collapses like a badly baked soufflé. Many phrases sound uninspired and silly (Ceres knows Juno "by her gait" [4.1.102]), the imagery is unoriginal, and the subject is as trivial as Marino's long epic *Adone* but without any of its graceful wit. The goddesses fail to convince even as baroque cardboard divinities. The ambiguity of Ferdinand's praise remains hidden to Prospero, who, like a proud amateur, cries out, "Hush and be mute" (4.1.126). When the frigid nymphs are invited to celebrate the marriage contract, forgetful Prospero suddenly remembers the "foul conspiracy" (4.1.139) and without more ado puts an end to all that nonsense. Here, as before in Milan, he has been betrayed by his enthusiasm for effects, his pedantry, and his penchant for shiny props. As artist-magician, Prospero seeks to entertain the present and future absolute rulers with courtly-baroque art, and he fails miserably, just as he failed as ruler of Milan.

The Tempest is thus not only a complex example of the change in aesthetic policy under James but perhaps also a self-reflexive comment on this change, an invitation by Shakespeare to ponder the values and functions of such courtly-baroque art. Is such art (including *The Tempest*) merely useful to obliterate time for an instant — like a maze or a masque? Should one avoid inquiring too deeply for fear of spoiling the entertainment? These are relevant final questions to leave students grappling with as we move on to the ideal play to discuss after *The Tempest*, Corneille's *Theatrical Illusion*.

Teaching *The Tempest* as the Art of "If"

Arthur F. Kinney

The Chief use then in man of that he knowes,
Is his paines taking for the good of all. . . .

. . . .

Yet *Some seeke knowledge, merely but to know,*
And idle Curiositie that is. . . .

— Fulke Greville

For more years than I care to remember, I attempted to clear the classroom air of any thoughts of Shakespeare's last play as merely a pageant or allegory by tackling that possibility head-on: "Can you have a work," I would ask, "based on these initial premises: Prospero controls everything; and Prospero is a good man." The obvious answer is no, but the next thought is that *The Tempest* is, in fact, *drama.* I wanted students to see that what *appears* to be a simple masquelike work (in a play about appearances) can stand variously, as John W. Velz notes, as (1) "the journey [of] Mankind from corruption to reform"; (2) a play about a father and a daughter coming of age together, a double (or even multiple) "rite of passage"; or (3) "Aeneas' journey, from Carthage to Italy by way of liminal experience" (321). These possible interpretations allow us to see that the play is both parable and not-parable, at once familiar and strange; but as tantalizing and even initially satisfying as these approaches are, they are simply not enough: they do not quite fit the play as we read it, discuss it, and study it.

For one thing, Prospero is not always in control; he can be distracted, frustrated, petty, even angry. And, in some ways, Miranda seems grown up before the play begins, even though she is inexperienced in the ways of humanity beyond the island's boundaries. Nor is Aeneas's heroic establishment of Rome a very exact fit, either for a usurped duke who lost his dukedom through negligence or for a young suitor about to inherit Milan; the "widow Dido" bears no resemblance to Claribel, the civilized Neapolitan matron abandoned to a black Muslim husband in African Tunis. Indeed, the ways in which Velz and I worked to get students to perceive as a drama a play that seems to strain toward being a parable of fall and redemption — of learning both justice and mercy — appear especially obscene in these days when we are aware of the great harm, as well as the awful seduction, of colonialist enterprise, in Shakespeare's time and in our own.

Such direct connections between Shakespeare's age and ours, both embarrassing and vitally enlightening, cannot be avoided. Showing how the age of exploration, discovery, and settlement, especially in the New World, could lead to greed, conquest, and exploitation — as it does with Prospero's disproportionate domination of Miranda and Ariel and his identical subordination of Caliban and Ferdinand into slavish log-carriers — aligns the play with possible source materials in sixteenth- and seventeenth-century voyage pamphlets that appear in the back of student editions (I use the Signet Shakespeare with undergraduates, the New Arden with graduate students). But I also teach *The Tempest* on occasion to huge numbers of freshmen and sophomores, in introductory courses on Shakespeare or world literature; to high school students, as a guest teacher; or to adults, in continuing-education classes or town or alumni meetings. These readers often want to stay close to the text itself in their first exposure. So with them I attempt, though more indirectly, to get at the same fundamental issue — How can a human being be so savage?

That Prospero is complicit in excusing misguided behavior and collusive in making the play feel like a pageant is superficially confirmed in the text, of course, all the way to the epilogue:

> Now my charms are all o'erthrown,
> And what strength I have's mine own,
> Which is most faint. Now 'tis true
> I must be here confined by you,
> Or sent to Naples. Let me not,
> Since I have my dukedom got
> And pardoned the deceiver, dwell
> In this bare island by your spell;
> But release me from my bands
> With the help of your good hands.
>
> (epilogue 1–10)

He knows confinement, too, then, but only fictional imprisonment that he can be freed from (and will doubtless be freed from) by the applause of those he addresses. His "insubstantial pageant" (4.1.155) which faded twice previously, is about to fade again, the "bare island" worth leaving not because (as a second thought) he has "pardoned the deceiver" but because (*this* is his first thought) he has his "dukedom got." While it is true that, with his charms overthrown, he is most faint, he nevertheless has no anxiety about returning to Milan or even about thinking of death; his position of power is transferable. All of us, he concludes, commit "crimes," and so we all "indulge" one another (epilogue 19, 20). If we anatomize the poetry, as Lear does to see what breeds about the hearts of his daughters, we will also be disappointed. It would seem that in this play of education — this drama of process — Prospero is as unrepentant as Antonio. Even Alonso, for all his generosity of spirit, distances himself: "I long / To hear the story of your life, which must / Take the ear strangely" (5.1.313–15).

For Prospero, Alonso, and Antonio, then, the story of Shakespeare's play has surprisingly *little* effect; it is as remote and detached as Gonzalo's dream of an ideal (but unrealizable) commonwealth (2.1.152–61; cf. 164–69). The easy composure they reveal is — in this play, anyway — the height of ignorance. For again and again, *The Tempest* is about dissension, betrayal,

disobedience, dis*belief*. The dramatic storm with which it begins is only
a gross signal for what is to follow more subtly — and excellent class discussions develop when I suggest that implicitly the whole play is tempest-tossed
(or, conversely, that the whole play is contained in the microcosmic,
metadramatic first scene) and then ask students to find examples that support
such a reading.

That storm in 1.1 is well worth close examination. In the first line, the
Master is out of control and seeks help from the Boatswain; his exit line
(4) shows his heightened anxiety. Even the Boatswain loses control (13–14)
and begins to command his superiors: "Silence! / Trouble us not!" (17–18).
The temperate Gonzalo chides the Boatswain for behaving rashly (19–20)
before he too loses faith (34). But rebellion spreads — to Sebastian ("A pox
o' your throat, you bawling, blasphemous, incharitable dog!" [41–42]) and
to Antonio ("Hang, cur! Hang, you whoreson, insolent noisemaker! We are
less afraid to be drowned than thou art. . . . We are merely cheated of our
lives by drunkards" [44–46, 56–57]). Others — the sailors, Gonzalo — do not
disobey the sea captain, they disobey God: they lose all hope (61–62, 66–67).
All order — of class, of rank, of trade — is overturned.

Students have no difficulty in seeing all this, although the reach of the
implications sometimes needs to be discussed. Yet what no student of mine
has ever noticed — and none of my colleagues, for that matter — is that no
matter how upsetting the first scene may be, it does not prepare us for the
opening of the second scene, which has one of the most astonishing lines
in all of Shakespeare. "If by your art, dearest father," Miranda says as possible *reprimand*, "you have / Put the wild waters in this roar, allay them"
(1.2.1–2). Touchstone has told us there is "Much virtue in If" (*As You Like
It* 5.4.103). And, looking backward, we are at once asked to make the storm
hypothetical. Why? More interestingly, Miranda's first reaction is not sorrow
or pity but blame: "If by *your* art, my dearest father, *you* have / Put the
wild waters in this roar, allay them." Why is Miranda's first instinct to accuse
her father? And why, more specifically, does she accuse his *art*? Is her father
fundamentally an evil magician? Is art by its nature — because it is not
natural — evil? Is any artist, therefore, potentially unnatural and potentially
evil (including, of course, Shakespeare)? This is not the customary Miranda
we read about, but it is, in fact, the Miranda Shakespeare gives us in her
transparent opening lines. And she goes on:

> The sky, it seems, would pour down stinking pitch
> But that the sea, mounting to th' welkin's cheek,
> Dashes the fire out. O, I have suffered
> With those that I saw suffer! A brave vessel
> (Who had no doubt some noble creature in her)
> Dashed all to pieces! O, the cry did knock
> Against my very heart! Poor souls, they perished!
> Had I been any god of power, I would

Have sunk the sea within the earth or ere
It should the good ship so have swallowed and
The fraughting souls within her.   (1.2.3–13)

The lines work verbally and aurally like certain optical illusions work visually — what one sees in the foreground of such pictures is two people kissing (or a rabbit); when one concentrates on the background, those pictures become candlesticks (or a duck). Emphasize the portrait, and Miranda teaches us mercy. Emphasize the pronouns, and she clearly blames her father without restraint ("O, *I* have suffered"; "Had *I* been any god of power"). This is where, in my classes, the play splits open, and discussion and often debate starts. Who will teach whom in this play? You can read the rest of the scene (and we try it aloud) to see Prospero finally, hesitatingly, tell the tale of their unhappy past, their joint biography, prodding Miranda from time to time to make certain she is awake, is paying attention. But you can just as easily (and in class we do) read the lines as so many promptings from Miranda, who cues, cajoles, reminds, interrogates her father, forcing him, it would seem, to *confess* not their joint past but his own personal negligence and pride: "You have often / Begun to tell me what I am; but stopped" (33–34); "Had I not / Four or five women once that tended me?" (46–47); "Sir, are you not my father?" (55) — this last question having the most reverberations of them all when we come to discuss fatherhood, parental responsibility, heredity, nurture. Miranda is probably working from instinct, for her father has deliberately kept her ignorant of his earlier rule in Milan. But he has not kept her ignorant of his treatment of Ariel and Caliban, which is mean and selfish. "How now? Moody? / What is't thou can'st demand?" he berates Ariel (1.2.244–45), the language at once excessive. And when Ariel answers, "My liberty," and reminds Prospero of his promise, what does Miranda hear? A father she has seen like this before? It would seem so, from Ariel's insistence that their bargain has been postponed and, perhaps, betrayed; and Miranda may begin to see the value of "liberty" for herself. What she actually hears from her father, though, is stern rebuke and a speech (1.2.261–93) that is a catechism of domination. Ariel's pitiful "I thank thee, master" (293) is in sharp contrast to Miranda's earlier accusation and command ("If by your art, . . . you have / Put the wild waters in this roar, allay them"). We are taken aback by Ariel's easy surrender, and we are the more prepared for (and perhaps half appreciative of) Caliban's insolence and defiance: "As wicked dew as e'er my mother brushed / With raven's feather from unwholesome fen / Drop on you both! A southwest blow on ye / And blister you all o'er!" (1.2.321–24). Beneath these opposed reactions, there is a rough parity in Prospero's treatment of his two servants. His possession of them is challenged by Caliban ("This island's mine by Sycorax my mother" [331]), who uses the same terms of natural inheritance in claiming the right to rule the island as Prospero does for Milan when reporting the past to Miranda. The wonderful thing about teaching

The Tempest is that such recognitions are instantaneous in class: they are at once apparent and at once important—and they raise very knotty issues indeed.

There is, for instance, that motif of Miranda's first word: the motif of "If." The hypothetical can explain actions, such as Prospero's causing the storm, or explain them away. In this instance, If involves a kind of parity, a kind of quid pro quo such as Cordelia uses in replying to Lear in the opening scene of that earlier play. It can also involve a kind of surrender to hypothesis as the displacement of reality—as Gonzalo illustrates when he describes his ideal commonwealth. If involves a kind of mutual trust, broken, it would seem, between Prospero and Ariel because Prospero has failed to keep his bargain—and has done so at a time when he must insist that Miranda trust his story of their joint past. If involves pledges toward the future—which must be how Ferdinand takes the boring job of chopping and hauling wood (and, by extension, Caliban may have too). If can be delusory, as when Prospero tempts the Neapolitans with a banquet, only to snatch it from them, an antecedent of the illusion that he can force Alonso and Sebastian and Antonio, all three, to repentance when, as with the masque of Ceres, he can only provide an opportunity or occasion but not legislate or guarantee a result. These interpretive possibilities the students soon come to see, though discussions in my classes have undergone strange sea changes of their own. What the classes generally do not see, however, is that If can also mean the lack of illusion, the admission of fact. This recognition is, I think, the play's last transposition of the word as basic signifier, and it is only fitting that once more Miranda, the island's first realist (as we are given the play), introduces it. The final introduction of If comes after Prospero gives what is perhaps his most arrogant and presumptive speech.

> In this last tempest, I perceive these lords
> At this encounter do so much admire
> That they devour their reason, and scarce think
> Their eyes do offices of truth, their words
> Are natural breath. But, howsoev'r you have
> Been justled from your senses, know for certain
> That I am Prospero, and that very duke
> Which was thrust forth of Milan, who most strangely
> Upon this shore, where you were wracked, was landed
> To be the lord on't.   (5.1.153–62)

Prospero's speech works precisely the way Miranda's opening speech does: read it for the facts, read the foreground, and it is an explanation that leads to the play's denouement; read the pronouns, the background, and the speech is as arrogant as ever: here Prospero is firmly in control again, by unallayed art. At just this point the stage direction tells us, "Here Prospero discovers Ferdinand and Miranda playing at chess" (5.1.171). Like the tempest, like the banquet, this revelation is another "show" he has "managed."

Or so he thinks. But once again, Miranda does not sit still; she is not (she is never) merely on display. She is, rather, by instinct, one of Shakespeare's strong, true feminists. Listen to her:

MIRANDA.   Sweet lord, you play me false.
FERDINAND.   No, my dearest love,
                I would not for the world.
MIRANDA.   Yes, for a score of kingdoms you should wrangle,
                And I would call it fair play.   (5.1.172–75)

Students can gloss the lines easily enough: she accuses Ferdinand of cheating; he denies it (shades of her other masculine partner, Prospero); she insists it is true; and then she *reconciles them both to it.* This If, the If of the truth of a cheater, is all right if those who do the cheating are devoted to each other so that no real betrayal takes place, so that cheating itself becomes not cheating.

Usually the class now jumps in to tell me where I am going. Where else in the play have others consented to an If they seemed to oppose? Ariel, in his continued service? Caliban, in his rueful way? Ferdinand and Miranda themselves, in their obedience? Alonso and Sebastian, in their request for forgiveness? Gonzalo, who may well know that a kingless kingdom is a paradox but more visionary for all that? Even, in the end, perhaps, Stephano and Trinculo, who know that Caliban is no god, and no useful citizen either, and that their attempt to establish their monarchy is as delusory as Gonzalo's, or Prospero's, or the usurping Antonio's.

What are we to make of this inherent storm of questions that the play keeps raising? I think *The Tempest* tells us that If can educate us, delude us, or disillusion us; that If, like any human endeavor or talent, like life, is always open to constant reinterpretation and negotiation. There is no way, finally, that Prospero can guarantee repentance from Antonio—or guarantee what repentance means from Alonso and Sebastian and *himself.* Ariel embodies this uncertainty, this need for openness to change, when he flies off to freedom: he flies off to—what? Caliban enunciates it: he will "seek for grace" (5.1.296), and though the absence of grace can make him, clearly, a "thrice-double ass" (296), the operative verb is still *seek.* Life may be education, process; but it is also exploration—and here the New World comes back into play—and constant negotiation and renegotiation. Even when we are sufficiently resigned to say that "Every third thought shall be my grave" (5.1.312), there are two other thoughts accompanying it. Touchstone, like Miranda, knew of the double-edged qualities, as well as the endless possibilities, of If. That is its virtue, its "much virtue."

That too is where the epilogue ends (and our class). While I have not glossed each scene in the play here—nor do I ever in my teaching notes, because I find that doing so leads discussion too closely and that students do not risk as much in their own quests for meaning—the direction of the class is clear enough. And it brings us back to where we began. Prospero's last lines — the final lines in *The Tempest* — are these:

> Gentle breath of yours my sails
> Must fill, or else my project fails,
> Which was to please. Now I want
> Spirits to enforce, art to enchant;
> And my ending is despair
> Unless I be relieved by prayer,
> Which pierces so that it assaults
> Mercy itself and frees all faults.
> As you from crimes would pardoned be,
> Let your indulgence set me free.
> (epilogue 11–20)

Unlike his opening lines, these words of Prospero are educated to a depth and complexity that was noticeably lacking in his early narrative. If his project succeeds because of our gentle breaths, we have become the Prospero of 1.2 and he the dependent sailors of 1.1. If he "wants" spirits and art, will he "despair"? He says he will despair without "prayer," but he offers no assessment or certainty of that claim, only the need for mercy to excuse (not dismiss or cover up) faults. We know this, his situation, because we too are guilty of crimes (19). We have to be, being human. Thus our indulgence for ourselves can also be an indulgence for him — or the other way around. Being indulgent, of course, is what Miranda was doing when she probed his narrative in 1.2 and what she openly tells Ferdinand as they play chess (for the Stuarts, the "game of life") in 5.1. A violent tempest opens the play; the quiet recognition of life as unending tempest closes it. Or ends it: the play never really closes, never really "ends." "Indulgence" is not an act, like "crimes"; it is a state of mind. It is ongoing, as mercy is, or prayer, or chess, or life. Or, come to think of it, the finest art.

Shakespeare's Magic and Its Discontents: Approaching *The Tempest*

Kay Stockholder

I teach *The Tempest* as Shakespeare's final effort to envision a dramatically probable world in which a perfectly benign authority might render the intransigent human passions that moved the play's tragic protagonists to their catastrophes amenable to a cosmic hierarchical order. To discern the relation of *The Tempest* to the canon, I emphasize the substantial differences between the naturalism and probable causality of the earlier plays and the more obvious symbolism of flattened characters and improbable events in the later plays. In line with Freud's insight that polarities conceal an underlying identity (*Lectures* 298–99), I give particular attention to the relationship in the plays between paired and polarized figures, such as good and bad women, and to the differences and omissions made significant by otherwise parallel plot sequences. In this way I can draw out the easily overlooked ideological and psychological dimensions of the play's formal qualities. The parallels among the themes, the conflicts, and the configurations of characters and action that are drawn symbolically in *The Tempest* and naturalistically in the earlier plays reveal the emotional implications of *The Tempest* and also illuminate the ideological undercurrents of the earlier works. In this essay, I concentrate on the forward direction to elucidate the significance of the magic that constitutes the single most striking feature of the play. An understanding of the genesis and components of Prospero's magic gives students access to the conflicts within Shakespeare's project that culminates in the breach between Prospero's entirely powerless subjects, for whom his magic constitutes their destiny, and Prospero's total power to shape his world.

By tracing the progression of magic from the providential happenings of the preceding romances, students can see that Prospero's magic is no mere device but rather the locus of the play's central meanings. There is no explicit magic in *Pericles*; here the author's controlling hand is transmuted into an ultimately benign fate made manifest in the fortuitous events that bring about the union and reunion of Thaisa, Pericles, and Marina. Unlike those of the early comedies, the coincidental meetings in *Pericles* are not perceived merely as a convention of the comic genre; instead they turn the play into a divine comedy in which the conclusion symbolizes a transcendent telos, or state of being that represents an ideal human state, permeated by divine authority. Though the play glances toward naturalistic causality in the deaths of Cleon and Dionyza at the hands of their enraged subjects, providence itself destroys the incestuous Antiochus and his daughter and ensures that the heroically good Pericles, as well as Thaisa and Marina, will be rewarded. In contrast to *Pericles*, *Cymbeline* partially obscures the providential hand by placing greater emphasis on human agency and by including more naturalistic characters who are not as clearly defined within the categories of good and evil as the characters are in *Pericles*. However, the seemingly less numinous accidental meetings that structure the plot appear in retrospect as instruments of a transcendent force, manifested finally in Posthumus's dreamed reconciliation with his dead family. This providential force functions now to administer a spiritual therapy by confronting the morally imperfect male characters with the apparently, but not really, irrevocable consequences of their actions. It allows them to transform their beings so that they will be morally worthy of happiness and become the means by which psychological, familial, civic, and political relations are aligned with divine hierarchical order.

However, both plays are somewhat messy and sprawling affairs, their action spanning the reaches of time and space. Their uneven quality has been widely noted, and students can readily identify the motifs from previous plays: *Pericles* combines motifs from *Hamlet* and *King Lear*, and *Cymbeline* combines motifs from *Othello* and *King Lear*, with shades of Lady Macbeth in the wicked Queen. Such comparisons highlight the degree to which the forces that wrest the characters from the tragically unalterable results of their actions lack a dramatic force commensurate with the gravity of these earlier works.

The Winter's Tale more clearly anticipates *The Tempest* in attempting to present magically transcendent events as though they were humanly possible and real. Here Shakespeare increases the dramatic energy by concentrating the action in two locales, allowing the sixteen years that separate the falling from the rising action to emphasize the benign power of time. He also intensifies the emotional effect in two ways: First, Leontes's paroxysm of jealousy and widening paranoiac vision give a fully tragic thrust to the action in Sicilia. Second, as Paulina controls action of the sort that the earlier plays left to time and circumstance, she becomes a kind of quasi magus, capable of turning art, the old tales and plays, and the statue into "life." Her role is to keep Leontes in an alchemical cauldron of agonized remorse on the implied assumption that sufficiently prolonged pain will transfigure his soul and he will become worthy of the restoration that waits in redeeming time. This fusion of evidently naturalistic human agency with a magical aura appears most vividly in Paulina's improbable but still naturalistic explanation for Hermione's "miraculous" resurrection. In this way Shakespeare asserts that the ostensibly irrevocable crimes and errors of the past can be revoked and that a transcendent fulfillment of the heart's deepest desires can indeed come to pass — that the real world can be a fairy tale. But the play remains a play; it cannot cross the boundary that divides the wonder of the onstage audience from that of its offstage audience, so that the more the play insists on the reality of its own transcendent vision, the more the multiplying references to art rebound as self-references, reinforcing rather than penetrating the invisible wall that separates the play from its audience.

These experiments with the quasi magical, whereby staged events simultaneously symbolize transcendent powers and purport to represent possible worlds, underline the import of the explicit magic with which *The Tempest* endows Prospero. The coalescing into Prospero's magic of the previously vague transcendental forces makes him into a representative of his author's shaping power who is entrusted with the task of turning his island kingdom into a microcosm of a transcendent world. While on the one hand Shakespeare abandons the representation of naturalistic causality in the events Prospero manages, on the other he portrays in Prospero a naturalistic psychology of a person capable of resisting the enormous temptations involved in wielding awesome power over the lives, hearts, and minds of others — power that in previous plays was bestowed on providential time and circumstance. To think of Prospero as an allegorical representation of providence is to ignore Shakespeare's attempt to paint a psychologically probable portrait of an uncorrupted ruler and to portray the human cost of the task the author has given him. The signs of personal stress that appear when Prospero acts irascibly, when he alternately shows impatience with and affection for Ariel, when he forgoes revenge, and when he sheds his power with mixed reluctance and weariness, are all designed to show Prospero as suffering the loneliness and burden of authority while resisting the enticement to misuse it in the service of self-interest.

While the play's tension arises from this internal drama, Prospero controls the comically reduced figures who are his pawns with an ease that conceals the emotional significance of the schematic action. However, just as the magnitude of Prospero's magic emerges in the context of earlier plays, so does the real intransigence of the problems he faces emerge when students place the figures subject to his magic in the context of Prospero's dramatic forebears. Moreover, the genealogy of Prospero's antagonists allows students to penetrate a darker side of the psychology of power, which appears as well in textual inconsistencies and omissions discussed below.

It is important for students to note that Prospero's most powerful antagonist is not any of the male figures he confronts; rather, it is Sycorax who, though banished to the past of the play, constitutes Prospero's only competitor for the magical control of the island. Though the cruelty of Sycorax and the compassion of Miranda cast them as polar opposites, both figures derive from the heroines of the early comedies. Portia makes her impassioned defense of pity as the "gentle rain" (*The Merchant of Venice* 4.1.183) that renews the world as she wittily orchestrates Shylock's humiliating defeat, and Rosalind both taunts Phoebe and toys with Orlando, but she faints with compassion at the thought of his wound. In *Twelfth Night* the two qualities unravel, so that Maria oversees Malvolio's discomfiture while Viola attends more to others' distress than,to her own and waits for comic time to untie the circumstantial knots. These two aspects of the feminine recombine in Isabel, who pleads that Angelo show Claudio mercy but shows little mercy herself when Claudio shrinks from martyring himself to her chastity. The gap widens in the tragedies. *King Lear* grounds the symbolic force of cruel women in the visceral response to the outrage of Gloucester's blinding, as does *Macbeth* in Lady Macbeth's assertion that she would have dashed out her infant's brains had she "so sworn" (1.7.58) as had Macbeth. These portrayals of female cruelty illuminate the depth of horror implied by, but hidden in, the flattened figures of Dionyza, who presides over a wasteland, a cannibalistic kingdom in which parents, like Lear's monsters of the deep, devour their young, and of *Cymbeline*'s Queen, who, with her beauty and sexual charms, initiates the hierarchical confusion of the entire action by seducing Cymbeline from his allegiance to Rome and whose foul sexuality generates her son, Cloten. The final avatar of this figure is Sycorax, whose description as the ugly witch of fairy tale represents her cruelty but whose evil magic derives from and cloaks not only the sexual allure of Goneril, Regan, and Lady Macbeth but also Cleopatra's bewitching charms.

As Miranda's progenitors become more polarized from Sycorax's, they become both more submissive and more subject to others' power. Desdemona's compassion for Othello's suffering defines their love—and extends even beyond the brink of death, when she exonerates him—but also makes her his victim. Cordelia's medicinal compassion for Lear can alone counteract the cosmic force of her sisters' cruelty, but the silence that defines her authenticity both leaves her defenseless against her articulate sisters and deprives her of dramatic force. Shakespeare maintains her aura of loving-kindness by banishing her from the stage while keeping her image present in the words of other characters, for whom she is a haunting memory. In *Macbeth* the figure of compassion forms a counterpart to Lady Macbeth's horrific imagination in Macbeth's image of "Pity, like a newborn babe / Striding the blast" (1.7.21–22). In *Coriolanus* Shakespeare almost makes muteness speak through Virgilia's silent agony at the sight of her husband's wounds, but Virgilia is powerless to shape events. In the romances this figure becomes Marina, whose radiant purity can cleanse brothels and heal, like Helena and Cordelia, Pericles's Lear-like catatonia. Miranda most completely incarnates compassion, but in being so fully constituted by, and an exemplar of, this single virtue that in more partial ways characterized her dramatic forebears, she becomes as one-dimensional, as fairy-tale-like, as her counterpart Sycorax.

By attending to these genealogies, students can see that Prospero's magic derives from, and is composed of, both the good and evil powers of female figures. On the one hand, Prospero takes from Sycorax and her forebears, along with shades of their cruelty, their power to cast the spells that make others subject to him and to shape events that constitute reality for them.

On the other hand, he aligns his magic with a cosmos that manifests its compassion in the winds and seas "whose pity sighing back again" did him and Miranda "but loving wrong." Shakespeare solves the problem of making female compassion an active principle while keeping female figures subservient to male authority by associating the active aspects of compassion with Prospero's magical powers. Therefore the magic that defines Prospero as an image of both his creator's shaping power and of a benign providence covertly derives from the women whose subordination it is designed to ensure.

On Prospero's control of women rests his success in containing the aspirations of those who would transgress the boundaries of correct hierarchy. Either the union of Ferdinand and Miranda will place Prospero's issue on the throne of a transformed Naples, or Sycorax's opposing kingdom will prevail, generated by the bad magic of her deceitful sexuality and peopled by the overreaching progeny, or dramatic ancestors, of Caliban and a befouled Miranda. Either a submissive Miranda will irradiate with her virtue the mind and soul of the man to whom she yields herself and generate virtuous children, or a reanimated Sycorax will, like *Cymbeline*'s Queen, pollute the being and the seed of men whose uneducated sexual passions enslave them to evil women. Only Prospero's commanding magic can protect the generative potency of a virtuous couple, necessary for a fertile kingdom, from the unruly and corrupting desires that will otherwise contaminate his world with the "pestilential vapours" that befouled Hamlet's.

As we have seen, Shakespeare's success in advancing so transcendent an ideal as an alternative to tragedy rests on creating in Prospero a psychologically probable exemplar of the psychic purity that Prospero inculcates in others by means of his punitive therapy. This project collapses should shades of Angelo's hypocrisy darken Prospero's image, allowing him to be seen as one who, like Lear's "rascal beadle," lashes the whore whom he "hotly lusts to use . . . in that kind / For which [he] whip'st her" (4.6.160–63). Overtly, the text eliminates the issue of Prospero's own sexuality by providing him with a long-dead wife and only a daughter for female companionship. But there are many grounds for seeing this absence arising from a textual concealment. The first is an argument from psychological probability, which would suggest that a person who, like Prospero, so concentrates attention on managing others' sexuality would also have disowned his own recalcitrant desires. Such a person would be subject to extreme tension. Desire for the divine Miranda would entail self-disgust, like Angelo's, for wanting to sully the good, but the only feminine alternative to her is Sycorax, whose image stands for the emasculating violence of her canonical predecessors and desire for whom would engender fear, as well as self-aversion for desiring the bad. Within the thought system implied by Prospero's banishment of Venus and her unruly son from the wedding masque, sexual desire itself, even within marriage, is corrupting (see Maclean 105n). Furthermore, unlike Lear, Pericles, and Leontes, Prospero has managed to keep his daughter with him, thereby characterizing any erotic desire as incestuous. The incestuous tensions that were suggested in various ways in these earlier plays were obscured by having the daughter given over to a benign providence, which in the guise of fortuitous circumstances also separated her from her father. Since Shakespeare's effort to embody transcendental powers in a human figure logically implies that Miranda be entrusted to her father's upbringing, Prospero must be one whose sexual passions are either extinct or entirely subordinate to his will. But signs that Prospero's sexual drives are neither extinct nor quiescent appear implicitly in his imprisonment and humiliation of even the virtuous Ferdinand, the pinches with which he torments Caliban, and the "beating brain" that afflicts him after the interrupted wedding masque—behavior that has led various critics to see the entire play as a critique of its central figure. Along with the textual lacunae, these details signify that Prospero's restraint of the unruly desires that are depicted in others derives from an equally severe and painful self-control. In psycho-analytic language, he can be seen as one whose ego ideal and passions are as radically polarized as are the figures he confronts.

This thematic emphasis on control is echoed formally in the contrast between the psychological naturalism of Prospero's character and the one-dimensional characters that people his world. This contrast, as well as the cancellation of ordinary causality, moves us toward a psychomachiac or oneiric reading in which aspects of the protagonist's psyche that he has repudiated to maintain his self-image are manifested in the figures whom he controls (see Garber; Stockholder). In this reading Caliban expresses Prospero's attitude toward his body. The imagery associates Caliban with standing water and earthiness, in contrast to Ariel, whose imagery involves moving waters and the "purer" elements of air and fire. Caliban's attempted rape of Miranda gives a sexual dimension to his insubordination to right authority, which in turn links him to the court party, and on Prospero's control of Caliban rests his ability to organize his island world as well as the Naples to which he will return. Ariel, the polar opposite of Caliban, represents the power by which Prospero ensures that the higher elements keep the lower ones in their places. However, the radical separation of sexuality from beneficent power becomes suspect in view of the common source for these apparently opposed figures. Caliban is born from Sycorax's womb, and Ariel is released by Prospero from her cloven pine, a distinctly genital image. That they are both in a sense born of Sycorax suggests a hidden affiliation between the sexuality Prospero governs and the cruel means by which he governs it.

The common birth of Ariel and Caliban suggests a quasi-fraternal relationship. As with the occulted ties between Sycorax and Miranda, one can discern underlying links between the polarized figures by attending to their dramatic ancestors, who are the good and bad brothers of previous plays. Ariel's supremacy over Caliban represents the rectification of the disordered passions depicted between brothers such as Oliver and Orlando, Duke Frederick and Duke Senior, Claudius and King Hamlet, Edgar and Edmund, and, of course, the two other fraternal pairs in this play. In earlier plays, good and bad brothers are opposed on the basis of their material and status versus spiritual and affectionate desires. However, in *Cymbeline* the fraternal pair acquires another range of associations, one that generates a new axis of signification. Like Caliban and Ariel, Cloten and Posthumus, being respectively foster son and stepson to the king, are also quasi-fraternal. To the previous value oppositions observed in other fraternal pairs, they add one between body and spirit that was anticipated, though without moral freighting, in the less obvious polarity between Puck and Bottom. Compared by Imogen to Posthumus's undergarments, Cloten becomes an allegorical symbol of the low desires from which Posthumus in time frees his more spiritual understanding. This new polarity is more fully realized in *The Tempest*, but the denied fraternal relationship of their dramatic predecessors suggests not only that it is Caliban in his "filthy mantled pools" (4.1.182) who represents his mother's rank sexuality but that the apparently antithetical figure of Ariel is a sublimated expression of the same desires.

The obscured relation between the figures is indicated in a second way. Though Prospero describes Caliban's past attempt to rape Miranda, in the present Caliban seems without sexual desire. Instead of seeking to repeat his attempt on Miranda, he offers her to Stephano, and for all Caliban is maligned, he is associated with the island's munificence. It is as though in the time between his attempted rape, in the image of the play's past, and his episode with Stephano he has been reduced to a kind of infantile or pre-genital psychological state (see Skura, "Discourse" 66–67, for a related approach to Caliban). The potency Prospero denies to Caliban he gives rather to his brother. In releasing his "tricksy spirit" (5.1.226) from Sycorax's power, Prospero acquires his magical powers, but only on condition of his denial of Caliban's, or his body's, sexual desires. (See N. O. Brown; Radin; and Kerényi for analogues in trickster myths to the view I argue here.) This configuration shows Prospero as one who is caught in a circular emotional argument. His assessment of his sexuality as evil is reflected in his vision of cruel and sexually foul women, which vilifies him for desiring them. Having entered Sycorax, in self-disgust he refuses to discharge the seed that will propagate more Calibans. He feels imprisoned by "her most unmitigable rage" (1.2.276), because he will not yield to orgasm and cannot lose his desire. The erect phallus is released only when transformed into the so "potent art" (5.1.50) that still sometimes does not "cleave" (4.1.164) to his thoughts and strains toward release. Once free, Ariel will display in benign (because nonhuman) form his genital source. "Where the bee sucks / There suck I" (5.1.88), he says, while an enervated and dreary Prospero will return to Milan with "every third thought on the grave" (5.1.312).

To serve his espoused hierarchical ideals, Prospero has transformed his sexual desire into the magic by which he restrains desire. His ideal is symbolized by, and made conditional on, the perfect subordination of a pure woman to a man in whom lust has been supplanted by affectionate appreciation of feminine spiritual radiance. However, not only does Prospero's victory over active and sexual women express his sexual fears; it also increases them by attributing to sexuality such vastly destructive powers. The pain of that escalating psychological dilemma is expressed in the image of Ariel's groans, vented for twelve years "as fast as mill wheels strike" (1.2.281). The only anodyne for Prospero's pain is to gain Ariel's release by changing his image of the sexually desirable woman into that of an ugly witch and channeling his frustrated phallic yearning into a will to power. Thus is Ariel comprised of the fused aggression and erotic drives that constitute Prospero's magic, while Prospero justifies his devious gratifications by recourse to the transcendent ideal in the name of which he punishes others for the desires he has so tortuously repressed in himself. The erotic passions with which Prospero tries to fecundate the otherwise sterile realm of the spirit never cease to rebel against and to permeate the restraints that were intended to render them benign. Insofar as Prospero's magical art is an image of Shakespeare's own art, the playwright's bestowal of creative force on an otherwise psychologically probable figure represents his effort to generate a vision of perfect authority so substantial that, like Hermione's statue, it might leap the ontological divide between life and art, between stage and audience. In this context the old idea that in Prospero's weariness Shakespeare expresses his own is both sanctioned and deepened, making it plausible to see Shakespeare as one desperately trying, with an explicitly psychological argument, to buttress a hierarchical value system that history was already washing from beneath his feet. Though his argument fails, in the process of mounting it Shakespeare created a moving image of the emotional dynamic involved in transforming libido into superego, or passion into the will to power.

CONTRIBUTORS AND SURVEY PARTICIPANTS

The editor thanks the following scholars and teachers of Shakespeare, whose generous help and support made this volume possible.

Michael Adams
Albright Coll.

Kristiaan P. Aercke
Univ. of Wisconsin, Madison

Linda Anderson
Virginia Polytechnic Inst.
  and State Univ.

James Andreas
Clemson Univ.

Louis R. Barbato
Cleveland State Univ.

Crystal L. Bartolovich
Drexel Univ.

Sharon Beehler
Montana State Univ.

Edward Berry
Univ. of Victoria

Eric Binnie
Hendrix Coll.

Stephen Booth
Univ. of California, Berkeley

Jean R. Brink
Arizona State Univ.

Thomas Bulger
Siena Coll.

Robert E. Burkhart
Eastern Kentucky Univ.

Margie Burns
Univ. of Maryland, College Park

Kathleen Campbell
George Mason Univ.

D. Allen Carroll
Univ. of Tennessee, Knoxville

Doris Clatanoff
Texas A&I Univ.

W. T. Colke
Univ. of the South

Dorothy Cook
Central Connecticut State
  Univ.

H. R. Coursen
Bowdoin Coll.

Jerry Crandall
West Valley Coll., CA

Karen Csengeri
West Georgia Coll.

Paul M. Cubeta
Middlebury Coll.

Peter Cummings
Hobart and William Smith Colls.

Earl L. Dachslager
Univ. of Houston, University Park

David O. Dickerson
Seattle Pacific Univ.

Michael Dobson
Indiana Univ., Bloomington

Joseph E. Duncan
Univ. of Minnesota, Duluth

Joyce East
West Virginia State Coll.

Peter Erickson
Williams Coll.

William R. Evans
Kean Coll. of New Jersey

Robert Fleissner
Central State Univ., OH

Charles R. Forker
Indiana Univ., Bloomington

Donald Foster
Vassar Coll.

John Freund
Indiana Univ. of Pennsylvania

Joanne E. Gates
Jacksonville State Univ.

Carol Gesner
Berea Coll.

Tapati Gupta
Calcutta Univ., India

Jay L. Halio
Univ. of Delaware, Newark

Donna Hamilton
Univ. of Maryland, College Park

Eugene D. Hill
Mount Holyoke Coll.

Delmar C. Homan
Bethany Coll., KS

J. Dennis Huston
Rice Univ.

Dorothea Kehler
San Diego State Univ.

Arthur Kinney
Univ. of Massachusetts, Amherst

Bernice W. Kliman
Nassau Community Coll., NY

Peggy A. Knapp
Carnegie Mellon Univ.

W. Nicholas Knight
Univ. of Missouri, Rolla

Stuart M. Kurland
Duquesne Univ.

Gregory Lanier
Univ. of West Florida

Alexander Leggatt
Univ. of Toronto, University Coll.

Gordon Lell
Concordia Coll., MN

Cynthia Lewis
Davidson Coll.

Stephen Lynch
Univ. of North Carolina, Asheville

Thomas McFarland
Princeton Univ.

Mary Ann McGrail
Kenyon Coll.

Philip C. McGuire
Michigan State Univ.

John Mebane
Univ. of Alabama, Huntsville

Michael E. Mooney
Univ. of New Orleans

S. S. Moorty
Southern Utah State Coll.

William Morse
Coll. of the Holy Cross

Michael Mullin
Univ. of Illinois, Urbana

Norman Nathan
Florida Atlantic Univ.

Rosemary Nudd, SP
Saint Mary of the Woods Coll.

Douglas L. Peterson
Michigan State Univ.

Vincent Petronella
Univ. of Massachusetts, Harbor
  Campus, Boston

Nicholas F. Radel
Furman Univ.

Robert Ray
Baylor Univ.

Constance C. Relihan
Univ. of Scranton

Hugh Richmond
Univ. of California, Berkeley

H. S. Rockwood III
California Univ. of Pennsylvania

David Rosen
Univ. of Maine, Machias

Gary Schmidgall
New York Univ.

Robert Schwartz
Oregon State Univ.

James Shapiro
Columbia Univ.

Michael W. Shurgot
South Puget Sound Community
  Coll., WA

William W. E. Slights
Univ. of Saskatchewan

Charlotte Spivak
Univ. of Massachusetts, Amherst

Kay Stockholder
Univ. of British Columbia

Edmund M. Taft
Kearney State Coll.

Frances Teague
Univ. of Georgia

Patricia Treanor
Graduate Center, City Univ.
  of New York

John W. Velz
Univ. of Texas, Austin

Gary Waller
Carnegie Mellon Univ.

W. G. Walton, Jr.
Meredith Coll.

William C. Watterson
Bowdoin Coll.

Barry Weller
Univ. of Utah

Helen Whall
Coll. of the Holy Cross

Paul W. White
Baylor Univ.

Robert F. Willson, Jr.
Univ. of Missouri, Kansas City

Douglas Emory Wilson
Anniston, AL

Paul Yachnin
Univ. of British Columbia

Bruce W. Young
Brigham Young Univ.

WORKS CITED

Books and Articles

Abel, Lionel. *Metatheatre: A New View of Dramatic Form*. New York: Hill, 1963.

Adams, Robert. *Shakespeare: The Four Romances*. New York: Norton, 1989.

Adamson, W. D. "The Calumny Pattern in Shakespeare." *REAL: The Yearbook of Research in English and American Literature* 4 (1986): 35–66.

Allen, Michael J. B., and Kenneth Muir, eds. *Shakespeare's Plays in Quarto: A Facsimile Edition of Copies Primarily from the Henry E. Huntington Library*. Berkeley: U of California P, 1982.

Anderson, Perry. *Lineages of the Absolutist State*. London: NLB, 1974.

Andrews, John, ed. *William Shakespeare: His World, His Work, His Influence*. 3 vols. New York: Scribner's, 1985.

Bacon, Francis. *Selected Writings of Francis Bacon*. New York: Modern Library–Random, 1955.

Baker, Herschel. *The Wars of Truth: Studies in the Decay of Christian Humanism in the Earlier Seventeenth Century*. Cambridge: Harvard UP, 1952.

Barber, C. L. " 'Thou That Beget'st Him That Did Thee Beget': Transformation in *Pericles* and *The Winter's Tale*." *Shakespeare Studies* 22 (1969): 59–67.

Barber, C. L., and Richard Wheeler. *The Whole Journey: Shakespeare's Power of Development*. Berkeley: U of California P, 1986.

Barker, Francis, and Peter Hulme. "Nymphs and Reapers Heavily Vanish: The Discursive Con-texts of *The Tempest*." Drakakis 191–205.

Barroll, J. Leeds, Alexander Leggatt, Richard Hosley, and Alvin Kernan. *The Revels History of Drama in English: Volume 3, 1576–1613*. London: Methuen, 1975.

Bartholomeusz, Dennis. The Winter's Tale *in Performance in England and America, 1611–1976*. Cambridge: Cambridge UP, 1982.

Barton, Anne. "Livy, Machiavelli, and Shakespeare's *Coriolanus*." *Shakespeare Survey* 38 (1985): 115–29.

Baudrillard, Jean. "The Precession of Simulacra." *Art after Modernism: Rethinking Representation*. Ed. Brian Wallis. New York: New Museum of Contemporary Art, 1984. 253–81.

Beaton, Roderick. *The Medieval Greek Romance*. Cambridge: Cambridge UP, 1989.

Beckerman, Bernard. *Shakespeare at the Globe, 1599–1609*. New York: Macmillan, 1962.

———. "Some Problems in Teaching Shakespeare's Plays as Works of Drama." Edens et al. 305–16.

Belsey, Catherine. "Disrupting Sexual Difference: Meaning and Gender in the Comedies." Drakakis 166–90.

Bennett, Tony. "Texts in History." *Journal of the Midwest Modern Language Association* 18 (1983): 1–16.

Berger, Harry, Jr. "Theater, Drama, and the Second World: A Prologue to Shakespeare." *Comparative Drama* 2 (1968): 3–20.

Bergeron, David M. "Plays within Plays in Shakespeare's Early Comedies." Edens et al. 153–73.

———. *Shakespeare: A Study and Research Guide*. New York: St. Martin's, 1975.

———. *Shakespeare's Romances and the Royal Family*. Lawrence: UP of Kansas, 1985.

Berry, Herbert. *Shakespeare's Playhouses*. AMS Studies in the Renaissance 19. New York: AMS, 1987.

Berry, Ralph. *Shakespeare's Comedies: Explorations in Form*. Princeton: Princeton UP, 1972.

Bethell, S. L. The Winter's Tale: *A Study*. London: Staples, 1947.

Bevan, Elinor. "Revenge, Forgiveness and the Gentleman." *Review of English Literature* 8.3 (1967): 55–69.

Bieman, Elizabeth. *William Shakespeare: The Romances*. Twayne's English Author Series 478. Boston: Twayne, 1990.

Bloom, Harold, ed. *William Shakespeare's* The Tempest. Modern Critical Interpretations. New York: Chelsea, 1988.

———. *William Shakespeare's* The Winter's Tale. Modern Critical Interpretations. New York: Chelsea, 1987.

Blum, Abbe. "Jane Howell's Statue Scene." Shakespeare Assn. of America Convention. Philadelphia, 14 Apr. 1990.

Boaden, James. *Memoirs of Mrs. Siddons*. London: Colburn, 1827.

Booth, Stephen. King Lear, Macbeth, *Indefinition, and Tragedy*. New Haven: Yale UP, 1983.

———. "Speculations on Doubling in Shakespeare's Plays." *Shakespeare: The Theatrical Dimension*. Ed. Philip C. McGuire and David A. Samuelson. New York: AMS, 1979. 103–31.

Bowers, Fredson. "Hamlet as Scourge and Minister." *PMLA* 70 (1955): 740–49.

Bradley, A. C. *Shakespearean Tragedy*. 2nd ed. London: Macmillan, 1905.

Braudel, Fernand. *The Perspective of the World*. New York: Harper, 1984. Vol. 3 of *Civilization and Capitalism: Fifteenth–Eighteenth Century*.

Breight, Curt. " 'Treason Doth Never Prosper': *The Tempest* and the Discourse of Treason." *Shakespeare Quarterly* 41 (1990): 1–28.

Brody, Alan. *The English Mummers and Their Plays: Traces of Ancient Mystery*. Philadelphia: U of Pennsylvania P, 1969.

Brower, Reuben A. "The Mirror of Analogy: *The Tempest*." *The Fields of Light: An Experiment in Critical Reading*. Ed. Brower and Richard Poirier. New York: Oxford UP, 1951. 95–122.

Brown, John Russell. *Shakespeare and His Comedies*. 1962. London: Methuen, 1968.

———. *Shakespeare's Plays in Performance*. New York: St. Martin's, 1967.

———. *Shakespeare's* The Tempest. Studies in English Literature 39. London: Arnold, 1969.

Brown, John Russell, and Bernard Harris, eds. *Later Shakespeare*. Stratford-upon-Avon Studies 8. London: Arnold, 1966.

Brown, Norman O. *Hermes the Thief: The Evolution of a Myth*. Madison: U of Wisconsin P, 1947.

Brown, Paul. "'This Thing of Darkness I Acknowledge Mine': *The Tempest* and the Discourse of Colonialism." Dollimore and Sinfield 48–71.

Brownlow, Frank Walsh. *Two Shakespearean Sequences:* Henry VI *to* Richard II *and* Pericles *to* Timon of Athens. Pittsburgh: U of Pittsburgh P, 1977.

Bullough, Geoffrey, ed. *Other "Classical" Plays:* Titus Andronicus, Troilus and Cressida, Timon of Athens, Pericles, Prince of Tyre. Ed. Bullough. London: Routledge, 1966. Vol. 6 of *Narrative and Dramatic Sources of Shakespeare*.

———. *Romances:* Cymbeline, The Winter's Tale, The Tempest. Ed. Bullough. London: Routledge, 1975. Vol. 8 of *Narrative and Dramatic Sources of Shakespeare*.

Bulman, James, and H. R. Coursen. *Shakespeare on Television*. Hanover: UP of New England, 1988.

Butcher, S. H. *Aristotle's Theory of Poetry and the Fine Arts*. London: Macmillan, 1907.

Calderwood, James L. *Metadrama in Shakespeare's Henriad*. Berkeley: U of California P, 1979.

———. *Shakespearean Metadrama*. Minneapolis: U of Minnesota P, 1971.

Calvino, Italo. *If on a Winter's Night a Traveler*. Trans. William Weaver. London: Harcourt, 1981.

Cartelli, Thomas. "Prospero in Africa: *The Tempest* as Colonist Text and Pretext." *Shakespeare Reproduced: The Text in History and Ideology*. Ed. Jean E. Howard and Marion F. O'Connor. New York: Methuen, 1987. 99–115.

Chambers, E. K. *The Elizabethan Stage*. 4 vols. Oxford: Clarendon–Oxford UP, 1951.

———. *William Shakespeare: A Study of Facts and Problems*. 2 vols. Oxford: Clarendon–Oxford UP, 1930.

Charney, Maurice. "Shakespearean Anglophobia." *Shakespeare Quarterly* 31 (1980): 287–92.

Clark, Cumberland. *A Study of Shakespeare's Henry VIII*. London: Mitre, 1938.

Clubb, Louise George. *Italian Drama in Shakespeare's Time*. New Haven: Yale UP, 1989.

Cohen, Robert. *Acting Power*. Palo Alto: Mayfield, 1978.

Coleridge, Samuel Taylor. *Biographia Literaria*. Ed. James Engell and W. Jackson Bate. London: Routledge; Princeton: Princeton UP, 1983. Vol. 7 of *The Collected Works*.

Colie, Rosalie L. *Shakespeare's Living Art*. Princeton: Princeton UP, 1974.

Colley, John Scott. "Disguise and New Guise in *Cymbeline*." *Shakespeare Studies* 7 (1974): 233–52.

Cook, Ann Jennalie. "Jane Howell's Manipulation of Distance in *The Winter's Tale*." Shakespeare Assn. of America Convention. Philadelphia, 14 Apr. 1990.

———. *The Privileged Playgoers of Shakespeare's London, 1576–1642*. Princeton: Princeton UP, 1981.

Cope, Jackson I. *The Theater and the Dream: From Metaphor to Form in Renaissance Drama*. Baltimore: Johns Hopkins UP, 1973.

Cressy, David. "Foucault, Stone, Shakespeare and Social History." *English Literary Renaissance* 21 (1991): 121–33.

Cruttwell, Patrick. *The Shakespearean Moment, and Its Place in the Poetry of the Seventeenth Century*. New York: Random, 1960.

Curry, Walter Clyde. *Shakespeare's Philosophical Patterns*. Baton Rouge: Louisiana State UP, 1937.

Curtius, Ernst Robert. *European Literature and the Latin Middle Ages*. Trans. W. R. Trask. New York: Pantheon, 1953.

Cutts, John P. *Rich and Strange: A Study of Shakespeare's Last Plays*. Pullman: Washington State UP, 1968.

Danby, John F. *Poets on Fortune's Hill: Studies in Sidney, Shakespeare, Beaumont and Fletcher*. 1952. Port Washington, NY: Kennikat, 1966.

Daniell, David. The Tempest. The Critics Debate. Atlantic Highlands: Humanities, 1989.

Dash, Irene G. *Wooing, Wedding, and Power: Women in Shakespeare's Plays*. New York: Columbia UP, 1981.

Davies, Godfrey. *The Early Stuarts, 1603–1660*. Oxford: Clarendon–Oxford UP, 1945.

Davies, Stevie. *The Idea of Woman in Renaissance Literature*. Brighton: Harvester, 1986.

Dean, John. *Restless Wanderers: Shakespeare and the Pattern of Romance*. Elizabethan and Renaissance Studies 86. Salzburg: Institut für Anglistick und Amerikanistik, Universität Salzburg, 1979.

Deleuze, Gilles, and Félix Guattari. *Anti-Oedipus: Capitalism and Schizophrenia*. Trans. Robert Hurley, Mark Seem, and Helen R. Lane. Minneapolis: U of Minnesota P, 1983.

Dent, R. W. *Shakespeare's Proverbial Language: An Index*. Berkeley: U of California P, 1981.

Dessen, Alan C. "The Supernatural on Television." *Shakespeare on Film Newsletter* 11 (Dec. 1986): 1+.

Dollimore, Jonathan, and Alan Sinfield, eds. *Political Shakespeare: New Essays in Cultural Materialism*. Ithaca: Cornell UP, 1985.

Drakakis, John, ed. *Alternative Shakespeares*. New Accents. London: Methuen, 1985.

Draper, Ronald P. *The Winter's Tale*. Text and Performance. London: Macmillan, 1985.

Drew, Elizabeth. "Language and Versification in *Cymbeline*." *Cymbeline*. Ed. C. J. Sisson. New York: Dell, 1964. 17–28.

Dunbar, Mary Judith. "*The Winter's Tale*: The Statue Scene." Shakespeare Assn. of America Convention. Philadelphia, 14 Apr. 1990.

———. "*The Winter's Tale*: The Trial Scene." Shakespeare Assn. of America Convention. Philadelphia, 14 Apr. 1990.

Eagle, M. N. *Recent Developments in Psychoanalysis*. New York: Basic, 1984.

Ebisch, Walter, with Levin L. Schücking. *A Shakespeare Bibliography*. 1930. New York: Blom, 1968.

———. *Supplement for the Years 1930–1935 to* A Shakespeare Bibliography. 1936. New York: Blom, 1968.

Edens, Walter, et al. *Teaching Shakespeare*. Princeton: Princeton UP, 1977.

Edwards, Philip. " 'Seeing Is Believing': Action and Narration in *The Old Wives Tale* and *The Winter's Tale*." *Shakespeare and His Contemporaries*. Ed. E. A. J. Honigmann. Manchester: Manchester UP, 1986. 79–93.

———. *Shakespeare and the Confines of Art*. London: Methuen, 1968.

Edwards, Philip, Inga-Stina Ewbank, and G. K. Hunter, eds. *Shakespearean Styles: Essays in Honour of Kenneth Muir*. Cambridge: Cambridge UP, 1980.

Eliot, Robert C. *The Shape of Utopia: Studies in Literary Genre*. Chicago: U of Chicago P, 1970.

Elton, William R. *Shakespeare's World: Renaissance Intellectual Contexts*. Garland Reference Library of the Humanities 83. New York: Garland, 1979.

Elyot, Thomas. *The Book Named the Governor*. Ed. S. E. Lehmberg. London: Scribner's, 1962.

Empson, William. *Some Versions of Pastoral*. London: Chatto, 1935.

Erickson, Peter. *Patriarchal Structures in Shakespeare's Drama*. Berkeley: U of California P, 1985.

Erickson, Peter, and Coppélia Kahn, eds. *Shakespeare's "Rough Magic": Renaissance Essays in Honor of C. L. Barber*. Newark: U of Delaware P, 1985.

Ettin, Andrew V. *Literature and the Pastoral*. New Haven: Yale UP, 1984.

Evans, Bertrand. *Shakespeare's Comedies*. Oxford: Clarendon–Oxford UP, 1960.

Farber, Stephen. "No Laughing Matter: Woody Allen." *Vis à Vis* 1.2 (Apr. 1987): 80.

Felperin, Howard. *Shakespearean Romance*. Princeton: Princeton UP, 1972.

Fenwick, Henry. "The Production." *The Tempest*. By William Shakespeare. BBC ed. New York: Mayflower, 1980.

Fiedler, Leslie A. *The Stranger in Shakespeare*. 1972. New York: Stein, 1973.

Fletcher, Anthony, and John Stevenson, eds. *Order and Disorder in Early Modern England*. Cambridge: Cambridge UP, 1985.

Foakes, R. A. *Shakespeare: The Dark Comedies to the Last Plays—From Satire to Celebration*. Charlottesville: UP of Virginia, 1971.

Forker, Charles R. *Fancy's Images: Contexts, Settings, and Perspectives in Shakespeare and His Contemporaries*. Carbondale: Southern Illinois UP, 1990.

Foster, Elizabeth Read, ed. *Proceedings in Parliament, 1610*. 2 vols. New Haven: Yale UP, 1966.

Fraser, Russell. *Young Shakespeare*. New York: Columbia UP, 1988.

Freer, Coburn. *The Poetics of Jacobean Drama*. Baltimore: Johns Hopkins UP, 1981.

Freud, Sigmund. "Family Romances." *The Standard Edition of the Complete Psychological Works of Sigmund Freud.* Vol. 9. Trans. and ed. James Strachey. London: Hogarth, 1959. 237–41.

———. *Introductory Lectures to Psychoanalysis.* Vol. 1. Trans. James Strachey. Pelican Freud Library'. New York: Penguin, 1973.

Frey, Charles. *Shakespeare's Vast Romance: A Study of* The Winter's Tale. Columbia: U of Missouri P, 1980.

Frye, Northrop. *Anatomy of Criticism: Four Essays.* Princeton: Princeton UP, 1957.

———. *Fables of Identity: Studies in Poetic Mythology.* New York: Harcourt, 1963.

———. *A Natural Perspective: The Development of Shakespearean Comedy and Romance.* New York: Columbia UP, 1965.

Garber, Marjorie. *Dream in Shakespeare: From Metaphor to Metamorphosis.* New Haven: Yale UP, 1974.

Gardiner, Samuel Rawson, ed. *Parliamentary Debates in 1610.* Camden Society 81. Westminster: Nichols, 1862.

Garner, Shirley Nelson. "Male Bonding and the Myth of Women's Deception in Shakespeare's Plays." Holland, Homan, and Paris 135–50.

Geller, Lila. "*Cymbeline* and the Imagery of Covenant Theology." *Studies in English Literature* 20 (1980): 241–55.

The Geneva Bible: A Facsimile of the 1560 Edition. Introd. Lloyd E. Berry. Madison: U of Wisconsin P, 1969.

Gesner, Carol. *Shakespeare and the Greek Romance: A Study of Origins.* Lexington: UP of Kentucky, 1970.

Gibson, William. *Shakespeare's Game.* New York: Atheneum, 1978.

Goffman, Erving. *Frame Analysis.* Cambridge: Harvard UP, 1974.

Goldman, Michael. *Acting and Action in Shakespearean Tragedy.* Princeton: Princeton UP, 1985.

———. *Shakespeare and the Energies of Drama.* Princeton: Princeton UP, 1972.

Greenblatt, Stephen J. "Learning to Curse: Aspects of Linguistic Colonialism in the Sixteenth Century." *First Images of America: The Impact of the New World on the Old.* Vol. 2. Ed. Fredi Chiappelli. Berkeley: U of California P, 1976. 561–80.

———, ed. *The Power of Forms in the English Renaissance.* Norman: Pilgrim, 1982.

Greene, Robert. *Pandosto: The Triumph of Time.* The Winter's Tale. By William Shakespeare. Ed. J. H. P. Pafford. Arden Shakespeare. London: Methuen, 1965.

Greenfield, Thelma N. "A Re-examination of the 'Patient' Pericles." *Shakespeare Studies* 3 (1967): 51–61.

Greenwood, John. *Shifting Perspectives and the Stylish Style: Mannerism in Shakespeare and His Jacobean Contemporaries.* Toronto: U of Toronto P, 1988.

Greg, W. W. *The Editorial Problem in Shakespeare: A Survey of the Foundations of the Text.* 3rd ed. Oxford: Clarendon–Oxford UP, 1954.

Greville, Fulke. *A Treatie of Humane Learning. Poems and Dramas of Fulke Greville, First Lord Brooke.* Ed. Geoffrey Bullough. Edinburgh: Oliver, 1939. 154–91.

Griffiths, Trevor R. " 'This Island's Mine': Caliban and Colonialism." *Yearbook of English Studies* 13 (1983): 159–80.

Gurr, Andrew. *Playgoing in Shakespeare's London.* Cambridge: Cambridge UP, 1987.

———. *The Shakespearean Stage, 1574–1642.* 2nd ed. Cambridge: Cambridge UP, 1980.

Halio, Jay L. "*Coriolanus*: Shakespeare's 'Drama of Reconciliation.' " *Shakespeare Studies* 6 (1972): 289–303.

———. "Hamlet's Alternatives." *Texas Studies in Literature and Language* 8 (1966): 169–88.

Hamilton, Donna B. *Virgil and* The Tempest: *The Politics of Imitation.* Columbus: Ohio State UP, 1990.

———. "*The Winter's Tale* and the Debate over the Union, 1604–1610." *Shakespeare Studies*: forthcoming.

Hartwig, Joan. *Shakespeare's Tragicomic Vision.* Baton Rouge: Louisiana State UP, 1972.

Haydn, Hiram. *The Counter-Renaissance.* New York: Scribner's, 1950.

Hayles, Nancy K. "Sexual Disguise in *Cymbeline*." *Modern Language Quarterly* 41 (1980): 231–47.

Hedrick, Donald. "The BBC *Winter's Tale*." *Shakespeare on Film Newsletter* 6 (Jan. 1982): 4.

Heise, Lori. "Crimes of Gender." *World-Watch* 2.2 (1989): 12–21.

Henderson, Katherine Usher, and Barbara F. McManus, eds. *Half Humankind: Contexts and Texts of the Controversy about Women in England, 1540–1640.* Urbana: U of Illinois P, 1985.

Herrick, Marvin T. *Tragicomedy: Its Origin and Development in Italy, France, and England.* Urbana: U of Illinois P, 1962.

Hill, Christopher. *Reformation to Industrial Revolution: A Social and Economic History of Britain, 1530–1780.* London: Weidenfield, 1967.

Hinman, Charlton. *The First Folio of Shakespeare: The Norton Facsimile.* New York: Norton, 1968.

———. *The Printing and Proofreading of the First Folio of Shakespeare.* 2 vols. Oxford: Clarendon–Oxford UP, 1963.

Hinson, Hal. "The Intensity of Being William Hurt." *Washington Post* 25 Jan. 1989: C1+.

Hirsh, James E. *The Structure of Shakespearean Scenes.* New Haven: Yale UP, 1981.

Hirst, David L. The Tempest. Text and Performance. London: Macmillan, 1984.

———. *Tragicomedy.* The Critical Idiom 43. London: Methuen, 1984.

Hoeniger, F. David. "Gower and Shakespeare in *Pericles*." *Shakespeare Quarterly* 33 (1982): 461–79.

Holland, Norman N., Sidney Homan, and Bernard J. Paris, eds. *Shakespeare's Personality.* Berkeley: U of California P, 1989.

Hull, Suzanne W. *Chaste, Silent, and Obedient: English Books for Women, 1475–1640.* San Marino: Huntington Library, 1982.

Hunt, Maurice. *Shakespeare's Romance of the Word.* Lewisburg: Bucknell UP, 1990.

Hunter, Robert G. *Shakespeare and the Comedy of Forgiveness.* New York: Columbia UP, 1965.

Hupka, Ralph B. "Cultural Determinants of Jealousy." *Alternative Lifestyles* 4.3 (1981): 310–56.

Ingram, William. *A London Life in the Brazen Age: Francis Langley, 1548–1602.* Cambridge: Harvard UP, 1978.

Jacobs, Henry E. Cymbeline: *An Annotated Bibliography.* Garland Shakespeare Bibliographies 3. New York: Garland, 1982.

James, D. G. *The Dream of Prospero.* Oxford: Clarendon–Oxford UP, 1967.

Jardine, Lisa. *Still Harping on Daughters: Women and Drama in the Age of Shakespeare.* Sussex: Harvester, 1983.

Johnson, Samuel. *On Shakespeare.* Ed. Walter Raleigh. London: Oxford UP, 1949.

Johnstone, Keith. *Impro: Improvisation and the Theatre.* London: Faber, 1979.

Jonson, Ben. *Ben Jonson: The Complete Masques.* Ed. Stephen Orgel. New Haven: Yale UP, 1969.

———. *Literary Criticism.* Ed. James D. Redwine. Lincoln: U of Nebraska P, 1970.

Joseph, Miriam. "*Hamlet*: A Christian Tragedy." *Studies in Philology* 59 (1962): 119–40.

Kahn, Coppélia. *Man's Estate: Masculine Identity in Shakespeare.* Berkeley: U of California P, 1981.

Kay, Carol McGinnis, and Henry E. Jacobs, eds. *Shakespeare's Romances Reconsidered.* Lincoln: U of Nebraska P, 1978.

Kellner, Douglas. *Jean Baudrillard: From Marxism to Postmodernism and Beyond.* Stanford: Stanford UP, 1989.

Kerényi, Karl. "The Trickster in Relation to Greek Mythology." Trans. R. F. C. Hull. Radin 173–91.

Kermode, Frank, ed. *English Pastoral Poetry: From the Beginnings to Marvell.* 1952. New York: Norton, 1972.

———. *The Sense of an Ending: Studies in the Theory of Fiction.* Oxford: Oxford UP, 1967.

———. *William Shakespeare: The Final Plays.* London: Longmans, 1963.

Kermode, Frank, and John Hollander, eds. *The Oxford Anthology of English Literature.* 2 vols. New York: Oxford UP, 1973.

Kernan, Alvin B. *The Playwright as Magician: Shakespeare's Image of the Poet in the English Public Theater.* New Haven: Yale UP, 1979.

Kirsch, Arthur C. "*Cymbeline* and Coterie Dramaturgy." *Journal of English Literary History* 34 (1967): 285–306.

Knight, G. Wilson. *The Crown of Life: Essays in Interpretation of Shakespeare's Final Plays.* London: Methuen, 1948.

———. *The Shakespearian Tempest, with a Chart of Shakespeare's Dramatic Universe.* 1932. London: Methuen, 1953.

Kott, Jan. *Shakespeare Our Contemporary.* Trans. Boleslaw Taborski. 1964. New York: Norton, 1974.

La Primaudaye, Peter de. *The French Academy*. Trans. T. B. London: Adams, 1618.

Lamm, Robert C., Neal M. Cross, with Dale Davis, eds. *The Humanities in Western Culture*. 8th ed. Vol. 2. Dubuque: Brown, 1968.

Leavis, F. R. *The Common Pursuit*. London: Chatto, 1952.

Leggatt, Alexander. "The Island of Miracles: An Approach to *Cymbeline*." *Shakespeare Studies* 10 (1977): 191–209.

Leininger, Lorie J. "The Miranda Trap: Sexism and Racism in Shakespeare's *Tempest*." Lenz, Greene, and Neely 285–94.

Lenz, Carolyn R. S., Gayle Greene, and Carol Thomas Neely, eds. *The Woman's Part: Feminist Criticism of Shakespeare*. Urbana: U of Illinois P, 1980.

Lindenbaum, Peter. *Changing Landscapes: Anti-pastoral Sentiment in the English Renaissance*. Athens: U of Georgia P, 1986.

Lockyer, Roger. *The Early Stuarts: A Political History of England, 1603–1642*. London: Longman, 1989.

MacCary, Thomas W. *Friends and Lovers: The Phenomenology of Desire in Shakespearean Comedy*. New York: Columbia UP, 1985.

Maclean, Ian. *The Renaissance Notion of Woman: A Study in the Fortunes of Scholasticism and Medieval Science in European Intellectual Life*. Cambridge: Cambridge UP, 1980.

Maguire, Nancy Klein. *Renaissance Tragicomedy: Explorations in Genre and Politics*. New York: AMS, 1987.

Mahler, Margaret. *The Psychological Birth of the Human Infant: Symbiosis and Individuation*. New York: Basic, 1975.

Mahood, M. M. *Shakespeare's Wordplay*. 1957. London: Methuen, 1979.

Mannoni, Octave. *Prospero and Caliban: The Psychology of Colonization*. Trans. Pamela Powesland. 1950. New York: Praeger, 1964.

Marcus, Leah S. *Puzzling Shakespeare: Local Reading and Its Discontents*. The New Historicism: Studies in Cultural Poetics 6. Berkeley: U of California P, 1988.

Marienstras, Richard. *New Perspectives on the Shakespearean World*. 1981. Trans. Janet Lloyd. Cambridge: Cambridge UP, 1985.

Marsh, Derick R. C. *The Recurring Miracle: A Study of* Cymbeline *and the Last Plays*. 1962. Lincoln: U of Nebraska P, 1969.

Marshall, Cynthia. *Last Things and Last Plays: Shakespearean Eschatology*. Carbondale: Southern Illinois UP, 1991.

Marx, Leo. *The Machine in the Garden: Technology and the Pastoral Idea in America*. New York: Oxford UP, 1964.

Maus, Katherine Eisaman. "Horns of Dilemma: Jealousy, Gender, and Spectatorship in English Renaissance Drama." *Journal of English Literary History* 54 (1987): 561–83.

Maveety, S. R. "What Shakespeare Did with *Pandosto*: An Interpretation of *The Winter's Tale*." McNeir and Greenfield 263–79.

McCavera, Tom. The Tempest. Twayne's New Critical Introductions to Shakespeare. Boston: Hall, forthcoming.

McDonald, Russ. "Poetry and Plot in *The Winter's Tale.*" *Shakespeare Quarterly* 36 (1985): 315–29.

————. "Reading *The Tempest.*" *Shakespeare Survey* 43 (1990): 15–28.

McFarland, Thomas. *Shakespeare's Pastoral Comedy*. Chapel Hill: U of North Carolina P, 1972.

McIlwain, C. H., ed. *The Political Works of James I*. Cambridge: Harvard UP, 1918.

McNamara, Kevin. "Golden Worlds at Court: *The Tempest* and Its Masque." *Shakespeare Studies* 19 (1987): 183–202.

McNeir, Waldo F., and Thelma N. Greenfield, eds. *Pacific Coast Studies in Shakespeare*. Eugene: U of Oregon P, 1966.

Mebane, John S. *Renaissance Magic and the Return of the Golden Age: The Occult Tradition and Marlowe, Jonson, and Shakespeare*. Lincoln: U of Nebraska P, 1989.

Metzger, Erika A., and Michael M. Metzger. "Courtly and Anticourtly Literature." *German Baroque Literature: The European Perspective*. Ed. Gerhart Hoffmeister. New York: Ungar, 1983. 250–69.

Michael, Nancy. Pericles: *An Annotated Bibliography*. Garland Shakespeare Bibliographies 13. New York: Garland, 1987.

Mitchell, Juliet. *Psychoanalysis and Feminism*. London: Pluto, 1974.

Moffet, Robin. "*Cymbeline* and the Nativity." *Shakespeare Quarterly* 13 (1962): 207–18.

Montaigne, Michel de. *The Complete Works of Montaigne*. Trans. Donald M. Frame. London: Hamilton, 1957.

Moretti, Franco. "'A Huge Eclipse': Tragic Form and the Deconsecration of Sovereignty." Greenblatt, *Power* 7–40.

Mowat, Barbara A. *The Dramaturgy of Shakespeare's Romances*. Athens: U of Georgia P, 1976.

————. "Prospero, Agrippa, and Hocus Pocus." *English Literary Renaissance* 11 (1981): 281–303.

Muir, Kenneth. *Shakespeare's Comic Sequence*. New York: Barnes, 1979.

————, ed. *Shakespeare's* The Winter's Tale: *A Casebook*. 1969. Nashville: Aurora, 1970.

Muir, Kenneth, and Samuel Schoenbaum, eds. *A New Companion to Shakespeare Studies*. Cambridge: Cambridge UP, 1971.

Mullaney, Steven. *The Place of the Stage: License, Play, and Power in Renaissance England*. Chicago: Chicago UP, 1988.

Mulvey, Laura. "Visual Pleasure and Narrative Cinema." *Feminism and Film Theory*. Ed. Constance Penley. New York: Routledge, 1988. 57–79.

Neely, Carol Thomas. *Broken Nuptials in Shakespeare's Plays*. New Haven: Yale UP, 1985.

————. "*The Winter's Tale*: The Triumph of Speech." *Studies in English Literature* 15 (1975): 321–38.

Nevo, Ruth. *Shakespeare's Other Language*. New York: Methuen, 1987.

Norbrook, David. "*Macbeth* and the Politics of Historiography." *Politics of Discourse: The Literature and History of Seventeenth-Century England*. Ed. Kevin Sharpe and Steven N. Zwicker. Berkeley: U of California P, 1987. 78–116.

Nosworthy, J. M. "Music and Its Function in the Romances of Shakespeare." *Shakespeare Survey* 11 (1958): 60–69.

Notestein, Wallace. *The House of Commons, 1604–1610*. New Haven: Yale UP, 1971.

Novy, Marianne. *Love's Argument: Gender Relations in Shakespeare*. Chapel Hill: U of North Carolina P, 1984.

Nuttall, A. D. *Two Concepts of Allegory: A Study of Shakespeare's* The Tempest *and the Logic of Allegorical Expression*. London: Routledge, 1967.

Olson, Glending. *Literature as Recreation in the Later Middle Ages*. Ithaca: Cornell UP, 1982.

Onions, C. T. *A Shakespeare Glossary*. 2nd rev. ed. Oxford: Clarendon–Oxford UP, 1949.

Orgel, Stephen. "New Uses of Adversity: Tragic Experience in *The Tempest*." In *Defense of Reading: A Reader's Approach to Literary Criticism*. Ed. Reuben A. Brower and Richard Poirier. 1962. New York: Dutton, 1963. 110–32.

———. "Prospero's Wife." *Representations* 8 (1984): 1–13.

Overton, Bill. The Winter's Tale. The Critics Debate. Atlantic Highlands: Humanities, 1989.

Palmer, D. J., ed. *Shakespeare's Later Comedies: An Anthology of Modern Criticism*. Penguin Shakespeare Library. Harmondsworth: Penguin, 1971.

———. *Shakespeare,* The Tempest: *A Casebook*. 1969. Nashville: Aurora, 1970.

Parten, Anne. "Cuckoldry in Shakespeare." Diss. Yale U, 1983.

Patterson, Annabel. *Shakespeare and the Popular Voice*. Cambridge: Blackwell, 1989.

Penrose, Boies. *Travel and Discovery in the Renaissance, 1420–1620*. Cambridge: Harvard UP, 1952.

Peterson, Douglas L. "Lyly, Greene, and Shakespeare and the Recreations of Princes." *Shakespeare Studies* 20 (1988): 67–88.

———. "*The Tempest* and Ideal Comedy." *Shakespearean Comedy*. Ed. Maurice Charney. New York: New York Lit. Forum, 1980. 99–110.

———. *Time, Tide, and Tempest: A Study of Shakespeare's Romances*. San Marino: Huntington Library, 1973.

Pettet, E. C. *Shakespeare and the Romance Tradition*. London: Staples, 1949.

Poggioli, Renato. *The Oaten Flute: Essays on Pastoral Poetry and the Pastoral Ideal*. Cambridge: Harvard UP, 1975.

Poisson, Rodney. "The 'Calumniator Credited' and the Code of Honour in Shakespeare's *Othello*." *English Studies in Canada* 2 (1976): 381–401.

Poster, Mark. *A Critical Theory of the Family*. New York: Pluto, 1978.

Primaudaye, Peter de la. *The French Academy*. London, 1607.

Puttenham, George. *The Arte of English Poesie*. Ed. G. D. Willcock and A. Walker. Cambridge: Cambridge UP, 1936.

Pyle, Fitzroy. The Winter's Tale: *A Commentary on the Structure*. London: Routledge, 1969.

Rabkin, Norman. *Shakespeare and the Common Understanding*. New York: Free, 1967.

——. *Shakespeare and the Problem of Meaning*. Chicago: U of Chicago P, 1981.

Radin, Paul. *The Trickster: A Study in American Indian Mythology*. New York: Philos. Library, 1956.

Raleigh, Sir Walter. *The Discovery of Guiana. Voyages and Travels, Ancient and Modern*. New York: Collier, 1910. Vol. 33 of *The Harvard Classics*. Ed. Charles W. Eliot. 321–94.

Reiss, Timothy J. *The Discourse of Modernism*. Ithaca: Cornell UP, 1982.

Richmond, Hugh M. "Performance as Criticism: *The Two Noble Kinsmen*." *Shakespeare, Fletcher, and* The Two Noble Kinsmen. Ed. Charles H. Frey. Columbia: U of Missouri P, 1989. 163–85.

——. "Peter Quince Directs *Romeo and Juliet*." *Shakespeare and the Sense of Performance*. Ed. Marvin Thompson and Ruth Thompson. Newark: U of Delaware P, 1989. 219–27.

——. "Shakespeare's Roman Trilogy: The Climax in *Cymbeline*." *Studies in the Literary Imagination* 5 (1972): 129–39.

Righter, Anne. *Shakespeare and the Idea of the Play*. Harmondsworth, Eng.: Penguin, 1967.

Rivers, Isabel. *Classical and Christian Ideas in English Renaissance Poetry: A Students' Guide*. London: Allen, 1979.

Rogers, Katherine M. *The Troublesome Helpmate: A History of Misogyny in Literature*. Seattle: U of Washington P, 1966.

Rose, Mark. *Shakespearean Design*. Cambridge: Belknap–Harvard UP, 1972.

Rousset, Jean. *La littérature de l'âge baroque en France: Circé et le paon*. Paris: Corti, 1954.

Sanders, Wilbur. The Winter's Tale. Twayne's New Critical Introductions to Shakespeare. Boston: Hall, 1987.

Schmidgall, Gary. *Shakespeare and the Courtly Aesthetic*. Berkeley: U of California P, 1981.

Schmidt, Alexander. *Shakespeare-Lexicon*. Ed. Gregor I. Sarrazin. 6th ed. 2 vols. Berlin: de Gruyter, 1971.

Schoenbaum, Samuel. *Shakespeare's Lives*. Oxford: Clarendon–Oxford UP, 1970.

——. *William Shakespeare: A Compact Documentary Life*. New York: Oxford UP, 1977.

——. *William Shakespeare: A Documentary Life*. New York: Oxford UP, 1975.

Schwartz, Murray M., and Coppélia Kahn, eds. *Representing Shakespeare: New Psychoanalytic Essays*. Baltimore: Johns Hopkins UP, 1980.

Shakespeare, William. *As You Like It*. Ed. Albert Gilman. Signet Classic Shakespeare. New York: Signet-NAL, 1963.

——. *The Complete Pelican Shakespeare*. Gen. ed. Alfred Harbage. Baltimore: Penguin, 1969.

——. *The Complete Signet Classic Shakespeare*. Ed. Sylvan Barnet. New York: Harcourt, 1972.

——. *The Complete Works*. Ed. Peter Alexander. New York: Random, 1952.

——. *The Complete Works of Shakespeare*. Ed. David Bevington. 4th ed. New York: Harper, 1992.

——. *Cymbeline*. Ed. Robert B. Heilman. Pelican Shakespeare. New York: Penguin, 1979.

——. *Cymbeline*. Ed. J. M. Nosworthy. Arden Shakespeare. London: Methuen, 1955.

——. *Henry VIII*. BBC ed. New York: Mayflower, 1979.

——. *The Late Romances:* Pericles, Cymbeline, The Winter's Tale, The Tempest. Ed. David Bevington. New York: Bantam, 1988.

——. *Pericles*. Ed. F. D. Hoeniger. Arden Shakespeare. London: Methuen, 1963.

——. *Pericles, Prince of Tyre*. Ed. Philip Edwards. New Penguin Shakespeare. New York: Penguin, 1976.

——. *Pericles, Prince of Tyre*. Ed. James G. McManaway. Pelican Shakespeare. New York: Penguin, 1977.

——. *Pericles, Prince of Tyre*; *Cymbeline*; *The Two Noble Kinsmen*. Ed. Ernest Schanzer, Richard Hosley, Clifford Leech, and Sylvan Barnet. Signet Classic Shakespeare. New York: Signet-NAL, 1988.

——. *The Riverside Shakespeare*. Ed. G. Blakemore Evans et al. Boston: Houghton, 1974.

——. *The Tempest*. Ed. David Bevington. New York: Bantam, 1988.

——. *The Tempest*. Ed. Northrop Frye. Pelican Shakespeare. New York: Penguin, 1970.

——. *The Tempest*. Ed. Frank Kermode. Arden Shakespeare. London: Methuen, 1954.

——. *The Tempest*. Ed. Robert Langbaum. Signet Classic Shakespeare. New York: Signet-NAL, 1987.

——. *The Tempest*. Ed. Stephen Orgel. Oxford Shakespeare. Oxford: Oxford UP, 1987.

——. *The Tempest*. Ed. Anne Righter. New Penguin Shakespeare. New York: Penguin, 1968.

——. *The Tempest*. Ed. Louis B. Wright and Virginia A. LaMar. Folger Library Shakespeare. New York: Washington Square, 1961.

——. *William Shakespeare: The Complete Works*. Ed. Stanley Wells and Gary Taylor. Oxford: Clarendon–Oxford UP, 1988.

——. *The Winter's Tale*. Ed. James C. Bulman and J. R. Mulryne. Manchester: Manchester UP, forthcoming.

——. *The Winter's Tale*. Ed. Frank Kermode. Signet Classic Shakespeare. New York: Signet-NAL, 1988.

——. *The Winter's Tale*. Ed. Baldwin Maxwell. Pelican Shakespeare. New York: Penguin, 1971.

——. *The Winter's Tale*. Ed. J. H. P. Pafford. Arden Shakespeare. London: Methuen, 1965.

——. *The Winter's Tale*. Ed. Ernest Schanzer. New Penguin Shakespeare. New York: Penguin, 1969.

——. *The Winter's Tale*. Ed. Louis B. Wright and Virginia A. LaMar. Folger Library Shakespeare. New York: Washington Square, 1966.

Shaw, George B. *On Shakespeare*. Ed. Edmund Wilson. New York: Dutton, 1961.

Sidney, Sir Philip. *The Defence of Poesie. Miscellaneous Prose of Sir Philip Sidney*. Ed. Katherine Duncan-Jones and Jan Van Dorsten. Oxford: Clarendon–Oxford UP, 1973. 59–121.

Simonds, Peggy Muñoz. *Myth, Emblem, and Music in Shakespeare's* Cymbeline: *An Iconographic Reconstruction*. Newark: U of Delaware P, 1992.

Skura, Meredith Anne. "Discourse and the Individual: The Case of Colonialism in *The Tempest*." *Shakespeare Quarterly* 40 (1989): 42–69.

Smith, Alan G. R. "Crown, Parliament and Finance: The Great Contract of 1610." *The English Commonwealth, 1547–1640: Essays in Politics and Society*. Ed. Peter Clark, Smith, and Nicholas Tyacke. New York: Barnes, 1979. 111–27.

Smith, Gordon Ross. *A Classified Shakespeare Bibliography, 1936–1958*. University Park: Pennsylvania State UP, 1963.

Smith, Hallett. *Shakespeare's Romances: A Study of Some Ways of the Imagination*. San Marino: Huntington Library, 1972.

———, ed. *Twentieth Century Interpretations of* The Tempest: *A Collection of Critical Essays*. Englewood Cliffs: Prentice, 1969.

Smith, Irwin. *Shakespeare's Blackfriars Playhouse: Its History and Its Design*. New York: New York UP, 1964.

Smith, Joan. *Misogynies*. London: Faber, 1989.

Sommerville, J. P. *Politics and Ideology in England, 1603–1640*. London: Longman, 1986.

Spevack, Marvin. *The Harvard Concordance to Shakespeare*. Cambridge: Belknap–Harvard UP, 1973.

Stockholder, Kay. *Dream Works: Lovers and Families in Shakespeare's Plays*. Toronto: U of Toronto P, 1987.

Stone, Lawrence. *The Crisis of the Aristocracy: 1558–1641*. Oxford: Clarendon–Oxford UP, 1965.

———. *The Family, Sex, and Marriage in England, 1500–1800*. New York: Harper, 1977.

Stone, Merlin. *When God Was a Woman*. San Diego: Harvest-Harcourt, 1976.

Styan, J. L. *The Shakespeare Revolution: Criticism and Performance in the Twentieth Century*. Cambridge: Cambridge UP, 1977.

———. *Shakespeare's Stagecraft*. Cambridge: Cambridge UP, 1967.

Sundelson, David. *Shakespeare's Restorations of the Father*. New Brunswick: Rutgers UP, 1983.

———. "(So Rare a Wonder'd Father): Prospero's *Tempest*." Schwartz and Kahn 33–53.

Swander, Homer D. "*Cymbeline* and the 'Blameless Hero.'" *English Literary History* 31 (1964): 259–70.

———. "*Cymbeline*: Religious Idea and Dramatic Design." McNeir and Greenfield 248–62.

Sypher, Wylie. *Four Stages of Renaissance Style: Transformations in Art and Literature, 1400–1700*. 1955. Gloucester: Smith, 1978.

Tanner, J. R. *Constitutional Documents of the Reign of James I, 1603–1625.* Cambridge: Cambridge UP, 1930.

Tayler, Edward. *Nature and Art in Renaissance Literature.* New York: Columbia UP, 1964.

Theweleit, Klaus. *Male Fantasies.* Trans. Stephen Conway et al. 2 vols. Minneapolis: U of Minnesota P, 1987–88.

Thomson, Peter. *Shakespeare's Theatre.* London: Routledge, 1983.

Tilley, Morris P. *A Dictionary of the Proverbs in England in the Sixteenth and Seventeenth Centuries.* Ann Arbor: U of Michigan P, 1950.

Tillyard, E. M. W. *The Elizabethan World Picture.* London: Chatto, 1943.

———. *Shakespeare's Last Plays.* London: Chatto, 1938.

Tobias, Richard C., and Paul G. Zolbrod, eds. *Shakespeare's Late Plays: Essays in Honor of Charles Crow.* Athens: Ohio UP, 1974.

Traister, Barbara H. *Heavenly Necromancers: The Magician in English Renaissance Drama.* Columbia: U of Missouri P, 1984.

Traversi, Derek A. *Shakespeare: The Last Phase.* New York: Harcourt, 1955.

Turner, Robert Y. "Slander in *Cymbeline* and Other Jacobean Tragicomedies." *English Literary Renaissance* 13 (1983): 182–202.

Uphaus, Robert W. *Beyond Tragedy: Structure and Experience in Shakespeare's Romances.* Lexington: UP of Kentucky, 1981.

Vaughan, Alden T. "Shakespeare's Indian: The Americanization of Caliban." *Shakespeare Quarterly* 39 (1988): 137–53.

Vaughan, Virginia. "The Forgotten Television *Tempest.*" *Shakespeare on Film Newsletter* 9 (Dec. 1984): 9.

Veeser, H. Aram, ed. *The New Historicism.* New York: Routledge, 1989.

Velz, John W. "From Jerusalem to Damascus: Bilocal Dramaturgy in Medieval and Shakespearean Conversion Plays." *Comparative Drama* 15 (1981–1982): 311–26.

Warner, Marina. *Alone of All Her Sex: The Myth and Cult of the Virgin Mary.* New York: Vintage-Random, 1976.

Warnke, Frank J. *Versions of Baroque: European Literature in the Seventeenth Century.* New Haven: Yale UP, 1972.

Warren, Roger. *Cymbeline.* Shakespeare in Performance Series. Manchester: Manchester UP, 1989.

Waugh, Patricia. *Metafiction: The Theory and Practice of Self-Conscious Fiction.* London: Methuen, 1984.

Wells, Stanley, ed. *The Cambridge Companion to Shakespeare Studies.* Cambridge: Cambridge UP, 1986.

———. " 'Goes out, Followed by a Furry Animal.' " *Times Literary Supplement* 20 Feb. 1981: 197.

———. *Shakespeare: A Bibliographical Guide.* Oxford: Clarendon–Oxford UP, 1990.

Wells, Stanley, and Gary Taylor, with John Jowett and William Montgomery. *William Shakespeare: A Textual Companion.* Oxford: Clarendon–Oxford UP, 1987.

Welsford, Enid. *The Court Masque: A Study in the Relationship between Poetry and the Revels*. 1927. New York: Russell, 1962.

Westlund, Joseph. "The Camera's View of the Baby in *The Winter's Tale*." Shakespeare Assn. of America Convention. Philadelphia, 14 Apr. 1990.

———. "Symbolic and Illusionistic Sets in the BBC-TV *Winter's Tale*." Shakespeare Assn. of America Convention. Philadelphia, 14 Apr. 1990.

Wickham, Glynne. "Romance and Emblem: A Study in the Dramatic Structure of *The Winter's Tale*." *The Elizabethan Theatre III*. Ed. David Galloway. Hamden: Archon, 1973. 82–99.

———. "*The Two Noble Kinsmen*; or, *A Midsummer Night's Dream*, Part II?" *The Elizabethan Theatre IV*. Ed. G. R. Hibbard. Hamden: Archon, 1974. 167–96.

Willems, Michèle, ed. *Shakespeare à la télévision*. Rouen: Université de Rouen, 1987.

Willey, Basil. *The Seventeenth Century Background: Studies in the Thought of the Age in Relation to Poetry and Religion*. New York: Columbia UP, 1950.

Williams, Raymond. *Key Words*. London: Oxford UP, 1975.

Williamson, Marilyn. *The Patriarchy of Shakespeare's Comedies*. Detroit: Wayne State UP, 1986.

Willson, Robert F., Jr. "The Plays within *A Midsummer Night's Dream* and *The Tempest*." *Shakespeare Jahrbuch* (Weimar) 110 (1974): 101–11.

Wilson, J. Dover. *The Meaning of* The Tempest. Newcastle upon Tyne: Lit. and Philos. Soc., 1936.

Wilson, Thomas. *The Arte of Rhetorique*. 1560. Ed. G. H. Mair. Oxford: Clarendon–Oxford UP, 1909.

Wither, George. *A Collection of Emblems*. 4 vols. London: Grismand, 1634–35.

Wölfflin, Heinrich. *Principles of Art History: The Problem of the Development of Style in Later Art*. Trans. M. D. Hottinger. New York: Dover, n.d.

Woodbridge, Linda. *Women and the English Renaissance: Literature and the Nature of Womankind, 1540–1620*. Urbana: U of Illinois P, 1984.

Wright, George T. *Shakespeare's Metrical Art*. Berkeley: U of California P, 1988.

Wrightson, Keith. *English Society, 1580–1680*. New Brunswick: Rutgers UP, 1982.

Yates, Frances A. *Shakespeare's Last Plays: A New Approach*. London: Routledge, 1975.

Young, Bruce W. "The Miracle of Faith, the Miracle of Love: Some Personal Reflections." *A Thoughtful Faith: Essays on Belief by Mormon Scholars*. Ed. Philip L. Barlow. Centerville: Canon, 1986. 259–76.

Young, David P. *The Heart's Forest: A Study of Shakespeare's Pastoral Plays*. New Haven: Yale UP, 1972.

Zitner, Sheldon. "Wooden O's in Plastic Boxes." *University of Toronto Quarterly* 51 (1981): 1–12.

Audiovisual Materials

Gorrie, John, dir. *The Tempest*. Video production. With Michael Hordern and Christopher Guard. BBC-TV/Time-Life, Inc., 1980. Col. videocassette. 150 min. Available for purchase only on ½" videocassette from Ambrose Publishing Co., 1290 Ave. of the Americas, Suite 2245, New York, NY 10104.

Greenaway, Peter, dir. *Prospero's Books*. Film. With John Gielgud, Michael Clark, and Michel Blanc. Miramax Films, 1991. Col. 129 min. Available for rental from Miramax Films, 375 Greenwich St., New York, NY 10013. Possibly available for rental on ½" videocassette from local video-rental stores.

Howell, Jane, dir. *The Winter's Tale*. Video production. With Jeremy Kemp, Anna Calder-Marshall, and Debbie Farrington. BBC-TV/Time-Life, Inc., 1980. Col. videocassette. 173 min. Available for purchase only on ½" videocassette from Ambrose Publishing Co., 1290 Ave. of the Americas, Suite 2245, New York, NY 10104.

Jones, David, dir. *Pericles*. Video production. With Mike Gwilym and Amanda Redman. BBC-TV/Time-Life, Inc., 1984. Col. videocassette. 177 min. Available for purchase only on ½" videocassette from Ambrose Video Publishing Co., 1290 Ave. of the Americas, Suite 2245, New York, NY 10104.

Mazursky, Paul, dir. *Tempest*. Film. With John Cassavetes and Gena Rowlands. Columbia Pictures, 1982. Col. videocassette. 142 min. Available for rental on ½" videocassette from local video-rental stores.

Moshinsky, Elijah, dir. *Cymbeline*. Video production. With Claire Bloom, Helen Mirren, and Richard Johnson. BBC-TV/Time-Life, Inc., 1982. Col. videocassette. 174 min. Available for purchase only on ½" videocassette from Ambrose Video Publishing Co., 1290 Ave. of the Americas, Suite 2245, New York, NY 10104.

Rylands, George, dir. *Cymbeline*. Recording. The Marlowe Society and Professional Players. 4 cassettes. Decca, London, forthcoming.

———. *Pericles*. Recording. The Marlowe Society and Professional Players. 3 cassettes. Decca, London, forthcoming.

———. *The Tempest*. Recording. The Marlowe Society and Professional Players. 3 cassettes. Decca, London, forthcoming.

———. *The Winter's Tale*. Recording. The Marlowe Society and Professional Players. 4 cassettes. Decca, London, forthcoming.

Sackler, Howard, dir. *Cymbeline*. Recording. With Claire Bloom. 3 cassettes. Caedmon, SWC 236, 1988.

———. *Pericles*. Recording. With Paul Scofield. 3 cassettes. Caedmon, SWC 237, 1988.

Schaefer, George, dir. *The Tempest*. Video production. With Maurice Evans, Lee Remick, and Richard Burton. NBC, 1960. Col. videocassette. 76 min. Available for rental or purchase on ½" videocassette from Films for the Humanities, PO Box 2053, Princeton, NJ 08543.

Smuin, Michael, chor. *The Tempest*. Ballet. San Francisco Ballet. PBS. 1 Apr. 1981.

Wilcox, Fred McLeod, dir. *The Forbidden Planet*. Film. With Leslie Nielsen, Walter Pidgeon, and Anne Francis. MGM, 1956. Col. videocassette. 99 min. Available for rental on ½" videocassette from local video-rental stores. Available for purchase on ½" videocassette from the Writing Company, 10200 Jefferson Blvd., Room K8, PO Box 802, Culver City, CA 90232-0802.

Wood, Peter, dir. *The Tempest*. Recording. With Sir Michael Redgrave. 3 cassettes. Caedmon, SWC 201, 1988.

———. *The Winter's Tale*. Recording. With Sir John Gielgud. 3 cassettes. Caedmon, SWC 214, 1988.

Woodman, William, dir. *The Tempest*. Video production. With Efrem Zimbalist, Jr., and William Bassett. Bard Productions, 1983. Col. videocassette. 127 min. Available for purchase only on ½" videocassette from Insight Media, 121 W. 85th St., New York, NY 10024-4401.

INDEX OF NAMES